W

with

and Ch

under

A
Fic
S

www.heinemann.co.uk
✓ Free online support
✓ Useful weblinks
✓ 24 hour online ordering

01865 888058

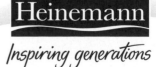

Heinemann

Inspiring generations

Heinemann Educational Publishers
Halley Court, Jordan Hill, Oxford OX2 8FJ
Part of Harcourt Education

Heinemann is the registered trademark of
Harcourt Education Limited

© Harcourt Education, 2006

First published 2006

10 09 08 07 06 05
10 9 8 7 6 5 4 3 2 1

British Library Cataloguing in Publication Data is available
from the British Library on request.

10-digit ISBN: 0 435987 31 3
13-digit ISBN: 978 0 435987 31 2

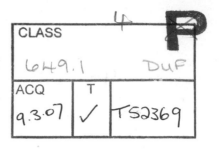

Edited by Jan Doorly
Typeset by Saxon Graphics Ltd, Derby
Original illustrations © Harcourt Education Limited, 2005
Cover design by Wooden Ark Studio
Printed in the UK by Bath Press
Cover photo: © Harcourt Education Ltd / Jules Selmes

Acknowledgements
Every effort has been made to contact copyright holders of material reproduced in this book.
Any omissions will be rectified in subsequent printings if notice is given to the publishers.

Photo acknowledgements
All photos © SureStart Local Programme Norris Green and SureStart Local Programme
Liverpool East except:
Harcourt Education Ltd / Jules Selmes – page 33
Getty Images / Digital Vision – pages 1, 110
Getty Images / PhotoDisc – pages 42, 140
Laura Dwight / Corbis – page 94
Lauren Shear / Science Photo Library – page 123

Text acknowledgements
Goleman, D (1996) *Emotional Intelligence*, Bloomsbury – page 95
Malaguzzi, L, 'No way. The hundred is there', from Edwards et al (1994) *The Hundred Languages
of Children*, Greenwood Publishing Group – page 161
Paley, V (1986) *Mollie is Three*, University of Chicago Press – page 142

Contents

Dedication

This book is dedicated to the children, families and early years practitioners of SureStart Local Programmes in Liverpool East and Norris Green. All SureStart royalties from the sales of this book will be used to fund and support professional development for early years practitioners in the SureStart areas.

Acknowledgements

Anna Duffy would like to thank the colleagues, practitioners and students with whom she has worked, who have been inspirational in their insights and their dedication to their work with children and their families. They have always been unfailingly generous in sharing their practice, and many of them have contributed directly to this book. She is also very grateful to her friends from outside childcare, who have given valuable insights into their particular areas of expertise. Finally, this book would not have been possible without the SureStart team in Liverpool who initiated this project and who have contributed so much to it by their vision, energy and enthusiasm.

The SureStart team (Fiona Chambers, Sally Croughan and Jill Stephens) would like to thank: Anna, for combining their ideas and experiences with her theoretical understanding and writing skills to produce the book; families and colleagues, past and present, for their contributions and support; the Steering Boards for their interest and encouragement; SureStart for the opportunity to explore new training and professional development issues; all those who have given technical support; photographers, Alan Edwards and Jonathan Turner, for their endless patience during the photo shoots; Sally Thomas for her valuable and thoughtful comments; colleagues at Heinemann and Gill Mason, Community and Society Advisor, City & Guilds.

Names of SureStart families, who have provided valuable information for this publication, have been changed to respect confidentiality.

About the authors

Anna Duffy

Anna Duffy has many years' experience of working with early years practitioners, first in a college of education (St Mary's College, Newcastle) and then from 1984 in the Department of Education of Newcastle University. Her work in the university included contributing to the primary PGCE course, running conversion courses for teachers wishing to move into early years work, supervising BPhils, Masters and PhD students and, since their inception in 1995, teaching on the university's ADE/BPhil courses, which are offered part-time to NNEBs, in both face-to-face and distance-learning modes.

In-service work has been her main focus for 30 years. Her work in Newcastle University also included working in the Education Department's Centre for International Studies in Education, teaching a full-time BPhil and Masters Early Years course for teachers from overseas. These teachers and administrators were predominantly from Africa and the Far East, though some came from the Middle East and Greece.

Anna retired from full-time work in the Department of Education in Newcastle University in 1996. In addition to the continuing work on the ADE/BPhil for Newcastle, she also contributes to the University of Northumbria's undergraduate degree in Childhood Studies. Her enthusiasm for early years work is undiminished and she is currently collaborating on the materials for Liverpool's SureStart training initiatives in Dovecot and Norris Green.

The SureStart team

The SureStart team, made up of Fiona Chambers, Sally Croughan and Jill Stephens, have a wide range of backgrounds in early years, community education and evaluation. Involved in developing learning programmes in family and public health agendas, they have worked at basic skills, further education and higher education levels. Individually, they have presented at international, national and local health, education and childcare conferences.

◆ **Fiona Chambers** is currently SureStart Local Programme Manager for the East

◆ **Sally Croughan** is currently SureStart Local Programme Manager for Norris Green

◆ **Jill Stephens** is Childcare and Early Learning Co-ordinator for the SureStart local programme in East Liverpool.

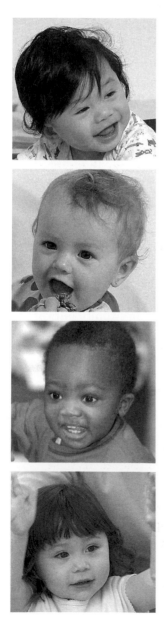

An open letter to a baby

Dear Baby

This book has been written for you. It outlines what is known about how children develop and it is written to help your carers reflect on the implications of this information for all that they provide for you when you are in the childcare setting.

This letter is to tell you about the principles that we bear in mind as we welcome you to our setting.

You are especially welcome because we know there is no one else in the world quite like you. Every person that is born is unique and irreplaceable. There never has been anyone quite like you, and there never will be anyone quite like you again. This is because we each have a personality that is a combination of internal (intrinsic) factors – your temperament, for example, is linked to the genes you were born with – and external (or extrinsic) forces which are often beyond anyone's control. These external forces include where you happen to live, the opportunities you are offered, and your position in your family – being the eldest, youngest or only child, for example.

Because you are so very special, we respect you. That means we take you seriously as an individual. We will listen to you and be aware of your particular needs. We are ready to help you to face the challenges ahead. We want to celebrate your talents. With us, you will never be seen as just one in a crowd. You are you.

We offer you these promises:

◆ we promise that you will be respected

- we promise we will support you as you learn in the way that suits you best, enabling you to follow your interests and develop your talents
- we promise to help you develop lots of ways to communicate with others
- we promise to help you learn with and through others
- we promise that we will respect your emotions and that you will have the opportunity to explore a range of emotions in safety through play and a range of rhymes and stories
- we promise to support your parents and the community in which you live, so that your need for a sense of security and belonging is satisfied
- we promise to co-operate with other professionals to ensure you get the help you need.

And, as the rest of this book shows, we will not stop striving for excellence in our provision for you.

With lots of love from all of us

What do these promises mean?

The focus of this book is on children from birth to roughly their third birthday. We do not always stop abruptly at the third birthday because we know that each child develops at a different rate. As our letter to the baby shows, we are interested in the child as a social and emotional being, an individual who is a learner and who will develop through being a communicator.

The first chapter explores the basic belief that young children are worthy of respect – for no other reason than the fact that they are unique human beings, as are their parents and the others who share their care with the parents.

Chapter 2 is about the child as a thinker and learner.

Chapters 3 and 4 examine the ways a child communicates. Chapter 3 discusses the ways children get their messages across in face-to-face encounters, and how much they pick up about how others are feeling. Chapter 4 looks at how children learn to use and understand other ways of sending, storing and receiving messages besides gestures and speech.

Chapters 5 and 6 are about professional childcare work. Chapter 5 examines the way the adults in the child's life interact with each other, working collaboratively to care for babies and young children. Chapter 6 looks at what it means to be professionally involved in working in childcare.

The purpose of this book is to make clear to early years workers the reasons that underpin recommended practice, so that they can reflect upon and develop their practice and be able to justify their actions to themselves, to parents and to other professionals.

The intention is to help them to reflect on their own practice, and also on that of other people. The format within each chapter is generally to begin with some theory, often followed by descriptions of the experiences of other people (these are the **Case study** sections), followed by an opportunity to examine some of the more practical implications of what has been described (these are the sections called **Focus**).

It is a good idea to have a notebook handy as you read the book so that you can record any ideas that may occur to you as you work through the chapters and begin to think about some of the implications of what you have read. Keeping your jottings in one place means you won't lose any of the insights that may occur to you as you read through the sections.

The **Reflect on your practice** sections are provided as a chance to pause for thought in a busy life, to help you become more aware of yourself and to begin to recognise what your current needs are in terms of your progress as a professional. Some of the tasks in these sections are quick examples for you to complete and then move on. However, those that begin with the words **It is a skill to…** pose some questions to help you to reflect and think more deeply about your practice. They are included to encourage you to act professionally by appraising yourself without waiting for someone else to tell you how you might improve.

Some of these reflections on your practice may make you decide to take action to change something you have been doing. Making and following an action plan for yourself is discussed at the end of Chapter 1.

Throughout the book, concepts that may be new to you are highlighted as **Key terms**, and these are also listed in the Glossary at the back of the book.

People whose research has been influential in developing our understanding of young children are mentioned in the text by name. You will find details about where you can read their work for yourself in the Bibliography at the end of the book. However, some particularly interesting books that are easy to get hold of are highlighted in the **Find out more** sections within the text, as well as appearing in the Bibliography.

In this book, children from birth to 12 months are referred to as babies; from 12–24 months they are called toddlers; twos and threes are called young children.

We hope that you will find the book useful in helping you to reflect on your practice. Do make notes on ideas that occur to you or your responses to those tasks you find interesting. When you look back over what you have written, you may well find that some themes are emerging which are important to you. Following these up could form the basis of a self-directed voyage of discovery and self-development.

Chapter 1

Respecting babies and young children

All early years work puts the child and his or her parent at the centre of the picture. This chapter considers the consequences of this belief for practitioners. The basic principle is that each child is to be respected because any human being has to be respected. Alongside this is the belief that what happens to babies and young children early in life has an immense effect on their fulfilment as an adult.

From birth, the child is a learner and a communicator. He or she is born with the instinct to make links to other people, and has as an equal right to respect.

This chapter is divided into the following sections:

- ◆ Respecting children
- ◆ Respecting parents
- ◆ Factors that make people who they are
- ◆ Implications for practitioners' development
- ◆ Basic tools for practitioners

Every child should be respected as a unique human being

Respecting children

It helps us to think about what respect means if we examine instances in our own experience when we have felt we are not respected. These instances may have occurred when you were a child, or today. They may have happened at home, or in public; when you were at work, or when you were supposed to be enjoying yourself. We feel we are not respected when we are ignored in a group or not included in a conversation. We feel lack of respect when our efforts are not appreciated, when we are patronised or not listened to. We feel hurt when we are not allowed to make choices or when competence or success is unrecognised, and opportunities to take responsibility are withheld. Judgements of disrespected people are usually made on an unrealistic basis.

On the other hand, when a person is respected he or she is consistently treated with kindness and courtesy. People who are respected are seen as individuals, spoken to, and made to feel cherished, their needs are acknowledged and met, and they are allowed to make choices and take decisions. People who are given proper respect are allowed to take initiatives, to tackle new challenges, given the time to get things right, and their successes are applauded. No unreasonable demands are made on them, and they are valued and understood.

REFLECT ON YOUR PRACTICE

Through analysing what people feel when they are not respected, we can begin to define the atmosphere and approaches necessary to make every child in the childcare setting confident that he or she is respected.

Think of private and public situations, at work and at leisure, when you have felt disrespected. When you are not respected, what emotions come over you? Now think of times and situations when you have felt you are being respected. What emotions come over you then?

Respect means that individuals are treated with courtesy, their opinions and needs are acknowledged, listened to and responded to.

REFLECT ON YOUR PRACTICE

There are implications for this in our practice whenever the children and their parents arrive and depart. How and where are they welcomed? How welcoming is the space? Is time taken to ensure that someone finds out how each parent and child is feeling today? Are the communications of parent and child listened to?

Staff need time and space to talk to parents

Every child needs to feel that there are people who are listening.

FOCUS

◆ Do we listen to the babies, toddlers and young children who are placed in our care?

◆ Babies communicate without language. Do we realise what they are communicating about? Are they afraid, do they feel abandoned, are they bored? Are their communications responded to?

◆ In the course of a day, how many opportunities are there for a one-to-one **conversation** with each child in the childcare setting? How could the opportunity to do this be arranged if it does not already exist?

◆ Are toddlers and 2- and 3-year-olds helped to develop their skills of communication? Are toddlers helped to learn the names of things and events? Do you meet the needs of 2- and 3-year-olds for explanations, and their need to recall and fix experiences? Do the children have the opportunity to initiate a conversation with an adult who has time to listen to them?

KEY TERM: Conversation

The exchange of ideas, feelings or information in speech between two or more people. Conversations require that the participants are aware of each other, listen to each other and respond to what they have heard. They require turn-taking. Babies begin to learn about how conversations work from a very early age, long before thay can speak.

Human needs

If a person is respected, his or her needs are known and responded to. Every human being, whatever his or her age, has needs that should always be respected.

The American psychologist Abraham Maslow ranked these needs in a hierarchy. He said that we all have the basic need for **food and shelter** to survive. Once that is taken care of, the next step is that we need **security**. Then we need to have a **sense of belonging** and of **achieving and being approved of**. Once all of these needs have been satisfied, there is a drive in us for **self-actualisation**, which means a sense that we are achieving our full potential.

> **KEY TERM: Self-actualisation**
>
> *The stage when an individual has an efficient and accurate perception of who they are, their strengths and weaknesses. It is marked by the courage to think independently, to resist pressure and to accept responsibility.*

Maslow's view of universal needs

Can you apply this framework to your own life? For example, does your place of work give you time to eat? Do you have a sense of belonging there? Do you feel your efforts are appreciated? Do you feel fulfilled in your work and the tasks you are given to do? Are there untapped strengths that could be used?

FOCUS

The implication of looking at needs in this way is that we should try our hardest to meet *all* of the child's needs. We are required to meet the child's basic needs for warmth, nourishment and rest. The provision of these can easily be checked. But does the child feel secure with us? How can we arrange things so that we give the child a sense of security? How do we ensure that the child feels that he or she belongs in the setting? How do we show each child that he or she is approved of? Most importantly, how do we build on the child's strengths and support his or her need for self-actualisation? What do you think self-actualisation is for a baby, a toddler, or a 2-year-old?

Respecting choices

Respect not only means that a person's needs are met, but that his or her wishes as to how they are met are also carefully considered. Adults have the responsibility to ensure that a child is fed, clothed and rested, and is at a comfortable temperature in safe surroundings. But everyone has to take appropriate responsibility for themselves if they are to achieve self-actualisation, to be as competent as their stage of development allows.

An appropriate responsibility for a young child in relation to food, clothing or rest might mean a choice of how much food to have, a choice of the colour or heaviness or lightness of a garment, and a choice about the length of sleep and when he or she needs it.

The childcare setting provides opportunities for a child to mix with other children, but any child needs to have opportunities to choose when to be social and when to be quiet. An appropriate responsibility for a young child would be to have a choice of companions for an activity. Toddlers and young children need the chance to practise physical skills such as walking, running, climbing, hopping, jumping and dancing. The childcare setting will provide for the development of these physical skills, but the appropriate choice for the child in this area might be to decide how long to practise these skills, and when.

Enjoying developing physical skills

People who are respected are allowed to take appropriate responsibility for themselves.

Working with Babies and Children Under Three

REFLECT ON YOUR PRACTICE

It is a skill to show respect to the children in a setting by planning opportunities allowing them to take appropriate responsibility for themselves.

Are the children in your setting given any opportunity to select companions, to choose when to rest or to be quiet, to practise a physical skill as long as they feel they need to, or to decide the order in which experiences are approached? Are things always cleared away as soon as the time allotted to them has ended? Can an unfinished construction be left out and returned to?

Any childcare setting provides activities for children, but it is not respectful to provide them with no choice of experience, no choice of when to start or finish it, and no opportunity to choose which resources to use, for example the range of colours to paint. Are children able to spend as much time as they need on a particular investigation?

The work produced by the child should also be treated with respect. It is an appropriate responsibility for toddlers and young children to have some say in what happens to work they have produced.

Over time, we as adults have devised routines that work for us. The problem is that very young children may not understand what is happening or why.

What are our unexamined reasons when we choose to treat all the children as a group rather than as individuals? What is preventing us from treating them as the individuals they are? Respect is shown when a person is seen as an individual and not just a member of a group, when his or her responses to what is happening are considered and not ignored. Respect is shown when a person is offered explanations as to what is happening, when he or she is informed about any changes of plan and given reasons for the change. There are many challenges for staff if they wish to ensure that all the children in their care are treated respectfully.

FOCUS

We should always consider how we can convey to children that they are respected as we carry out our routines. How is a baby treated with respect? How is respect shown to a toddler? How is respect shown to a 2-year-old? In answering these questions, consider your routines at arrival and departure times, meal times, toileting times, transitions between activities, and choices of activity. When is there a chance for privacy for the child? When is there an opportunity for him or her to be treated as an individual? When are efforts, however small, recognised?

6

Respecting parents

A young child must be considered in relation to his or her parents. Working alongside parents will be discussed in Chapter 5, but it is important to recognise that all of the principles of respect and consideration that are relevant to young children also apply to our relationship with their parents.

Listening to parents and carers

REFLECT ON YOUR PRACTICE

It is a skill to let all parents with children attending the setting see that they are respected.

Which procedures could you adopt so that parents feel more respected at the setting? Consider arrival and departure times, how information is passed to the parents, what information is asked for, where and when is it requested, why and by whom. What happens to the information they give you? What information is given to them, and how?

Are you aware of situations outside the setting where you consider that parents could be treated with greater respect? How could you improve the practice in these situations?

Sometimes, especially in the past, respect has been understood to involve an unquestioning acceptance of someone's position and wishes. But respect really means openness to and acceptance of a person, consideration of people's feelings, acceptance of their individuality, and response to their needs. Each person has his or her own strengths, and these are to be celebrated.

It is important that every individual is respected because everyone is unique. Next, we shall consider which factors contribute to an individual's uniqueness.

Factors that make people who they are

In the Introduction, the letter to the baby (page vi) said that everyone is special and that our personalities are made up of a combination of **intrinsic factors**, which are linked to generic inheritance, plus the impact of **extrinsic forces**, which arise from outside circumstances. The intrinsic factors and the extrinsic forces will now be considered in turn.

Intrinsic factors

A basic factor that makes the differences between us is our temperament. We do not all have the same way of approaching life. **Temperament** is not so much about what you do as the way you do it.

> **KEY TERM: Temperament**
>
> *A characteristic approach to life.*

At a party, one child may dash about and shriek with delight, while another may shrink in a corner. Their temperaments are different.

Differences in temperament show early. Babies are often described as falling into one of three categories: easy, difficult or slow to warm up. An **easy** baby has regular patterns of eating, sleeping and toileting. He or she is ready to approach new objects or people. A **difficult** baby is less predictable. He or she dislikes changes and withdraws from new experiences, and is often ill at ease and tense. A baby who is **slow to warm up** takes time to adjust to new experiences, but becomes increasingly positive or adaptable as experiences become more familiar. He or she is typically less active than children in either of the other two categories.

CASE STUDY:
AMINA'S CHILDREN

Amina writes:

My children are now grown up, but as young children they were very different. All three were brought up in the same environment with the same family values, yet each child displayed very different characteristics and reacted to situations in very different ways.

As a baby, my first son was very difficult. He was unpredictable, temperamental, disliked change and was quite tense. He was very impetuous and quick to learn, but found many everyday situations unsettling and difficult to cope with.

My daughter, the middle child, was an easy baby. She slept for long periods of time, was always contented and coped easily with new people and situations. She was easy-going and fitted into the everyday family routines.

My younger son was quite different from the other two. He was a baby who was slow to warm up. He took his time to learn to do things, and to us as parents it appeared that he sat back and watched and did not attempt anything new until he felt he could do things well. He did not begin talking until he was almost three. As a third child, he had less need to talk than his older siblings – they talked for him. However, he missed out many of the preliminary stages of speech, and when he began to talk he spoke in long sentences, as if he had been watching and waiting until he could do it well.

As adults they all show signs of the same temperament that they had as babies. My elder son has grown up to be a troubled soul who does not seem at ease with himself. He is frequently tense and finds many new situations difficult. He has, however, developed a quick wit and great charm.

My daughter, as an adult, shows similar characteristics that she showed as a very young child – she is calm, contented and copes well with new or difficult situations. She is the person in the family we all turn to when there are problems. She is an easy person to be with and fits in with many different social situations.

My younger son is still slow to warm up; he stands back and doesn't make rash decisions. He watches and likes to feel confident before he tries new things.

When I first became a parent I didn't imagine that my children would turn out so differently. In essence, each child had the same experiences and opportunities, but each had a different temperament and coped in different ways. Each has developed a unique personality.

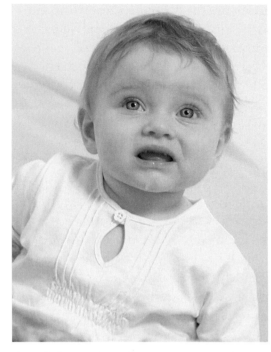 

Many babies are apprehensive in new situations…   *but most of them quickly gain confidence*

Key components of temperament

There have been several attempts to identify the key areas of temperament – those that really make the difference.

One research team, led by Robert Plomin and working in the US in the 1980s, identified emotionality, activity and sociability as the key components of temperament. Their model is therefore called the **EAS model**.

◆ **Emotionality** means how quickly a negative response is expressed. Plomin believed some children have a quicker physiological response to unpleasant situations. Their bodies easily release high levels of the stress hormone cortisol. During the first few months, emotionality is seen in a baby who readily cries in unpleasant or frightening situations and takes a long time to settle down afterwards. Later in life this quick, short-fuse response develops into an immediate flare-up of either fear or anger, depending on what has been learned from early experiences.

◆ **Activity** describes the baby's energy and tempo. Is the baby always on the move, or is he or she more relaxed?

◆ **Sociability** refers to the baby's preference for being with other people. Does the baby obviously prefer people to things? Does he or she dislike being left alone? Does he or she react positively to strangers, or show wariness of them at first? Is the baby content with his or her own company?

Shyness has often been added as a fourth component to Plomin's three dimensions of emotionality, activity and sociability. However, the word *shyness* covers a whole range of behaviours. In some cases the word might mean being able to be self-sufficient, or being involved but usually rather quiet in social situations. In others it might mean tending to blush or feel nervous as a response to being noticed. It might mean always being ill at ease in company, or anxious about anything or anyone unfamiliar. Shyness does not necessarily mean a lack of interest in people; it arises as the result of stress and anxiety and it is due to wariness rather than a lack of sociability.

In one important study the American researcher Jerome Kagan followed up a group of children from infancy. His findings led him to believe that shyness is part of a broader spectrum, which he labelled **inhibition**. This means a general wariness shown in all challenging or unfamiliar situations, as well as a reaction of withdrawal from unfamiliar people. About half of the children he observed were characterised as being **uninhibited**. They were outgoing, sociable and interested in new situations. On the other hand, **inhibited** children were wary, quiet and subdued when faced with a new situation, becoming anxious if any pressure was put on them. Kagan noted that this characteristic shows as early as 4 months. At that age, when children encountered an unfamiliar experience, such as a balloon popping, the inhibited babies cried and moved their limbs vigorously, while the uninhibited babies showed little distress and little motor activity. In their second year, when encountering a stranger, such as Santa Claus, inhibited children showed signs of anxiety and withdrew, whereas the uninhibited group were fearless and interested.

> **KEY TERM: Inhibition**
>
> *A general wariness in all challenging situations (Jerome Kagan), being ill at ease in society (Avshalom Caspi).*

However, Kagan's research also showed that changes in the level of inhibition can occur in all children except for those at the two extremes: those who were very outgoing or very shy. He noted that, over time, changes can occur in either direction according to influences children encounter in their social environment.

REFLECT ON YOUR PRACTICE

It is a skill to be aware of one's own habitual ways of responding.

Can you trace any of these elements (a quick-fire reaction; always on the go; outgoing or rather more reserved) in your own temperament? Are you aware of any changes in your responses now compared to when you were younger? As an adult, how have you learned to cope with your own negative reactions to certain situations?

Development of temperaments

The Dunedin Study in New Zealand (reported by Avshalom Caspi) also investigated whether temperaments were set for life. This study followed over 1,000 children from when they were 3 years old to when they were 21. The research found it was possible to describe three groups of people with constellations of related temperaments which tended to persist.

Those labelled **under-controlled** were at three impulsive, emotionally volatile, irritable, impatient, restless and distractible. At 21 they were described as impulsive, aggressive, thrill seeking, unreliable and restless. The group labelled **inhibited** were at three socially ill at ease, fearful, easily upset by strangers and shy. At 21 they were over-controlled, cautious, non-assertive, socially isolated and depressed. The **well-adjusted** group were at three self-confident, friendly after initial wariness, tolerant of frustration and self-controlled. Aged 21 they were described as normal, average, mentally healthy. However Caspi, like Kagan, warned that the predictions could only be stated in terms of probabilities rather than certainties. Like Kagan, he found that there were plenty of examples of change.

The implication of this is that practitioners should be aware that some children need more help than others to meet the demands we put on them. Supporting children in managing their fears or their impulsiveness can help them enormously.

Self-regulation

Other ways of describing temperament have been suggested. Mary Rothbart, working in the US in the 1990s, concentrated on only two basic aspects of temperament. The first was **reactivity** – this is rather like Plomin's emotionality but, unlike Plomin, Rothbart included positive reactions as well as negative ones.

The other trait that Rothbart felt was important was **self-regulation**. The ability to have some sort of control over one's reactions is a crucial aspect of human development. Children develop the ability to control their behaviour to take account of others. To become a mature adult, a person has to make a transition from being controlled by others to being able to exercise self-control. The process (which few really ever truly complete – we all need the support of others in a crisis) begins in early childhood.

> **KEY TERM: Self-regulation**
> *The ability to control one's actions and emotional responses.*

Even young babies have reflex responses that enable them to self-regulate their sensory input. For example, babies squint when facing bright sunlight. Babies also control how long they will look at an interesting stimulus before turning away.

Down they go!

Babies' approaches to unfamiliar experiences vary. One study examined the extent of the link between reactivity and self-regulation. Linda LaGasse and her team showed that babies who sucked harder to get more sweetened water at 2 days old also reacted strongly to both pleasant and unpleasant situations when they were 18 months old. These babies wanted more of the good experiences and vigorously rejected less pleasant ones. Early ways of self-regulating feelings of discomfort in a baby include finger sucking or looking away from too strong a stimulus. In their first year, infants will also orient towards their main care-giver for comfort when they feel distressed.

By 12 months it can be seen that a child acts purposefully, making a grab for a toy or knocking over a tower of bricks, but at this age babies' ability to monitor (and consequently to modify) their behaviour is limited.

However, as the toddler begins to move about, carers watch and warn whenever a risky situation presents itself: *Don't go near the road, Keep away from the hot stove, Don't do that to the cat.* Being able to exercise self-control at this stage means that the toddler is conscious of the demands of the external world and what is considered appropriate behaviour, and begins to adjust his or her actions accordingly. A baby who is beginning to be a mobile toddler is constantly hearing *No!* as he or she learns to adapt to the customs of the culture. One researcher counted and found *No!* was said to the child he observed on average every 9 minutes.

REFLECT ON YOUR PRACTICE

It is a skill to recognise the expectations we have of children.

What is your idea of a 'good' baby or a 'good' child? Is it the baby who is no trouble, and makes no demands? Go through the sections of your day and write down what you expect a 'good' child to do, for example to settle quickly after coming in, to play happily, to change activity without protest, to go to sleep on demand, to be cheerful when waking up, and so on.

Selecting a favourite toy

A child's self-regulation involves **compliance** with care-givers' wishes and expectations. As we have seen, temperaments differ and some children (particularly those whose temperaments are fearful or inhibited) find being compliant easier than others.

> **KEY TERM: Compliance**
>
> *A child's willingness to go along with a care-giver's expectations, which Mary Rothbart saw as an important element in a child's temperament.*

Grazyna Kochanska believes there are some children who have a **receptive stance**. She says that the children in those **dyads** (parent/child relationships) which are marked by a happy mood, with parent and child being responsive to each other, are more likely to be compliant. She argues that children of all temperaments who have been sensitively treated, children whose needs for comfort have been met and whose bids for attention and social overtures have been responded to, are the ones who are more likely to be responsive to their care-givers' wishes.

> **KEY TERM: Dyad**
>
> *A close pair, e.g. mother and child.*

Other researchers have investigated mother–child interactions in Japan, where the mother–child relationship is particularly close and indulgent and is marked by a deep reluctance on the part of the parent to engage in any confrontations or contests of will. This happens because the adult's intention in Japan is to encourage the child to learn to desire to adhere to parental values. The researchers found that children there are in fact more willing to comply and less inclined to pick a fight than children generally. The result of the Japanese approach is that the stage of 'the terrible twos' is unheard of in Japan.

FOCUS

Babies should be respected as the individuals they are; they all need a loving and sensitive response, even those who are more demanding. Children are born with a particular response to life and it is the interaction with their care-givers that can make the difference. Shyness and timidity can be diminished if the care-givers are sensitive, responsive and highly involved with the child. A 'difficult' baby cannot help being stressed and scared, but it doesn't help if he or she is responded to with irritation by someone whose own temperament prefers regularity and order. The care-giver must be mature enough and flexible enough to be responsive. If a highly-strung baby is not helped and supported in reactions to stress, he or she may go on later to become aggressive and have low self-control.

In another American study Kochanska followed a group of children from 14 months to their fourth birthdays to observe how self-regulation developed. In the second year of life, she found, toddlers began to comply with adults' directives, though at first they would more usually refuse or ignore instructions. However, between 18 and 24 months their compliance to 'don't' instructions increased dramatically. At this age toddlers were beginning to internalise their care-givers' warnings and to become committed to them. By the time they were 4 years old, this happened about 80 per cent of the time.

It is an important developmental task for toddlers to develop what is known as the **parasympathetic nervous system**, that is a bodily reaction that warns the child (or adult) to stop doing something if past experience has shown that that behaviour is dangerous or is regarded as unacceptable. When this holding-back system is aroused, the body responds with a drop in blood pressure and the breathing becomes shallow. It is a very obvious physiological signal, and if the activity is continued in spite of the danger signals, a sense of shame or guilt follows. These self-conscious and self-judging emotions are related to a sense of self which begins to emerge about the age of 18 months. Shame results from the self evaluating the self. The standards that are being used are acquired from the people in contact with the child.

KEY TERM: Parasympathetic nervous system

The system producing bodily sensations when a person is thinking of transgressing a code he or she has accepted.

Besides being told not to do certain things, 2- and 3-year-olds are also told about what they *ought* to do. Compared to the 'don'ts', the 'dos' (for example, saying *Please* or *Thank you*, cleaning teeth, sharing toys, tidying away toys) take longer to learn. Learning what you ought to do requires a lot of adult support, in the form of gentle reminders, or with the task being presented as a game.

From the age of two onwards, children show that they are monitoring some activities, for example their physical skills or the constructions they have built. By 24 months children pay attention to simple standards – and react if they fail to meet them. Self-regulation is also used when a child deliberately alters strategies that he or she finds are not working. Using self-regulation, 2- and 3-year-olds begin to be able to avoid things they have been told they must avoid, and they begin to be able to wait for things they cannot have straight away. Now their self-regulation is based on measurement of self against external standards.

The implication is that the way adults support a child in developing self-regulation (as opposed to blind obedience) are crucial. The effectiveness of any intervention is related to the amount of respect and consideration shown to the child.

REFLECT ON YOUR PRACTICE

It is a skill to support children to learn to control their responses.

Write out the names of the children in your charge. How would you describe each one's temperament? How do you adjust to their responses? How do you support a toddler to learn to control his or her responses, both the 'don'ts' (such as restraining aggression) and the 'dos' (such as tidying up or sharing)?

Make an audit of how many prohibitions you utter and what you prohibit over one session. Make another audit of occasions when you helped a baby, a toddler or an older child to become aware of his or her emotions in order to control them. When do you think a child is a spoilt child? What might you say to help a parent who was shouting at a young child?

Individual strengths

A further factor that makes a difference between individuals is that people all have particular strengths. Three types of response are commonly recognised in the shorthand **VAK**, which stands for visual, acoustic (or auditory) and kinetic. Visually oriented people are those whose preferred thinking style uses things they can see or visualise. Acoustically oriented people are those more sensitive to sounds and rhythms. The kinetic group register physical and emotional feelings strongly.

> **KEY TERM: VAK**
>
> *Short for the visual, auditory and kinaesthetic modes of experiencing, remembering and representing experience.*

Salesmen and managers are trained to identify these groups and to respond using the preferred thinking style of the person they are dealing with. A visually oriented person will say things such as *I see the problem*; an acoustically oriented person will say *It sounds like a good idea*; a kinaesthetic person will say *I feel upset about this* or *We'll run with this idea*.

In a more comprehensive discussion of the range of differences between people, Howard Gardner argued that we are born not with a once-and-for-all IQ but with more or less of each of a **range of intelligences**. This is his list.

Gardner's types of intelligences	
Type	**Revealed in**
Linguistic	Sensitivity to words, poetry and stories
Logico-mathematical	Ability to use logic and to solve problems
Musical	Interest in patterns of sound and rhythms
Kinaesthetic	Good bodily control and skills
Spatial, visual	Ability to see spatial relationships and patterns
Naturalist	Interest in the variety of types of plants and animals
Interpersonal	Interest in people and an ability to understand their intentions
Intrapersonal	Ability to understand oneself and one's feelings (emotional intelligence)

Most adults show a distinct leaning to one of these frames of mind. Some people like words and literature and perhaps enjoy word puzzles; others are good at calculations and enjoy puzzles that involve logic or numbers. Some are artistic, others musical. Some people are able to be very sensitive to others' feelings and responses. Others are interested in living things and will enjoy gardening and pets. Footballers, dancers and athletes have a large dose of kinaesthetic intelligence.

Musical, visual and kinaesthetic intelligences tend to show early. Not all of these intelligences are equally valued by the formal education system, but recognising and exercising the ones you have strengthens your enjoyment of life and possibly influences your choice of occupation.

Extrinsic forces

A child's personality is also shaped by external pressures. The people surrounding the baby, both in the home and in the community, have an impact on how the child develops. Pressures are felt both from the parents / carers and from the community at large.

It is obvious that each stage of development from lack of awareness to self-regulation involves an adjustment. Each adjustment is a challenge. The adults close to the child have to support the child to meet the challenges of these adjustments.

The ultimate challenge we all face is to find ourselves as a human being, that is reach Maslow's summit of self-actualisation. The psychologist Erik Erikson conceptualised all of life as a series of challenges that must be successfully overcome in order for us to be at ease with ourselves. In Erikson's view, life is about a quest for identity, and as we mature physically each stage brings a challenge which arises from where we stand in relation to others. The timing of the stages is fixed in our genes, but the influences that challenge us at each stage come from the people around us. If we succeed in facing the challenge of one stage, we can move on to the next. If we fail the challenge we are stuck, and further development is impaired, Erikson argues.

Developing trust

As you will see in the table on page 20, Erikson says that healthy development has to begin in babyhood with the development of trust. If we have no trust, we can have no confidence in ourselves or others; if we have no confidence we can take no initiative; if we take no initiatives we do not try things out; if we do not try things out, we never learn to put in effort; if we do not put in effort we do not know the sort of person we can be... and so on.

This baby is learning to develop confidence

The first challenge for children is to learn that they can trust others to attend to their needs. A child instinctively seeks the attention of others from birth, instinctively forming a particular **attachment** to the main care-giver. Whether this works out well depends on the care-giver's response to the child.

> **KEY TERM: Attachment**
>
> *A long-enduring, emotional tie to a specific individual. The baby's urge to form an attachment has a biological function – the need to survive. The urge also has a psychological function – the need for security.*

Erikson's stages of development		
Ages	**Choice**	**Challenge**
Birth to 18 months	Basic trust v mistrust	Infants must form trusting relationships with carers. They can then be secure and open to new experiences.
18 months to 36 months	Autonomy v shame	As they master more skills (walking, toileting, etc.) children begin to feel more independent and in control. They begin to develop self-control.
3 to 6 years	Initiative v guilt	As children develop a sense of independence there may be conflicts with care-givers.
6 to 12 years	Industry v inferiority	Children begin to realise they must put in effort to learn and acquire skills.
12 to 18 years	Identity v role confusion	Teenagers must confirm a sense of self as a unique individual in various areas such as talent, skills, temperament and gender, or risk role confusion in adulthood.
Young adult	Intimacy v isolation	The challenge of forming emotional commitments to other people (where there has to be give and take) must be met.
Adult	Generativity v stagnation	Adults face the challenge of taking care of the next generation as a parent and / or in the workplace as a passer-on of skills or knowledge.
Older adult	Ego integrity v despair	Older adults need to feel a sense of satisfaction about how they have coped with the circumstances and people in the life they have led.

Developing attachments

Attachments are defined as being an enduring emotional tie to a specific person. These people offer the child comfort and security. In young children, attachments involve wanting to be near the person – **proximity seeking** – and they produce **separation upset** when proximity cannot be obtained. Attachments are often very long-lasting. The work studying the development of attachment was led by John Bowlby, who published his first book in 1969. Bowlby identified four stages in the development of attachment.

◆ **Stage 1 Pre-attachment** (birth to 2 months). The baby responds to anyone.

◆ **Stage 2 Attachment-in-the-making** (2 months to 7 months). The baby recognises the main care-giver and enjoys practising the basic rules of interaction – being pleased to see the care-giver, and (with the care-giver's support) baby and care-giver respond to each other in turn.

◆ **Stage 3 Clear-cut attachment** (7 months to 24 months). At this time there are protests when the main care-giver leaves, there are attempts to gain the care-giver's attention and to be close, there is a wariness of strangers.

◆ **Stage 4 Goal-corrected partnership** (from 24 months). The child begins to be aware of the care-giver's needs and begins to make adjustments and allowances for these in order to enjoy their continued emotional support.

A mother with her new baby

Just six months later, attachment and interaction are developing well

From Bowlby's work, the belief has arisen that it is vital for children to learn to trust the person who is their main carer. This has to happen very early in life. Bowlby wrote: 'Even good mothering is almost useless if delayed until after the age of two and a half years.'

Other researchers have examined this claim. In England, Barbara Tizard undertook a long-term study of children who were in a children's home from an early age (and so with shift patterns in operation, hardly had the opportunity to form an attachment with anyone). She showed that after being adopted, the children had been able to develop close attachment bonds with their adoptive parents. However, these children tended to be aggressive and unpopular with other children when they went to school.

Another English study of children adopted from a Romanian orphanage showed that even those who had stayed there till they were four or five were able to develop emotional bonds with their adoptive parents. However, they were not easily comforted when distressed and, like the children in the Tizard study, they were inclined to be overfriendly with strangers. So it could be argued that the normal stage of the extension of trust to others beyond the main care-giver had perhaps been unsupported.

The implication of these studies is that those who share the care of young children with parents have to work hard to provide the child with the opportunity to extend his or her trust to others besides the main care-giver.

REFLECT ON YOUR PRACTICE

It is a skill to help a child to develop trust in the carers at the setting.

Can you recognise the urgency of a particular child's need for a familiar face in the setting? What arrangements are made in your setting to ensure that a child can develop secure relationships with staff? (In one system, in Italy, the same group of staff remain with the same children for their first three years in the nursery.)

There have been many studies of the way babies form attachments. Mary Ainsworth worked from 1969 to find a way of assessing how much security children found in their main attachment relationship. Through using her **strange situation procedure** (a strictly organised and timed session during which a mother leaves her 12- to 18-months-old child in a playroom with toys with an adult stranger for a short while before she returns), Ainsworth described four basic attachment patterns.

KEY TERM: Strange situation procedure

A procedure devised by Mary Ainsworth to test the response of a child aged 12–18 months to being left alone with a stranger. The child's response when the mother returned gave an indication of the child's relationship with the mother.

A child was judged to be **securely attached** if in the strange situation he or she showed a moderate level of proximity seeking, was upset when the mother departed and greeted her positively on her return. The assumption was that such children had had positive initial experiences, with their mother meeting their needs, comforting them whenever they were distressed and enjoying playing with them. This consistent behaviour conveys a caring and interested attitude and babies learn that people can be trusted. This means that they can be expected to form confident relationships with other adults. This will lead to an assured self-image that will stand them in good stead in life. About 40 per cent of children are in this group.

A second group was described as **insecurely attached – avoidant**. Here, the toddlers avoided contact with the mother on her return, and were not greatly upset when left with a stranger.

In the **insecurely attached – resistant** group, the toddlers were greatly upset on the mother's return. They were difficult to console, both seeking comfort and, at the same time, resisting it.

The toddlers in the two insecurely attached groups did not seem to have acquired a built-in expectation that they could rely on their main carer, and had not been able to learn to trust. Ainsworth suggested that their future relationships and adjustment may be at risk.

Ainsworth also had a small group which was categorised as **disorganised**. This group had no coherent way of coping with the stress of the very demanding structured experience. The toddlers responded to the mother with contradictory behaviour, with proximity seeking being followed by avoidance. It was believed that this indicated confusion and fear about the relationship and was a warning of future psychopathic problems.

There have been criticisms of Ainsworth's work. The study only looked at children in a narrow age band (12–18 months old). Follow-up studies showed that some children remained in their original category, but others moved categories. This may have been due to a change for the worse in family circumstances, or an improvement that may have come about through extra support for a parent. In addition, Ainsworth only assessed attachment to the mother, whereas children can have a range of people to whom they are attached – not least their fathers and siblings.

The implication of this is the immense importance of all adult–child relationships for helping a child to meet the challenges of his or her own temperament and achieve some measure of the emotional competence that is needed for effective social functioning.

Developing emotional habits

More recently Sue Gerhardt, using the growing understanding of the physiological processes involved in emotional reactions, has explained the mechanism through which emotional habits develop. She argues that every newborn child is programmed to seek help to have his or her basic needs met in order to survive. Every mother's hormones prime her to respond to these pleas for help. The baby feels stress when hungry, thirsty or tired. Sensing danger, the baby's system responds with a signal from the brain to the adrenal glands, which produce **cortisol**.

> **KEY TERM:** Cortisol
>
> *A substance produced by the body from the adrenal glands in response to stress.*

Cortisol readies the body for the reflex actions involved in the **flight or fight** response to danger, but producing too much cortisol too soon and too often is dangerous. The body either limits cortisol production or keeps on producing a lot of it even when it is hardly needed. The babies whose systems have adapted by producing less cortisol are those whose attachment responses are described as **avoidant** (they are already learning to ignore their feelings). Those who produce it in excess are those whose attachment responses are described as **resistant**. These children have learned that drama and exaggeration may be a help in obtaining attention.

There are further dangers with cortisol. It can inhibit brain growth, especially that part of the brain that is still developing in the months after birth, which deals with the ability to respond to social and emotional cues and underpins the way we respond to others. An excess of cortisol can also destroy cortisol receptors in the brain. Having plenty of these receptors helps you to cope with stress in later life: if there are not many of them, cortisol will remain in your system with nowhere to go and you will remain stressed.

The way to deal with increased levels of the hormone cortisol is to calm down. But babies are unable to do this for themselves. They need someone to meet their needs and then to calm them down. Babies need a care-giver who will respond to them – they cannot learn to manage emotional states for themselves unless they learn that discomfort can pass. They only learn this through having the experience of being calmed down to a comfortable level. At first, this has to happen with outside help.

Babies are not 'playing up' when they cry. Something is upsetting them and they need someone to remove the cause of the distress and help them back to their normal state of feeling. It is vital that there is someone who is tracking their emotional state and can restore them to an even keel as quickly as possible. It is also important that this person has learned to deal with the negative states of anger and hostility in his or her own life.

Children – and adults – need to learn that in certain circumstances they become angry or afraid or ashamed. It helps to be able to name these emotions and, as language develops, to be able to talk about them. Children are aware of pleasure and pain from birth and they begin to be able to name some emotions (happy, sad, afraid) before they are two. After two, there is a great increase in references to emotional states in themselves and in others.

Daniel Goleman, who coined the term **emotional literacy** to describe the ability to recognise and deal with one's own and others' emotional states, believes awareness of one's emotions is far more important than high intelligence. It is important for a person to learn that people not only have emotions, for example aggression, but that emotions can be controlled or channelled in ways that are not disruptive to others. It is also necessary to be able to recognise emotions in others.

> **KEY TERM:** Emotional intelligence, emotional literacy
>
> *Terms describing the ability to recognise and deal with one's own and other people's emotional states.*

The implication of this is that we must recognise children's emotions and talk about them with the child, even before the child can talk. We must support children and help them to understand the feelings they have.

REFLECT ON YOUR PRACTICE

It is a skill to be able to manage one's emotions.

How do you calm yourself down? How do you keep calm? To extend your repertoire of methods for calming yourself, talk to other people about what they do to calm themselves when they feel stressed.

FIND OUT MORE

Gerhardt, S (2004) *Why Love Matters*, Brunner-Routledge

Goleman, D (1999) *Emotional Literacy*, Bloomsbury

Society's expectations

Besides the immediate family, another extrinsic pressure forming a person's outlook comes from the beliefs and expectations of society in general. These are taken on board (to a greater or lesser extent) by parents and carers. One of these beliefs is about how men and women should behave.

Between 18 months and 24 months, a child begins to acquire **gender identity**. This means that everyone, including themselves, is recognised as a member of one of two groups, boys or girls, men or women. From the end of the second year on at least, when asked 'Are you a boy or a girl?', the child will answer correctly. From the beginning of the third year the child can discern whether another child is a boy or a girl. From about three the child begins to understand that an individual's sex remains a constant feature throughout life. After four, children can use this information to predict whether they will be a mother or a father in adulthood.

> **KEY TERM: Gender identity**
>
> *Recognising oneself as male or female.*

The society to which we belong has deeply ingrained expectations of the behaviour of members of each group. In general, and without much hard evidence, males are thought to be dominant, active, confident and aggressive, while females are thought to be nurturing, caring and gentle.

FOCUS

The Baby X experiment illustrates this. Take a baby dressed in white or a neutral colour and introduce the child to someone who does not know him or her. Tell some people you introduce the child to that the child is a boy; tell others that the baby is a girl. Note the way the adults interact with the child. Many adults will play with a child they believe is a boy quite vigorously. If they believe the baby is a girl, they will be gentler. If there are toys available nearby, adults will select the toys they believe suitable: a car for a boy or a doll for a girl, according to the information you have given them. If there is a sudden loud noise, the adults will comfort the baby differently according to whether the infant is thought to be a boy or a girl.

From very early, children come to know that certain kinds of behaviour are expected from boys and from girls. In general, boys are expected to play with trucks, blocks and guns. Girls are expected to play with dolls and domestic articles. The information the child acquires (**gender role knowledge**) comes from parents, together with other adults providing for children, from educational establishments to shopkeepers and the media.

> **KEY TERM: Gender role knowledge**
>
> *Knowing what is expected of a boy or girl, man or woman.*

There are definite pressures on children to conform to the expected norm. Gender-stereotyped toys are provided, and boys are encouraged to be active while girls are discouraged. Parental talk differs: boys are encouraged to be tougher and more decisive, girls to be gentler and more compliant. Girls are spoken to more about feelings and emotions. Boys are encouraged to suppress expressions of emotion.

Does this play challenge gender stereotyping?

CASE STUDY:
AISLINN

Aislinn writes about what she saw at the mother and toddler group which met in her school.

Just observing them with their young babies and toddlers emphasised what I had read about differing expectations and attitudes. The boys in the mother and toddler group were allowed to walk around freely in the area set aside for the group. They were given much freer access to the toys and allowed to throw toys around and make a noise. The girls, on the other hand, were restricted to sitting beside their mothers and playing with one or two toys. They were discouraged from wandering about and from shouting out. The girls' mothers appeared to be much more protective, while the boys' mothers seemed proud of their sons' more aggressive behaviour.

Aislinn discussed her observations with a friend. She continues:

When I asked Susan if she had different expectations of her children (a boy now ten and twin girls of six) when they were little, she said: 'Well, I knew the girls would be quieter. You expect boys to be noisy. I think boys need more space. Keith always questioned everything I said. He always wanted to know what was the logic behind everything, and I respected that. You had to respect him; after all he was a boy.' When I queried what she meant by respect she found it hard to reply, but eventually said she thought it summed up the difference between Keith and the girls, and how she treated them. She went on to describe a situation where two of her friends had encouraged their little sons to fight and be aggressive because they were boys and should be able to stand up for themselves. She had felt very sad at this and was sure she had not wanted this for Keith or that it was the correct way for children of either sex to behave.

Interestingly, there appears to be an inbuilt preference from the third year on for boys to choose boys as companions and girls to choose girls. This persists throughout adolescence and beyond. It appears to happen in all cultures, and even in monkeys. Peer pressure then reinforces the earlier socialisation (and perhaps explains it: fathers are often very protective of their sons' masculinity).

FOCUS

The implication is that practitioners should beware of carelessly reinforcing stereotypical behaviours, which may prevent fulfilment of the individual's need for self-actualisation. Do we unthinkingly reinforce **gender stereotyping** in the provision we have for children? Are boys given one sort of treatment and girls another? What about the toys and equipment provided?

KEY TERM: Gender stereotyping

Having fixed expectations of how boys and girls are likely to behave and encouraging them to behave in these ways. Gender stereotyping may inhibit a child's potential by closing off areas of activity.

REFLECT ON YOUR PRACTICE

It is a skill to be aware of the prevalence and potency of gender stereotyping.

Look at the adverts on television. How are boys portrayed? How are girls portrayed?

Go to a shop that sells toys. What is on offer for boys, and what is on offer for girls? Are the toys mixed together, or are they separated?

Look at the provision in your setting. Do you reinforce gender stereotypes? Try to make a list of what you expect from, and reinforce in, boys, and then do the same for girls. What can you do to ensure you reduce any unconscious bias you have discovered?

Implications for practitioners' development

If we promise a child that he or she will be respected, allowed choices, allowed to take risks in safety, allowed access to the inherited wisdom and tools of society and be given help to grow emotionally, it follows that he or she must be in contact with adults who have respect for themselves and others. It means that they have the emotional resilience to withstand the surges and tempests of babies' and young children's passions. People who care for young children in groups must be aware of each child's temperament, the demands and joys of that temperament, and ways to help the child's development through an awareness of attachment theory and the toddler's increasing self-awareness.

The fulfilment of the promises that were made to the baby in the Introduction to this book makes heavy demands on the practitioners who work with children.

First, the practitioner has to understand the theories behind children's development as they make relationships and develop knowledge and skills. Secondly, the practitioner has to have professional skills. The basic skill is to be able to observe children.

Basic tools for practitioners

Recording observations

If you believe that all children build their own minds in their own way and at their own pace, the basic professional skill you need to develop is to be able to observe children and to record precisely where they are in their development at the time you do the observation. The information you obtain will not be a picture of where they were a week ago, and they will have moved on by next week. Each observation is precious and it deserves your best effort.

The type of observation that is recommended is an attempt to capture the essence of the child – energy levels, responses to experiences and people, character and temperament, what he or she can do and what he or she knows. Observations should be signed and dated and should record the child's name, the time and place they were made, and the context (e.g. was the child alone or in a group). Each observation should have three sections – what you saw, how you interpret this, and what action you intend to take as a consequence of what you have seen.

The technique is to watch the child intently and without interruption for 10 minutes – without writing anything down. This is so as not to miss something while you are writing notes. Focus on the child to the exclusion of everything else. Put other thoughts out of your mind so that you can tune into the child's experiences and feel the ebb and flow of his or her emotions. Then straight afterwards take at least 10 minutes to write down everything you saw and were aware of, including your own feelings and responses. Make the account as full and detailed as possible.

Be objective in the sense of leaving nothing out, even though you might think it is unimportant or unflattering. Make what you write as vivid as possible. If the child is mobile, what word would best describe how he or she moved across the room? Did the child dash, tiptoe, stumble, stagger, stroll, saunter, run or dawdle across the space? Did he or she do things eagerly, gingerly, carefully, easily, with concentration, abstractedly, effortlessly or with difficulty? How did he or she respond to other children and other adults?

F. Laevers suggests that it is very important to capture the quality of children's involvement in what they are doing, rather than merely writing down what they do. His list of signs of involvement includes facial expression, composure and concentration; energy; persistence; precision; reaction time; and satisfaction.

The Children's Centre at Pen Green has its own framework for reporting. In every observation they make a comment on the child's patterns of behaviour, well-being, involvement in the activity and level of engagement with the adult(s).

Sally Thomas has developed an alternative framework – the 5Ds of observation – based on the Te Whariki model. These are *describe*; *distinguish* – i.e. using the Birth to Three framework decide what the activity demonstrates (e.g. making connections, listening and responding, showing a sense of belonging, etc.); *discuss*; *decide* what is appropriate for you to do next to extend and support the child's interest, and *document*.

After 10 minutes observing, write down your impressions or speak about them into a recording device, making an effort to avoid professional jargon. Steer clear of references to learning goals or milestones. Instead, capture as vividly as you can the essence of the child as it was shown in your 10 minutes of close attention. In your account, don't be afraid to let your feelings show as you record what you saw and heard.

Doing observations in this way will feed your own growth as a person, because observations should lead to action. Your observations need to be shared with colleagues, and in doing this you function as a team member. They should form the basis for your team's planning for this child. They should be done for each child about once a fortnight, and they should be shared with parents.

Narrative observations give much richer information than checklists. If you use checklists for observations, there is a danger that you will record only what you expect to find, and will regard the child less as an individual than as a member of a group. It is dangerous to look for milestones that you expect, and to want every child to meet these in a particular sequence.

Another practice to be avoided when doing observations is to write in the presence of the person being observed. Toddlers or young children may become aware of being under surveillance, and whether or not they change their behaviour as a result of noticing this, such an awareness may be uncomfortable or oppressive.

FOCUS

The suggested method of observing has implications for the organisation of the setting. What does it mean in terms of staff deployment? What would be the advantages of using this style of observation for staff development?

If this style of observation is new to you, plan to try it out as soon as possible. Then compare it with the last observation you made. What differences do you notice between the two? If possible, discuss your experiences in trying the two types of observation with a colleague who has also tried the new method.

FIND OUT MORE

Elfer, P 'Observation Matters' in Abbott, L and Langston, A (2005) *Birth to Three Matters*, Open University Press

Miller, L (2002) *Observation Observed: An Outline of the Nature and Practice of Infant Observation* (Videos and Booklet), The Tavistock Clinic Foundation (Tavistock Centre, 0207 435 7111)

Making an action plan

An action plan is a resolution to take some action; any good intention needs to be made a reality. The way to do this is to write down your intention, then to monitor how well you are succeeding in putting it into practice for a given length of time. Finally, you need to decide when you will check the impact of your new behaviour.

When you write an action plan, make sure you cover these points, summed up in the word **SMARTI**. Your plan must be:

◆ **Specific.** This means that you should not write 'I want to be a better practitioner.' Look at the **It is a skill to…** tasks you have done, or choose to work on other ideas you have read about. An example of a specific plan is: 'I will work on speaking to children about their emotions.'

◆ **Measurable.** Select how often you will attempt to measure your success. Perhaps you might decide to do this three times a day.

◆ **Achievable.** Be realistic. It might be better to decide to put your plan into action once a day, or twice a week, or to focus on only one child.

◆ **Resourced.** Think about the resources you will need. Will you need a colleague's help so that other children can be attended to, or a quiet place, or do you need to read more information before you begin? If so, specify what you need – which book, how and when it will be obtained, and how long you will give yourself to read it.

◆ **Timed.** Decide how long you will try out your resolution – perhaps a fortnight, or a month at most.

Finally, your plan must have:

◆ **Impact.** At the time you have set, decide what the impact of your initiative has been.

Conclusion

This chapter has discussed what respect means in relation to childcare. Respect is due to children because they are unique. A person's uniqueness derives from his or her temperament and the external forces at work.

Some of a carer's professional responsibilities in the light of this have been mentioned. The following skills have been highlighted.

◆ It is a skill to show respect to the children in a setting by planning opportunities allowing them to take appropriate responsibility for themselves.

◆ It is a skill to assess how much our practice allows us to show respect to children.

◆ It is a skill to analyse the way in which parents are treated.

◆ It is a skill to let all parents with children attending the setting see that they are respected.

◆ It is a skill to be aware of one's own habitual ways of responding.

◆ It is a skill to recognise the expectations we have of children.

◆ It is a skill to support children to learn to control their responses.

◆ It is a skill to recognise people's strengths.

◆ It is a skill to help a child to develop trust in the carers at the setting.

◆ It is a skill to be able to manage one's emotions.

◆ It is a skill to be aware of the prevalence and potency of gender stereotyping.

Chapter 2

How babies and young children learn

This chapter will examine how a child's brain develops and how adults can provide experiences that nurture the child's instinct to learn. It is written from the constructivist viewpoint, which respects a young child as an active learner who literally builds his or her own brain.

This chapter is divided into the following sections:

◆ The brain – how it grows and develops

◆ Babies' learning

◆ Sensory experiences for babies

◆ How thinking develops in toddlers

◆ Learning experiences for toddlers

◆ How thinking develops in 2- and 3-year-olds

◆ Learning experiences for 2- and 3-year-olds

◆ Barriers to learning

Babies and young children are constantly learning

Brains and learning

It is not unusual for many adults to think that babies have a sort of subhuman existence. They glance at babies who are unable to move about or talk, and think of them as existing in a state of passive waiting – waiting to be able to move around by themselves, waiting to be able to talk, waiting to be taught. The commonly held view is that after children achieve these milestones of walking and talking, they become more interesting. This is a sad misunderstanding. With the technology that is now available to us, a new picture is emerging of the very young baby's competence as a thinker and a learner. It is now obvious that it takes skilled and knowledgeable practitioners to meet the needs of these rapidly developing and vulnerable human beings. Parents with children of this age may need the support of capable and informed practitioners.

Just as a plant has an inner drive to grow, so a child has a drive to learn. A baby's capacity and energy for learning is phenomenal. Babies seem to realise that they need to learn about the world in which they find themselves and, totally undaunted, set about the task of doing so.

This is rather different from the conditions most adults associate with learning. Typically, adults have been led to think of learning as something that happens when we receive direct instruction from a person who knows things that we don't know. The instruction is usually given in a special place at a specific time. But learning also takes place when, for example, we meet a new acquaintance, or get to grips with a new job or a new washing machine or car. This independent type of learning happens through processing our own experience – it does not rely on an instructor. We are in charge, we rely on our senses and each of our actions brings about a change in our understanding.

Babies and very young children learn whenever they process input from their senses. They do not rely on an instructor. They learn anywhere, at any time, whenever they respond to an experience. As young people process their experiences, they are literally building their own minds. Feeding the brain with experiences and using it will make it grow stronger and more flexible. Starving the brain of experience will stop its development. It's as simple as that.

So what is the brain like, and how does it develop?

Every experience counts

The brain – how it grows and develops

It is very important for people who work with young children to realise that the period from conception to 3 years of age is extremely important for the development of the brain. The brain grows fastest in the first few years of life, and what happens in these early years affects the child's ability to learn throughout the rest of his or her life. The brain works harder at this stage than at any other period. In fact by the time they are three, children's brains are working twice as fast as those of adults. In these first 3 years the pathways between the sensory organs and the brain, and between one part of the brain and another, become firmly wired up and the connections made are available for further use. The more the connections are used, the faster the processing is done in the brain, and the speed of action, reaction, feeling and recognition increases.

The brain is central to every area of development. It controls our movements and our emotions, our ability to communicate and our responses to the environment. One area of development where learning is very apparent is the young child's increase in physical skills. At 3 months, a baby is clumsy and relatively immobile, but can lift his or her head. By the first birthday, a child can pick up a small object and may even be able to walk. By three, the child can walk and run, jump and balance.

The baby communicates eagerly and efficiently from birth, but not by using words. The 1-year-old is learning to talk. The 3-year-old is fluent. These developments are obvious to the observer. What is less obvious is that the brain begins developing in the womb and continues to do so for several years after birth.

Parts of the brain

The human brain co-ordinates the operations of every organ and tissue in the body. It is also the physical basis of all mental activities, consciousness, feelings and sensations, thinking, speech, memory, emotions, character and skills. It has three major parts: the brain stem, the mid-brain and the outer cortex or cerebrum. Each component is responsible for various functions.

◆ The **brain stem** develops first. It is sometimes called the old brain or the reptilian brain. This is the portion of the brain closest to the spinal cord. It is chiefly a relay station for the pathways between the higher parts of the brain and the rest of the body, and it is also responsible for regulating core bodily functions such as breathing, body temperature, heart rate, blood pressure and digestion. It controls eating and sleeping patterns. This part of the brain does not make decisions but it contains the amygdala, which instantly reacts to danger. It takes over when threats are sensed and it pumps adrenaline into the system to provide the power for either fight or flight. This part of the brain also includes the **cerebellum**, which is near the top of the spinal column controlling skilled muscular co-ordination, including balance, walking and articulation of the organs of speech. These are activities that require the co-ordination of a sequence of steps.

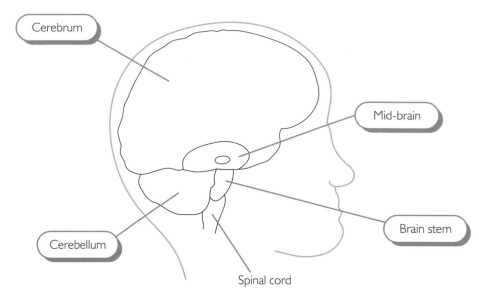

Cerebrum

Mid-brain

Cerebellum

Brain stem

Spinal cord

The major parts of the brain

◆ The second area is the **mid-brain**, sometimes called the mammalian brain, the emotional brain or the limbic system. It is where a person's long-term memory, habits, behaviours and memories of emotional experience are housed. These traits help to make people who they are. This part of the brain filters incoming information and decides whether to relay it up to the next level or down to the reflex response centre. This section of the brain bridges the areas above and below it. It can hold the emotions in check and consider alternative courses of action.

◆ The outer layer, the **cerebrum**, is the highest and most complex part of the brain. It is crucial for intellectual functioning, sensory perception and voluntary movement. It consists of two halves, the right and left cerebral hemispheres. The left hemisphere controls the right side of the body. The right hemisphere controls the left side of the body. The right and left hemispheres have different specialities. The left is more oriented to words and concepts and is used mainly for analytical thinking, speech, reading, sequencing and logic. In contrast the right cerebral hemisphere responds in a more holistic way and is more oriented to creativity, musical and spatial awareness, imagination and rhythm. It responds to the general feel of things, the whole picture. The two hemispheres are linked by the **corpus callosum**, which transfers learning from one side to the other. Scans show that the left hemisphere is the more active in language tasks and the right in maths and quantitative tasks. At birth the left hemisphere is more developed in females and the right in males. In males, language processing tends to be localised in the left hemisphere. Females use both hemispheres to process language.

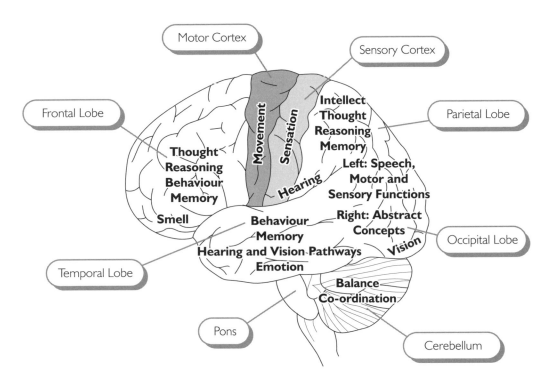

The brain viewed from the side

As you can see from the diagram of the brain, deep indentations divide each hemisphere into four lobes.

◆ The **frontal lobe** of each hemisphere controls voluntary muscle movements on the opposite side of the body. Other frontal lobe activities include intellectual functioning, especially for creativity and the organisation of ideas, thought processes, behaviour and memory.

◆ The **parietal lobe** receives and interprets sensations. These sensations include pain, touch, pressure and body part awareness, plus visual–spatial thinking. Other functions involving the parietal lobe are hearing, mathematical reasoning and memory.

◆ The **temporal lobe** is involved in the understanding of sounds and spoken words, as well as in emotion, memory and spatial organisation.

◆ The **occipital lobe** at the back of the head is involved in the understanding of visual images and in the interpretation of written words.

Development within the brain occurs at different times. For example, the occipital lobes, which deal with vision, mature well before the frontal lobes, which are concerned with functions such as planning and attention. These frontal lobes are still developing in adolescence.

The brain is made up of approximately 10 billion nerve cells, or **neurons**. Neurons are not like other cells. Like all cells they have a nucleus and a cell body. But neurons are unique among cells because they grow with extensions on opposite sides. On the incoming side the extensions are called **dendrites**. They are branching strands, which look rather like the roots of plants.

> **KEY TERM: Neurons**
>
> *Nerve cells that pass information from nerves, glands and muscles to the brain. The most important are those in the brain and in the spinal cord.*

> **KEY TERM: Dendrite**
>
> *In the brain, branching strands extending from one side of a neuron which receive information for that neuron across a synapse from the axons of a neuron nearby.*

At the other side of the cell the outgoing extension is called an **axon,** and it is more like a single strand, which can be quite long.

> **KEY TERM: Axon**
>
> *A strand in the brain extending from the neuron, which carries information out from the nerve cell.*

It is covered with a sheath of a white substance called **myelin** which is both a protection and a food, so that it speeds the passage of information from one cell to another.

> **KEY TERM: Myelin**
>
> *A white substance coating the axon which speeds the flow of information from one neuron to another in the brain.*

The axons do not quite touch the dendrites of the next cell. The axons and the dendrites are separated by fluid-filled gaps called **synapses**.

> **KEY TERM: Synapses**
>
> *In the brain, junctions or fluid-filled gaps between dendrites of one neuron and the axon of another. Information is passed from cell to cell by chemical activity in this fluid. Those synapses that are frequently used grow in size.*

Chemicals called **neurotransmitters** transmit electrical activity from one cell to another across the synapse.

KEY TERM: Neurotransmitter

A chemical substance released to aid the transmission of messages across synapses from nerves, glands and muscles to the brain. It usually works in the presence of substances released either by hormones or the endocrine glands.

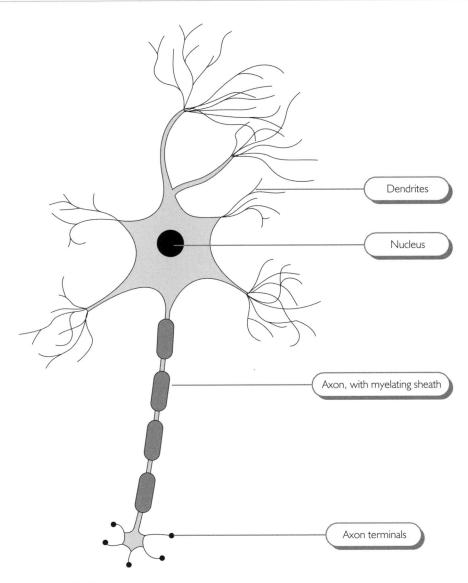

A neuron with its dendrites and axons

The outer layer of the cerebrum is covered with a layer of grey matter, known as the **cerebral cortex**. This covering of the brain develops last, and continues to develop through childhood. It is literally the thinking cap – a thin sheet of grey matter 3 mm thick, folded in on itself, which covers the brain and controls the higher-level brain functions. It is crucial for the functioning of the senses, language, memory and thought. It also controls decision-making and planning. It has more than 40 functional areas.

It can be visualised as a fisherman's net made of horizontal and vertical cords knotted together at the intersections. The intersections are the synapses. The synapses (or junctions) that are most often used increase in size. Their increased size accounts for the increase in weight of the child's brain by the age of two.

FOCUS

You will have noticed from the brief description above how many parts of the brain are concerned with the emotions. The effective development of emotional reactions is intricately linked to general brain development. Jean Piaget, the first to trace in detail the development of thinking from birth to maturity, regretted that usually psychologists tended to keep their discussions of thinking and emotions separate. He said that it was impossible to think without feeling and impossible to feel without thinking.

How the brain develops

During pregnancy the baby's brain grows faster than any other part of the body. In the first stage of its development the brain begins as a hollow tube and the neurons are generated along its inner walls. Between the sixteenth and twenty-fourth weeks of pregnancy the weight of the baby's brain increases fourfold, and there is a surge in cell production. Most of the 10 billion neurons that make up the brain are produced between 10 and 26 weeks after conception, at the rate of about 250,000 a minute. They are to last a lifetime, because neurons are not produced after this time.

Once the neurons have been produced near the centre of the brain, they have to migrate to their specific locations. By the third month of pregnancy the brain is already organised into the functional subdivisions of seeing, hearing, touch, smell and thinking. Scientists do not yet understand how the neurons know where they have to go, but cell migration is complete by the seventh month of pregnancy.

When the neuron has found its home, the third stage of brain development begins. This stage is called cell elaboration, and at this time axons and dendrites form synapses with other cells. In the last three months of pregnancy the brain demands increasing amounts of resources – it uses a third of all the baby's calories and oxygen as the areas that control memory and language start to grow. Towards the end of pregnancy, the cells that will eventually control consciousness and judgement also begin to grow.

This process of linking neuron to neuron continues for years after birth, but those pathways that are left unused appear to wither away. Scientists treating babies born with cataracts find that the children never learn to see properly, unlike adults whose sight is restored when cataracts are removed. The brain cells linked to the eye all have specific functions: some cells respond to vertical edges; some react to horizontal edges; some 'like' angles or diagonal lines. They need to learn to fire in synchronism so that the eye can see a box as one object. The time in which the cells can learn to act in unison in this way is short.

> ## CASE STUDY:
> ### GENIE
>
> Russ Rymer tells the story of Genie, a sad instance of the brain losing cells that are not used at the vital time. Genie was a child who, from the age of 18 months until she was rescued at 13, was kept by her parents locked away from human contact and auditory stimulation. Despite intensive instruction after her rescue, she never developed competence in language. However, her right brain made up for this. She could pick up the feel of a situation and make her desires and feelings known without a word.

Other windows of opportunity that close early are those for emotional control and habitual ways of responding (this happens by around the age of two). Is the child's general approach to life to be one of openness and confidence, or wariness, or resentment? The possibility of easily grasping the concept that there is value and interest in the use of symbols (that is using words, learning the purpose of writing or numerals, 'reading' pictures, interpreting the emotions caught in music and dance) begins to lessen when the child is about three. The ability to learn another language with ease fades at about four.

Learning before birth

The eyes, ears, skin and spinal cord of the foetus develop early. At just 7 weeks into pregnancy, the nerve connections between the brain and the muscles are complete and the foetus can be seen gently moving its arms and legs. At first the whole body moves, but just 3 weeks later the baby can move the hands on their own. At 16 weeks the baby can turn somersaults. The kicking that the mother feels at about 20 weeks indicates that the baby is capable of controlling the limbs. This control over movement is a significant indication of how much development has taken place over these 3 months.

The first working components to develop inside the brain are the ones that manage basic needs such as hunger, thirst and sleep. From 26 weeks it becomes possible to discern distinct patterns of waking and sleeping states in the foetus – patterns that repeat about once every 40 minutes. At 32 weeks it is possible to distinguish between the two types of sleep, active sleep with rapid eye movement (REM) and non-REM sleep (quiet, deep sleep). In the next few weeks of the pregnancy, researchers can also discern states of drowsiness as well as deep sleep, shallower sleep and active alertness.

At 28 weeks of gestation, the baby opens his or her eyes and starts to see. If at this time a bright light is shone onto the mother's abdomen, the baby inside the womb will respond by an increased heart rate and perhaps by moving around. But babies are also observed opening and closing their eyes when there is no extra light.

We know that the baby begins to be able to distinguish sounds about the twentieth week.

CASE STUDY:
LEILA'S PREGNANCY

Leila writes:

I had heard of the many widely reported benefits of exposing babies to music both before and after birth; therefore at the earliest stage of pregnancy my radio alarm clock was placed on my 'bump' and the sounds of Classic FM provided a constant bombardment. This provided much amusement when, after the twentieth week, the radio would jump up and down as the baby kicked, I hoped with enjoyment.

Straight after birth, newborn babies provide evidence that they have been learning. They show that they recognise their mother's voice. If they have heard a piece of music, story or poem regularly (played to them about twice a day, in the last 2 months of pregnancy) they respond to these sounds after birth and can be soothed by the familiar music.

Babies' responses can go beyond merely finding comfort in sound. Tessa Livingstone (2005 page 56) reports that 2 weeks before a baby was born, a functional magnetic resonance imaging (fMRI) scan, which shows which areas of the brain are active in response to a certain stimulus, showed not only that the hearing areas of the brain were active when the baby in the womb was hearing a familiar story being read, but that there was also activity in the frontal cortex, which is the area of attention and consideration. So the child has been learning before birth.

KEY TERM: MRI scan

A medical scan making use of the properties of magnetism to look at areas of activity within the body's tissues.

By the time the baby is born, the brain has grown to be a quarter of the size of an adult's. In contrast, the baby's whole body is only about 5 per cent of the adult weight. After birth, the child's brain continues growing rapidly.

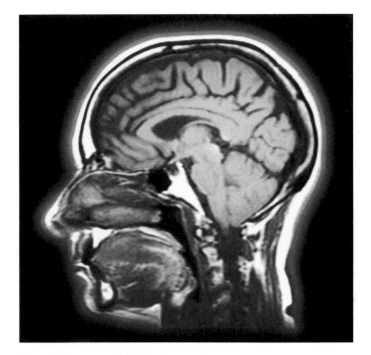

Brain scans can tell us which parts of the brain are active

Babies' learning

At birth the child is using two different neural systems. The reflexes of sucking, crying, breathing and temperature regulation (sometimes called the experience-expectant system) are already established at birth. Other neural pathways (which are sometimes labelled the experience-dependent system) emerge according to the sensory experiences the child processes. The connections of this system are acquired slowly and will continue to develop through life according to a person's lifestyle.

CASE STUDY:
LONDON CABBIES

An example of the development of neural pathways is what happens to the brains of London taxi drivers. Before they can be licensed, London cabbies must learn 'the Knowledge' – they must prove that they know their way around all the streets of the capital so that they will always choose the most efficient route. Scans of their brains show that the part of the brain dealing with spatial relationships is far more developed in them than in other people.

Another instance is that when the eminent physicist Albert Einstein's preserved brain was examined it was found that his parietal lobe was 15 per cent wider than those of men who had died at a similar age.

Several techniques have been developed that enable scientists to know more about the growth and activity of the brain. By using the images from scans and electron microscopes, scientists can now see the functioning of a newborn baby's brain. It is now a simple matter to use apparatus to time how long babies spend looking at a stimulus. That's how we can discover what babies find interesting. It is also possible to monitor babies' heart rates to measure their interest in particular features.

Another technique is to give the baby a pressure-sensing dummy. The baby sucks on the dummy and finds that it can produce an interesting sight or sound. If the stimulus is switched off for a moment, the baby can call it back by sucking harder. A similar technique is to put a pressure-sensitive pad under the baby's pillow. The pad can be set so that by turning the head in a particular direction the baby can call up a stimulus that interests him or her. Using these methods, scientists have discovered babies' responses, their preferences and how they think. We are sure that the child learns and remembers from a very early stage.

What interests babies?

We now know that newborn babies have definite visual preferences. Scientists studying what babies pay attention to have found that young babies prefer patterned to plain surfaces, and solid rather than two-dimensional objects. Babies are more interested in things that move rather than in stationary things. They like high-contrast rather than low-contrast colours, prefer curves to straight lines, and symmetrical rather than asymmetrical stimuli. Babies are very interested in edges and boundaries.

From birth, babies are interested in the human face. The researcher R. L. Fantz showed newborn babies three stimuli – a picture of a face, a picture of a 'scrambled' face, and an abstract shape. The children looked longest at the recognisable face. This response appears to be a reflex action based on the primitive parts of the brain; responding to a human face obviously helps to ensure a child's survival. The higher functions of the brain which develop at about 2–3 months after birth enable the child to notice differences and so to recognise individual faces.

Face   Scrambled face   Abstract shape

The stimuli used by Fantz

The type of sound most likely to attract a newborn's attention is the human voice. Among voices, newborns prefer the voices of adult females. They prefer their mother's voice to a stranger's. In one study, if the babies were given a choice between the sound of their mother speaking on a normal tape recording or their mother speaking on a tape that had been doctored to imitate the way it would have been heard in the womb, they went for the 'inside the womb' version. In another study, at the age of 2 days, children born to English-speaking or Spanish-speaking mothers heard samples of both languages. They preferred to listen to their mother's language.

Neural pathways

As the child experiences the world, messages pass through the brain from dendrites to axons so that neural pathways are set up. At 6 months the child's brain has doubled in weight and has become half the weight of an adult's – something the baby's body as a whole does not do until the child is aged about ten. This growth in weight is not the result of an increase in neurons but is entirely due to the growth of the connections (synapses) between neurons. By the time the child is two, any single neuron may have connections to 10,000 other cells. But many remain unused. Around this age a 'pruning' process takes place which eliminates those synapses that are not required by the individual, and the pathways are reorganised to fit in with the living patterns of the child.

In the first months of life the child learns about the people he or she is in contact with. The baby becomes familiar with the routines of feeding, sleeping and being changed and cared for. The baby is talked to, hears music, and shares the pleasure of books. He or she may notice the difference between night and day, and learns through the sense of touch that some of the things are soft, others are hard; some things are rough, others are smooth. Young babies have to get to know everything around them through their senses of taste, touch, smell, sight and hearing.

FOCUS

The first two years of life have been named the **sensorimotor stage**. This word reflects Piaget's observation that what children at this stage learn comes into their brains through their senses of sight and hearing as they watch and listen, and through the way they act on their environment by sucking, grasping, biting, smelling, touching and feeling the objects that surround them.

KEY TERM: Sensorimotor stage

Jean Piaget's name for the way the child operates in the first two years of life. It is the time when the baby or toddler gathers information through the senses of taste, smell, touch, sight and hearing, and through his or her actions.

Exploring by touch and sight

Thinking in babyhood

Learning depends on fixing and reflecting on experiences. It depends on remembering and then organising the experiences into groups so they can be dealt with more easily.

How long can babies remember? Care-giving routines are initially organised by the adult in response to the baby's rhythms, but by end of the first year the baby makes a contribution to them, showing that he or she has internalised the routine, and remembers sequences such as the game of Peekaboo or Peep-o. Ross Vasta reports studies showing that after a 2-week gap, a child of 5 months can recognise a photograph of a face that had initially been viewed for only 2 minutes. Babies who were only 3 months old at the age of exposure still remembered a moving stimulus after 3 months.

Carolyn Rovee-Collier reported an experiment in which a ribbon was attached to a baby's ankle and to the mobile above the cot. Kicking gave the baby the power to make the mobile jump. At 2 months the baby remembered what had to be done to make the mobile jump 3 days later. At 3 months the memory was alive for 8 days, and at 6 months it was recalled after 3 weeks.

By the time they are 12 months old most children show that they can remember permanent locations of familiar and valued objects. At 12 months they can remember sequences of three items or steps, for example bathing a doll (place the doll in a bowl, wash it with a sponge, dry it). By the time they are 2 years old they remember five actions. At 30 months they can carry an eight-step sequence in their heads.

Learning also depends on the ability to make connections and to develop categories.

Grouping ideas into categories by linking similar things together makes thinking more efficient. Piaget used the word **assimilation** to describe the process of noticing that the event or the experience can be fitted into an existing category. For example, we categorise the elements of our world into two large categories, animate and inanimate – things that have life and things that do not. We have a category called clothing, and we can divide it into indoor and outdoor clothing, clothes for work and clothes for leisure.

> **KEY TERM:** Assimilation
>
> *Named by Jean Piaget, the process of recognising a similarity and allocating a new object easily into an already existing category.*

Piaget used the word **accommodation** to describe the situation where the experience does not exactly fit in to an existing category and the category has to be redefined.

> **KEY TERM:** Accommodation
>
> *The word given by Jean Piaget to the process of having to take account of an example not exactly similar to those you already have. This leads you to adjust your mental categories.*

REFLECT ON YOUR PRACTICE

It is a skill to encourage the process of accommodation.

An example would be the category of *dogs*. All the four-legged creatures we meet that have hair, that bark, respond to whistles and are led about on leads are put into this category. If a child comes across a type of dog that has no hair or cannot bark he or she will have to use the process of accommodation to extend the *dogs* category.

This ability to develop categories is evident in very young children. If infants at about 3 months are shown a series of pictures of animals, they will show surprise when a picture of a piece of furniture is included in the sequence. There appears to be an internal category of living things and inanimate things.

By 4 months, if babies have been shown a series of pictures of dogs, they will look longer at a picture of a bird when it is shown. The baby is recognising categories within living creatures.

This capacity to form categories develops over time. Between 12 and 24 months, if children have been shown a series of pictures of various kinds of food and then are given the choice of seeing an apple or a chair, they will look longer at the picture of the chair because it is a member of what they realise is another category.

Developing a wider perspective

Through his or her experiences in the first 2 years of life (the years of the sensorimotor stage) the child moves from treating each item or event as a one-off, self-contained item to being able to link situations together and to see events and situations in a wider perspective.

Piaget tracked this development, from the baby's focus on the immediate environment to the ability to consider a wider perspective. He was a trained scientist and he started to use his observational skills to record the mental development of his own children. He noticed that their development proceeded through several increasingly complicated stages before the age of two.

The steps in this expansion of experience and comprehension identified by Piaget were as follows.

Sub stage 1: 0–1 month

At this stage the child is exercising reflexes, that is inborn responses. These responses include sucking and grasping. The newborn suckles when a nipple rubs across the lips or grasps when an object grazes the palm. At first a very young baby will grasp an object only if his or her hand comes into contact with it. No attempt is made to move the object or to look at it.

Sub stage 2: 1–4 months

The child now develops these basic reflex actions into schemas that can be used with skill in a range of situations. For example, the child can be seen adapting the grasp to use it for different purposes. The grasp used for holding a rattle will be modified for holding a finger or a toy. At this time also, separate movements begin to be co-ordinated – the child can look at an object and then move to grasp it.

Sub stage 3: 4–8 months

Now the child is discovering procedures and paying more attention to exploring the environment. At this stage the child is more interested in the toy being grasped than in the act of grasping it. The child may discover that a particular action brings about an interesting result, and so will repeat the action.

Sub stage 4: 8–12 months

This is the stage when intentional behaviour becomes evident. The child can be seen deliberately taking action to bring about an intended outcome. This development shows us that now the child is able to hold two ideas in the mind simultaneously. For example, babies will realise that they need to move an object aside if they want to reach a toy they know is behind it. In doing this they have to think simultaneously about their **purpose** (to get the toy) and envisage the **means** or method of doing this.

Encouraging brain development in babies

Babies need to be given lots of opportunities to explore their surroundings. Being able to touch things and use their senses of taste, smell, sight and hearing not only expands their knowledge of the world they live in, but at the same time it has the effect of activating and strengthening the neural pathways in the brain.

Sensory experiences for babies

Babies are born with the senses of taste, touch and smell well developed.

Taste

An ultrasound scan late in pregnancy will show a baby opening and closing the mouth. The baby is drinking **amniotic fluid**, and by the end of pregnancy may drink 4 pints a day. Amniotic fluid has the same sweet taste as milk and it is not surprising that babies are born liking the taste of a sweet, warm solution. Vasta reports research with newborns which showed that at 2 hours, newborn babies make different expressions when they taste sweet and non-sweet fluids, and they can also differentiate between sour, bitter and salty tastes.

> **KEY TERM: Amniotic fluid**
>
> *The fluid that surrounds the foetus in the womb.*

This implies that children come into the world with established likes and dislikes about food. In some cases this may be caused by having been exposed to strong-tasting foods in the womb, thus establishing a preference for certain flavours.

It is also known that some people are endowed with more taste buds than others. About 25 per cent of the population are very sensitive to strong tastes and the feel that food has in their mouths; consequently their diets are often more limited. At the other end of the spectrum, another quarter of the population can eat almost anything. The advantage for these people is that their diet can be very varied. The rest of us are in between.

After about 4 months, babies may be gently introduced to a range of flavours, and later to a range of textures of foods.

Smell

This sense is very well developed from birth. As adults we make less conscious use of this sense, although you may have noticed that a scent can powerfully evoke a memory, or that when we have a cold we cannot taste our food.

Newborns definitely respond to smells. They will turn their head away from an unpleasant smell. At 3 days old, infants respond to a pad moistened with their mother's amniotic fluid rather than another woman's. At 6 days old they turn more to their mother's breast pad than another woman's.

FOCUS

The implication of this is that we should pay more attention to the smell of the setting and the linen used for babies. Consider providing oils in a burner and use aromatic cloves or oranges to scent the room. Grow lavender, thyme or mint outside and make sure the babies are able to get near them in the summer. For indoors, make a scented mobile (scented cotton wool balls or lavender bags inside socks hung above the cot, within the baby's reach and on elastic so that the child can grasp them). It is very important to avoid synthetic scents or air fresheners in the room and to avoid strongly-scented washing powders.

Touch

The baby in the womb responds to touch as early as the second month following conception, and touch sensitivity increases over the first days after birth. A baby can feel even the gentlest stroke. The touch receptors are spread more liberally across the skin than an adult's, but they are not as precise in their response. The neural pathways are still in the process of being wired up. However, it is clear both that a baby feels pain and that touch comforts a crying baby. The use of touch is vital for the social interaction the baby craves. For older infants, touching increases positive emotional reactions and reinforces visual response to the care-giver.

FOCUS

Babies use touch to explore the environment. They can feel the shape of things more easily with their mouths than with their hands, because the nerve endings in the mouth are more sensitive than the finger pads. It is natural for babies to want to explore objects by using their most sensitive parts – their mouths and hands. Care should be taken to keep sharp-edged objects, or small objects that could cause choking, well out of reach.

Exploring using the mouth

Babies rely on touch for healthy development. **Baby massage** (from birth to about 18 months) has been used for centuries in the East to promote good health and prevent disease. It is said to aid digestion and elimination and encourages muscular co-ordination and joint flexibility. In the West, where it was introduced in the 1990s, baby massage is more prized for its psychological effects. It reduces tension, restlessness and irritability in the baby. It relaxes the child and promotes deeper and longer sleeps. The close physical contact promotes the baby's emotional and mental growth; the baby has the experience of being cared for, loved and respected.

> **KEY TERM:** Baby massage
>
> *Used with babies under 18 months to soothe them with gentle touches. Some believe it aids their digestion.*

Baby massage aids the parents too. The parents talk gently to the baby throughout the session and feel closer to the child as they see how well he or she responds to the experience. Parents may be helped by having the opportunity to be instructed in baby massage and being told about a CD called *Mother and Baby* (www.newworldmusic.com).

FOCUS

Babies should be touched lovingly. Touching can be used to soothe or to stimulate – play gentle tickling games such as 'This little piggy or 'All around the garden'. Rhythmic verbal communication should accompany the touching. Think about making tactile floor mats using corduroy or furry fabrics. Buy feely books – or make them yourself using emery paper, sand paper, card and corrugated paper as well as fabrics such as silk, velvet, suede, fleece, artificial fur, blankets or towelling.

Hearing

It is known that babies like being talked to gently. They focus well on sounds that fall within the frequency range of the human voice. They don't like noises that are too loud. On the other hand, unlike adults, they can't hear whispers from about 4 feet away.

The baby's ability to localise sounds is present at birth and then fades somewhat, to reappear in a more efficient way at about 4 months. This ability becomes more precise during the first 18 months of life.

Babies enjoy being sung to. They prefer lullabies to other songs, and according to S. E. Trehub and J. Henderson can tell the difference between a lullaby and an adult-focused song, even when these are from another culture. Don Campbell (2002 page 178) reports that infants as young as 2 months are able to match the pitch, loudness and melodic contours of their mother's songs. Babies are intrigued by varying rhythms, whether in music or other improvised sounds or the language of **nursery rhymes**.

FOCUS

Besides talking and singing to the child, carers should also soothe babies and every carer should have a repertoire of at least three lullabies.

Other ways to feed the baby's interest in sounds include hanging wind chimes of wood or metal near an open window. Rattles and shakers engage a baby's attention. These may be bought or improvised – for example by putting grains of rice, dried peas or lentils in a small container, such as the container of film for a camera. Each makes a different sound. Babies pay attention to the intensity (loudness), frequency (pitch), and duration of sounds. Sounds presented to the baby should enable this power of discrimination to be practised in each of the three dimensions. Musical 'wallpaper' from a radio station does not always allow this to happen, because babies need to have adult interaction as they listen.

Classic FM produced a CD called *Music for Babies* in 2005.

Sight

Babies are attracted by light and movement. They like colours, and they like strong contrasts such as black and white.

FOCUS

Practitioners should think of their lighting and colour schemes. Consider having some stained glass or light catchers in the windows. Utilise the movement of mobiles, and net curtains at an open window. Provide bubble lamps and real bubbles, and play tracking games with a young baby. Install mirrors above the changing table and at floor level for babies who are able to crawl. Out of doors, provide the baby with the opportunity of watching the movement of leaves and branches, people passing, traffic going by.

CASE STUDY:

BABY AND TODDLER UNITS IN REGGIO EMILIA

Reggio Emilia is a town in the north of Italy that has earned world-wide respect for its provision for its children up to the age of six (when children in Italy begin formal schooling). Here are four accounts of the provision for babies in nurseries at Reggio, written by practitioners who have visited. They all visited different settings, and at different times, but the Reggio style shines through.

Panyin writes:

The first thought that came into my mind on entering the baby room was 'lack of clutter'. It was a spacious environment with minimal storage units. The resources available for the children were accessible at the children's level, allowing them to make their own decisions and choices. It was bright and clean, yet it did not have a clinical appearance. There was a warm, inviting and welcoming aura to the room.

I was most impressed by the abundance of mirrors, lights and resources to encourage the babies to investigate and explore. There were no barriers to deter the children from exploring. The babies' own natural instincts appeared to act as an inborn barrier. They seemed to recognise their own safe limitations even at an early stage. The baby room gave me the impression of a room designed with much research behind the planning, to allow the children freedom of movement and the opportunity to investigate without restricting their need to explore.

I began to question our own need in this country to put up barriers to our children's development in the name of safety.

Inger writes:

The first thing I noticed was the light. There were views of plants outdoors at the children's level; the light was filtered by blinds at the window. Blinds, either cloth or made of natural materials, were coming from the ceiling at different angles, making variation in the light all around the very plain, calm room. Sources of electric light were also available in the room – a light table, a projector, a reading lamp and an overhead projector.

Enhancing all this, the room had mirrors at child level so it became quite a different environment in each corner. The ceiling was unusual but so was the floor; in one corner there were really chunky turquoise-covered foam shapes as a soft play area for the babies to roll around and explore; in another, an area of cool marble tiles. Other areas were carpeted and along one wall, beneath a worktop, there were curtains that could be opened or drawn back to create a couple of dens or Peekaboo places. The sleeping area was created by having very large, low-walled baskets on the floor with entry gaps like the ones on dog baskets so that the babies could crawl into them when they wanted to sleep. Each one had the baby's photograph on it.

The equipment consisted of mobiles; natural objects; rattles and drums; soft, hard, rough objects. There were comfortable chairs for an adult and child to sit together, a mirror above the changing mat and cupboards for a small, plain home corner.

Emily writes:

When I entered the baby unit the first thing I noticed was the soothing environment with a vast amount of natural lighting and space. Within the unit there was a large hanging hammock which unusually created a harmonious and home-like feel. The babies had space to gradually gain mastery over their own bodies and to be able to move freely.

The walls had varying shades of calm colours which looked slightly bare; this is done so that the best balance is reached when the space is inhabited. Cots and sleep resources were in a separate room within the unit. There appeared to be only a couple of room dividers which also doubled up as shelves to hold the treasure baskets and a book display cabinet.

The unit provided plenty of sensory stimulation. This is more important in babyhood than any other time. There were treasure baskets that contained a variety of objects for tactile exploration, and mirrors to give the babies the opportunity to become aware of who they are. On the walls and floor there were tactile things to give babies the chance to feel things with their hands and feet.

Equipment was available for climbing, pushing and pulling. Within the area there was only one small child-sized table and set of chairs.

This very different and unique baby unit left a big impression on me.

Catrin writes:

As an English early years practitioner I was amazed by the lack of colourful toys, bright paintwork and the general clutter we tend to have in settings in Britain. In Reggio Emilia the rooms are light, airy and spacious and they give the babies opportunities to explore and discover in an interesting but safe environment. The light levels and general use of light are an integral part of the Reggio baby rooms. Some areas of the room are darker than others. Children who are mobile can move in and out of these areas as they wish. There are also 'dens' they can choose to hide in if they wish.

Treasure baskets

Treasure baskets were suggested by Elinor Goldschmeid for those babies who can sit up but who are not yet mobile. The treasure basket is intended to give the child a rich range of sensory experiences that will stimulate the growing brain.

Babies enjoy and learn from treasure baskets

KEY TERM: Treasure basket

A low, handle-less basket filled with a variety of natural and everyday objects for a sitting or supported baby to explore.

FOCUS

The intention of the treasure basket is to allow babies to explore the materials we use in daily life. You will need a shallow basket within the baby's reach. The basket should be without handles or sharp edges. Each child should have one, or at the very most one may be shared between two babies. The contents of the basket need to be changed from time to time, and since everything goes to the mouth at this age, the materials need to be kept hygienic as well as being checked for safety – no sharp edges, nothing that might be swallowed, nothing painted or breakable.

The basket should contain only objects made from natural materials. The reason for explicitly excluding plastic is that all plastic objects feel the same and there is little variation in weight.

To use the treasure baskets clear the floor, put the babies on a rug, prop them up with cushions if necessary and allow them to explore the contents of the basket until they want to stop. The adult needs to remain close by, but should refrain from interacting with them and breaking their concentration. This is a good time to make an observation of a child.

Items for a treasure basket

Objects from nature	Wooden objects	Metal objects	Leather, fabrics
Large pebbles, a piece of pumice stone, a piece of loofah, a small natural sponge, avocado pear stones, large chestnuts, large walnuts Bone spoon, bone napkin ring, bone egg cup, bone shoe horn Big feathers Coloured marble eggs Small brushes – a toothbrush, a nail brush, a blusher brush, a shaving brush	Egg cup, curtain ring, napkin ring, bobbin cotton reel, wooden spoon, peg Small turned bowl, small boxes Coloured beads safely on a string, wooden cubes, cylinders, rods	Spoons, keys on a ring, bangle, costume jewellery chain, small bells, rattles, tin lids, tea strainer, tea infuser, small closed tins to shake (containing rice, pebbles, dried pulses), a bottle brush, a small whisk, brass curtain rings, bath plug with chain, a small hand mirror	Small rag doll, small teddy, leather purse Swatches of silk or velvet, fake fur Small cloth bags containing cloves, lavender, rosemary or thyme Tennis ball, golf ball, a ball made of fake fur, woollen pom-poms

A treasure basket

REFLECT ON YOUR PRACTICE

It is a skill to provide a full range of opportunities for babies to develop their brains through sensory experiences in the childcare setting.

Go through each sense in turn, answering the following questions in relation to each child:

◆ What resources exist?

◆ Are these resources available at an appropriate level for the child in one-to-one situations in each session?

◆ What is recorded about the child's response?

◆ Are these records shared with colleagues?

◆ Are they shared with the parents?

It is a skill to support the child in his or her learning by providing a treasure basket.

List at least four words that you as an adult would use to describe (not just label) each item in your treasure basket. It may be helpful if you think of each sense in turn and see whether a word occurs to you in relation to it.

How often are the treasure baskets available? Is there a variation in the contents of each basket? How often are observations recorded about each child at the treasure basket?

FIND OUT MORE

Campbell, D (2002) *The Mozart Effect*, Hodder and Stoughton

Goldschmeid, E and Jackson, S (1994) *People Under Three: Young Children in Day Care*, Routledge

McGuinness, H (2003) *Baby Massage*, Hodder and Stoughton

How thinking develops in toddlers

When children become mobile, towards the end of their first year of life, their field of experience widens further. In their second year of life, toddlers have a great drive to use their new mobility to explore their environment. The more toddlers explore and experiment, the more they understand and the more effective they feel.

Piaget called the period from 12–18 months the stage of novelty and exploration. At this time the child experiments for the sheer delight of experimentation, for example dropping a spoon from a high chair in several different ways. The child deliberately tries out new behaviours to create new effects.

Children at this exciting stage begin to connect cause and effect. They are fascinated by switches, taps, door handles, and the placing of objects in and out of containers. They recognise sequences of actions – laying the table means food, preparing the buggy means going out.

Children now begin to build an understanding that although an object may look different from different angles, it still remains the same object. Crawling round a table or armchair enables the child to see it from different angles and to realise that the different views still reveal the same object. This realisation that objects can be viewed from different angles and still retain their identity makes for more efficient mental processing, and redundant neural pathways can be pruned.

FOCUS

At this time the setting must offer plenty of opportunities to explore materials and their properties. **Heuristic play** was developed by Goldschmeid. The word *heuristic* comes from the Greek word for discovery. The intention of heuristic play is to allow toddlers (children who can walk but are still acquiring speech) the opportunity not only to explore the properties of the materials we use in everyday life (as they did in their sessions with the treasure basket), but also to investigate the similarities and differences of a collection of objects and the way these objects and materials behave. Are they made of the same material? Do they stack? Do they roll? Can they be poured?

KEY TERM: Heuristic play

Sessions recommended by Elinor Goldschmeid to enable toddlers to examine the properties of a range of materials.

Preparing for heuristic play sessions

In preparing for heuristic play sessions, care is taken to provide a range of types of object that will support the toddler's developing discrimination and ability to see similarities. A child may want to make a collection of similar shapes or of things made of the same material. The child may want to see whether the same action can be applied to every object.

The collection should also include objects that may be combined. For example, a child may place pegs round the rim of a container. The purpose may be to place objects beside each other, inside each other or on top of each other. In heuristic play the child is completely in control as he or she tests out and expands the range of categories. While engaged in this type of learning there is no one directing the child's attention. Children are actively learning at their own pace and there is no fear of failure.

Prepare a carpeted empty area without distractions during the half-hour session. Prepare between 20 and 50 cloth bags, each about half the size of a pillow case, one for each of your types of objects or materials. To avoid conflicts, each bag should contain about 50 identical items – or near identical in the case of keys, napkin rings or shells. Vary the experiences the children can have by putting out a different selection of your collection of bags each session. The children will need containers of various shapes for their collections of the objects that interest them. These containers may include small baskets, empty catering-size jam jars or coffee tins, plastic containers (such as margarine or ice-cream boxes), cylindrical containers (such as empty containers for bottles of spirits), plus cylinders that will allow things to pass things through them – kitchen roll centres, or rolls that have held cloth or carpets. Children may need more than one container during the session; allow sufficient containers for each child to have three.

Bags may contain natural or man-made materials, things that make sounds, things that roll or things that move in an interesting way. For example, a child might notice the difference between the movement of ribbons, chains and a length of tubing as they are held or shaken, or the difference between spheres, cones and irregular shapes.

Contents for the bags could include the following.

◆ Collections of unused winemakers' corks, wooden pegs, plastic clip pegs, wooden curtain rings, napkin rings, bobbins, spools, brass curtain rings, bottle tops, keys, spoons, tin lids, shakers, ash trays, hair rollers

◆ Balls made of crunched silver foil, woollen pom-poms, plastic spheres for the slow release of soap powder in washing machines, baubles, large marbles, pine cones, nuts in their shells

◆ Scraps of cloth of various types, pieces of leather or fake fur, scarves, transparent and translucent materials, lace

◆ Lengths of coloured ribbons, lengths of chain (fine and stronger), longer and shorter strings of beads, coils, tubing

◆ Large feathers, shells, pine cones, largish pieces of tumbled stones

◆ Plastic containers for reels of film, small boxes, purses of different types, small transparent or opaque bags, net containers

◆ A collection of small cylinders and cones

◆ Small brushes, pan scrubbers, sponges

◆ Sound sources – a whistle, a pair of unpainted castanets, a tambourine, small bells, small drum, scraper, small rain stick

In these sessions the empty carpeted area or room is prepared with the contents of the selected bags emptied out. They are left in heaps on the floor with as much space as possible between the heaps. The adult sits in a comfortable chair at the edge of the room. The adult encourages the children with evident attention but does not interact with them unless they approach. The adult does not speak to the children about what they are doing – the words would distract them from their own exploration and discovery. This appears hard at first for many practitioners, but this self-restraint is necessary for these intensive sessions.

At times the adult may unobtrusively re-order the materials if they have become too scattered. At the end of the session the adult encourages the children to replace the materials in the appropriate bags. It is also useful to have a large cardboard box to hand in case a child begins to kick or throw the materials about; this disruptive activity may be redirected to the more purposeful one of placing items in the box.

In these sessions there is often very little interaction between the children, but their actions give an interesting insight into the growth of their mental categorisations, their concentration span and their interests. One of these sessions is a good opportunity for a key worker to make an observation of a child.

Object permanence

An important development in young children's thinking powers emerges during the months covered by Piaget's sub stages 3 and 4 (from 4 months to about 12 months). The process of developing the notion of **object permanence**, which began in babyhood, continues into toddlerhood. It is important for a child to come to an awareness that we as adults take very much for granted – that objects continue to exist even when they are out of sight.

This understanding has to be constructed by each child through his or her own experience. If a 2-month-old lets go of a toy and it rolls out of sight, he or she will behave as if the toy no longer exists; out of sight is out of mind. At this age if a child is looking at an apple and sees you cover the apple with a cloth, the child will not look for the apple under the cloth.

A few weeks later, some time around 4–8 months, the child will recover an object if it is *partially* covered by a cloth. In the earliest part of this stage, most of the object has to be visible. Later the child can cope when far less is seen. Between 6 and 12 months the child is able to recover an object that he or she has watched being completely hidden under a cloth.

On the way to the stage of finding the object no matter where or how it has been hidden, children go through a further intermediate stage. This is usually between 12 and 18 months, when if the child has been successful in finding a hidden object and then sees it being hidden again, and also sees that the adult goes on to move the hiding place, he or she will only look for it where it was first hidden. This is known as an A-not-B error. From the children's point of view it is logical to go to the place where they know they found the object last time. However, when a child has fully grasped the notion of object permanence (usually about the age of 18 months), you cannot trick him or her even if you move the concealed object (for example a coin in your closed hand) from one hiding place to another. The child can think about the object when it is not visible. Problem-solving can now happen internally.

The fact that objects continue to exist even when they are out of sight. Adults take this idea for granted. Jean Piaget traced the way the idea gradually dawns on the child, usually between 6 and 18 months of age.

1. Object in view

2. Object is covered

3. Cloths are transposed

4. No further action

5. 'Where's the car?'

Object permanence: The A-not-B error

Time and place

Once the child is convinced that objects continue to exist even when they are out of sight, it is possible to begin to develop the idea of *now* as opposed to *then* – the child develops the idea of **time** – and of *here* as opposed to *there*, the idea of **place**. Two ideas are kept in the mind at once.

Learning experiences for toddlers

Toddlers need the full range of sensory experiences which were offered to babies – opportunities to listen to music, rhymes and stories; opportunities to explore colours, light and reflections; opportunities to touch and to construct; opportunities to taste and smell. The brain is coping with a massive input of sensory experiences and if the experiences are not to fade they must be processed.

FOCUS

Toddlers need to be gently encouraged to concentrate. Praise the child for sticking at an interesting activity until it is finished. This means that they should be given time to remain at an activity if they are deeply involved in it. Practitioners should think twice about interrupting a toddler's concentration for the sake of a rigid schedule.

Toddlers benefit from interacting with carers as they examine something. They will spend longer with a toy and manipulate it in more complex ways if they are with an interested adult than when they are playing alone.

If the adult knows what the child has been experiencing, opportunities can be seized to praise the child when there is evidence that he or she is remembering. A child of 12 months can remember a vivid experience for up to 3 months, especially if he or she has been reminded of it.

It is also helpful if adults make their planning ahead explicit, to help the toddler to build an understanding of the usefulness of this type of thinking. For example, say 'We'll get the things ready for dinner before we go out.'

Developing physical skills

Toddlers have increasing mobility and physical control.

FOCUS

The obvious implication of this is that they need plenty of opportunities to practise and develop their increasing skills of walking, running, dancing, balancing, and jumping up and down. They need to have space to do this, indoors and out.

With more access to other people through their increasing mobility, toddlers become more aware of others' intentions and actions. Toddlers watch other children and like to share their activities. Early in this stage they will copy another toddler's actions – if one bangs on the table with a spoon, the other will do the same. Becoming aware of adults going about their jobs, toddlers like to help. **Gender identity** generally appears in the second half of the second year of life (18 months to 24 months).

Toddlers need a chance to run

FOCUS

Toddlers need opportunities to watch and interact with other children. They need consistency and they need opportunities to be helpful to adults. They need to be able to make choices and to feel that their personality is respected. Practitioners must watch out to see whether children's awareness of gender becomes a barrier to extending learning.

The psychologist Erik Erikson pointed out that the toddler's new-found physical abilities, such as walking and bladder control, give the child a sense of autonomy. On the other hand, these advances often lead to conflict in the child's social world, the family and the setting, leading at times to the new emotions of shame and doubt which begin to emerge around 30 months.

FOCUS

Practitioners must support toddlers as they face this dilemma. The child's confidence can easily be damaged by either too few opportunities to make decisions or too permissive a response. Parents with their first toddler may need advice from practitioners as the cuddly baby begins to turn into a more assertive person.

It is a skill to encourage a toddler's sense of self.

Are you aware of the particular talents of each child in your care? Do you take steps to encourage a range of activities for the child to enjoy? Do you ensure each child has the opportunity to play with toys which unthinking gender stereotyping might otherwise prevent him or her from experiencing?

It is a skill to support a toddler's sense of mastery.

It is important for the child to develop physical skills. Are time and space allowed for **gross motor** skills? Are you aware of each child's progress in **fine motor** skills? Are there opportunities for children to make choices about activities, to revisit activities they find satisfying, or to be appropriately supported in attempts to try something new or difficult? Is your praise focused on what the child has done?

It is a skill to foster a toddler's awareness of others.

Are there opportunities to watch other children and adults, to play alongside peers, to help adults in everyday tasks?

How thinking develops in 2- and 3-year olds

At two the child's brain has grown to about 70 per cent of adult size. So far the child has been learning through the experience of interacting with the environment and observing how things work. Children between two and three are avid learners. With greater mobility and a wider range of experiences at their disposal, children of this age move from focusing on individual items of experience to linking a greater range of experiences together, and so they become able to detect patterns and similarities in the various elements of their environment.

Once they have spotted the repetition of a phenomenon, they look for further examples of it wherever they can find them and, more importantly, they begin to represent them. Their understanding is always expressed first through their actions, and the adults in a child's life need to be on the lookout for signs of the child's involvement with a particular idea.

Schemas

Piaget saw that very young children could adapt a basic movement (for example grasping or sucking) according to what they were trying to suck or grasp. He called this basic pattern which can be adapted a **schema**.

As adults we recognise patterns in events and operate on the basis of expecting them. For example, you may have a schema about going on holiday. You collect brochures or look on the Internet and select a holiday. You book and pay. You prepare, pack and set off. You live a different type of life for the duration of the holiday, then come back to normality. In every case the details will differ but the underlying structure remains the same.

> ### KEY TERM: Schema
>
> *Jean Piaget noticed that children have schemas or patterns of action, e.g. sucking or grasping, which they adapt in various ways as appropriate. Chris Athey followed up this idea and watched how young children focus for a while on a particular phenomenon, which can be seen repeated in many guises in the world around them, e.g. circles or enclosures.*

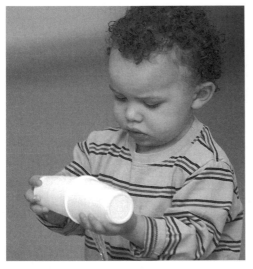

This child is showing evidence for the schema of 'transferring'

CASE STUDY:
CHRIS ATHEY

This aspect of Piaget's work was followed up by Chris Athey in a childcare setting in London in the 1980s. After analysing thousands of close observations of children between the ages of one and four in a nursery at the Froebel Institute, Athey was able to identify many more schemas. She and her colleagues noticed that the children appeared to become fascinated by various characteristics of the world around them. Once a child noticed that an interesting phenomenon could be spotted in various circumstances, he or she sought it out and picked it up everywhere.

For example, the child may notice that the space contains horizontals and verticals. In some cases (as in fencing, ladders, paving stones, oven trays, goal posts, doors and window frames) these can be seen intersecting. Gradually the child becomes very familiar with the phenomenon and uses it in constructions or drawings. By the time this has happened, the child will be moving on to pick up on something else that can be found in a lot of places.

One of the outstanding schemas that Athey noticed in her study of children from 12 to 48 months was the children's interest in **enclosures**. It is hardly surprising that children fasten onto this aspect of the world we live in because human beings make a lot of use of enclosures. We live in an enclosure (a house or flat) that is divided into smaller enclosures (rooms). Inside the rooms we have smaller enclosures (cupboards) that are often filled with even smaller enclosures (boxes). Cars, trains and buses are also types of enclosures. We write using enclosures because sentences, paragraphs, chapters and books are all enclosures. The idea of enclosure, of being within a boundary, is one that is basic to human existence.

Athey found that children crawling and learning to walk were interested in the horizontal and vertical. Children aged two to three were interested in intersections and grids. They were fascinated by fences, ladders, railway lines and oven shelves (all showing intersections where the horizontal and vertical lines meet). Experience of the diagonal comes through experiencing ramps in slides, entrances to buildings, or toy cars rolling down planks.

Experimenting with schemas

Children can be seen experimenting with their current schema in various places. For example, a child interested in enclosure would, on different occasions, make a den in the garden, creep behind the sofa, put a doll into a pram, put up fences for miniature animals, pack bricks into a box, paint a border round a picture, put bricks or tiles round the edge of a table. Some children can be seen repeatedly placing objects on top of others or next to others. This is positioning. Some children are fascinated by connections – the vacuum cleaner to a socket, a dog to a lead, a handset to a phone.

An understanding of schemas explains much of children's behaviour. A child emptying the pans out of a cupboard or dropping things behind a radiator is not just being naughty. Through a fascination with transferring things from one place to another the child is reaching an understanding that will stand him or her in good stead when it comes to learning about place value in addition or bookkeeping. Dropping things is an exploration of the law of gravity.

It is up to the adult to devise a less irritating opportunity for the child to pursue a fascination with the particular phenomenon that is interesting him or her. Naturally, much schematic behaviour happens at home and parents find it helpful to have the idea of schemas explained to them. We can share our observations with the parents, and as Chris Athey wrote, 'Nothing gets so much under a parent's skin more quickly and more permanently than the illumination of his or her own child's behaviour' (1990 page 66). We can share our professional expertise with parents by helping them to devise other ways to support their child's investigation of phenomena, to displace the annoying way the child may have first developed.

FOCUS

Many schemas involve movement. Prams are pushed backwards and forwards across the nursery. Toys are dropped. These are examples of trajectories. Dolls are wrapped up; dressing-up clothes are put on. There is a fascination with wrapping up parcels (enveloping). Objects are joined together or pulled apart. Rotation is seen when wheels or helicopter blades, dials or windmills turn, in turntables and washing machines and on the roundabouts at the fair. Farm animals are lined up or put in enclosures. Dolls and presents are wrapped up and paintings painted over (enveloping). Careful observation often shows that what might at first sight be seen as purposeless movement in a nursery is in fact a consistent, purposive exploration of the various manifestations of a phenomenon the child has noticed and is interested in.

Athey's schemas

The following two tables list the schemas Athey found. They suggest the sources of the schemas and give a brief indication of their use later in developing the concepts that underpin various fields of study.

The first table includes fixed phenomena in the environment. The second list includes schemas that involve movement. It must be stressed that schemas cannot be taught. There is no fixed order in which children go through them, and some children deal with an idea briefly, which for others might be a life-long interest. The adult's role is to observe the occurrence of the interest and to support the child by providing appropriate resources.

Table 1 Static schemas			
Schema	**Seen in**	**Child's actions**	**Future value**
Horizontal	Floors, beds, shelves, road markings	Block play	Drawing, literacy, numeracy
Vertical	Buildings, lamp-posts, trees, external lifts, scaffolding	Building towers, using climbing frame	Literacy, numeracy, construction
Intersection	Doors, windows, fences, paving stones, nets	Construction, climbing frame	Letters E, F, H, L, T, X Numeral 4 Graphs, timetables
Diagonal	Slides, ramps, escalators, road signs	Sliding, rolling cars or balls down ramps	Letters A, K, M, N, R, V, W, Y, Z Numerals 2, 4, 7 Graphs, engineering

Enclosure	Houses, boxes, teams, fenced areas	Dens, miniature world play	Categorising, organising, paragraphing, algebra
Boundaries ('in' meets 'out')	Gates, entrances, river banks, colanders	Indentations in play dough, digging	Form filling, legal and financial procedures, caving
Circles, curves	Coins, biscuits, lids of jars, road signs, the moon, gardens, plants	Scribbles, drawings, hoops, wheels, following paths	Letters B, C, D, G, J, O, P, Q, R, S, U Most lower-case letters Numerals 2, 3, 5, 6, 8, 9, 0

Table 2 Dynamic schemas (involving things moving)			
Schema	**Seen in**	**Child's actions**	**Future value**
Horizontal trajectory	Buggies being pushed, traffic moving, the wind blowing, birds in the air	Pushing prams, wheeled toys, toy cars, running, dancing	Sport, e.g. football, billiards, racing Recognising beginnings and ends
Vertical trajectory	Lifts, taps running, rain, hail, snow	Dropping things, demolishing towers, games that involve falling to the ground	Sport, e.g. rugby, basketball, tennis, archery, shooting Air transport Recognising sequences
Transferring	Filling, emptying, shopping, packing	Filling, emptying, playing shops	Maths – place value Translating, finance
Connecting	Overhead power lines, plugs and sockets, trains, bridges	Using string and sticky tape, opening and closing doors, zips	Adding, multiplying Stories, history, detection and diagnosis Electronics
Separating	Cutting, slicing, dismantling, harvesting	Taking things apart	Subtraction, division, analysis, dissection, logic, law, finance

➡

Rotating	Wheels, windmills, tops, dials, helicopters, CDs, revolving doors	Spinning round, more interested in the wheels than in riding the bike, circle games	Engineering, astronomy
Positioning	Car parks, table settings	Setting out objects in rows or under or on top, block play, patterns, stripes	Maths, geography Construction, design Architecture, planning
Enveloping	Wrappings, pies, pasties, sandwiches	Dressing up, wrapping up dolls or presents	Fashion, design Food preparation Acting
Transporting	Transport of people and goods	Pushing prams, bags packing for 'picnics'	Transport and delivery systems
Going through a boundary	Buttons and buttonholes Taps, plugs, travel, tunnels, burrows, rites of passage e.g. starting nursery, birthdays	Digging, splashing Stories about rabbits, magic tricks	Literature Diving, caving Archaeology, exploration, history, anthropology

As the tables show, the ideas that the children focus on are the basis of much of human activity and learning. Ideas of enclosure, joining, separating, connecting and transporting underpin maths and literacy. Rotation and trajectory come into science and sport. All the ideas children develop arise from their own thinking about the phenomena they notice or the experiences they have.

We will look more closely at the schemas that occur in children's drawings when we talk about creativity in Chapter 4.

FOCUS

Careful observation is necessary to know what is interesting a child at a specific time. The adult has to have ways of extending the child's interest, through further activities that will enhance the child's understanding. The practitioner needs to be aware of the potential for supporting particular schemas in each piece of apparatus or each area of the setting. The adult should be able to call upon a knowledge of relevant local visits and appropriate songs or stories for each schema.

The only appropriate curriculum for children under three is one that is based on supporting their schemas as they work through them. Children tackle the common schemas in their own order and at their own pace. So the provision for each child must be based on close observation of what the individual child is finding interesting at present.

CASE STUDY:
KAREN'S DAUGHTER

Karen writes about her daughter:

Frances first became fascinated by rotation and circularity when she was about 18 months old. She spent much of her time playing with her doll's buggy, her tricycle and her lawn mover. However, much to the frustration of her Daddy, she never pushed them anywhere. They were always on their sides and Frances loved to spin their wheels and watch them go round. Her favourite game was Ring-o'-roses and the three of us, along with three toys (to make the circle bigger!), spent lots of time each day playing this game and hoping no one looked into the house and saw us.

Frances loved going into the local town to watch the wind turbines, and she demonstrated an uncanny ability to sense when we were within a few miles of the town, always insisting on a detour. (She also sustained a number of bruises as a result of spinning herself round in circles.)

When she revisited this schema some time later her interests had changed. She liked to beat eggs to make scrambled egg for tea and produced tens of circular finger paintings. These activities enabled me to introduce many mathematical terms to Frances in a meaningful context, for example, *circle, round, round and round, spiral, fast* and *slow*, to name but a few.

This activity coincided with her interest in enveloping, and many mathematical concepts were explored as Frances attempted to wrap everything in sight with whatever came to hand. Concepts such as *too much, not enough*, and *too many*, the language of comparison associated with size and the skill of estimation were all apparent at this time. I have found it incredibly interesting and exciting to observe her play and spot the underlying schema – to watch the theories I have read about coming to life before my eyes.

FIND OUT MORE

Athey, C (1990) *Extending Thought in Young Children*, Paul Chapman Publishing

Bartholomew, L and Bruce T (1993) *Getting to Know You*, Hodder and Stoughton

Nutbrown, C (1999) *Threads of Thinking*, Paul Chapman Publishing

REFLECT ON YOUR PRACTICE

It is a skill to share your knowledge of schemas with the parents of the children in your care.

Since children spend most of their time at home, we need to share our knowledge of a child's current schemas with the parents.

Make a list of the points you will make to a parent about the idea of schemas. How will you share the information about schemas in general with parents? Parents have a lot to tell us about their child and his or her current interests. How and when will you get this valuable information? Can you devise a record sheet about schemas to be shared between the setting and home? There is an example of a 'Running record' at the back of this book (Appendix 1).

It is a skill to support a child's current schema.

This can be done by seeing that relevant resources are available at the setting. For example, a child who is interested in rotation would be fascinated by a globe. Playing Ring-o'-roses will appeal to a child interested in rotation as well as to one who is taken by the idea of vertical trajectory. If you made a wormery or went outside to dig for worms, it would fascinate those interested in going through a boundary.

Turn to the 'Schema support grid' at the back of the book (Appendix 2). Alongside each of the schemas listed there, can you suggest a resource you have or could easily acquire, a local visit you could make, and a story or rhyme featuring a particular schema that you could use to support and extend a child's interest? It may be helpful to do this exercise with a colleague.

Learning experiences for 2- and 3-year-olds

As children begin to extend their mobility, adults can encourage them to notice elements within their environment, indoors and out. The adult's responsibility is to help the child to look carefully at the world. At the same time the child's power over language is growing and adults should take every opportunity to introduce words that capture or define the experience the child is having. Developing the habit of paying attention to sensory impressions is very important for brain growth. If an experience 'passes over the child's head', no connections will be made in the brain, the neural pathways will not be developed and quite quickly the facility to learn will be lost.

The particular sensory features that are important at this time are sight, hearing and the development of physical skills.

Sight

At this stage the adult needs to encourage the child to look closely at what he or she sees and to notice the relationship between parts and the whole – the petals as well as the whole flower, the component features of the car, its paintwork and its wheel hubs as well as its make. Besides learning the colour names, words should be used to describe the variations in colour in fruits and leaves, the intricacies of naturally occurring patterns, in the grain in wood or pigeons' wings, or man-made patterns in townscapes or landscapes. Examples of symmetry can be drawn to the child's attention, as can for example the differences in scale between jeans for a toddler and an adult, or a doll's house and a real one. Attention can also be drawn to the effect of distance on perceived size, the train at the station platform and the one seen from afar.

Opportunities to look at the appearance of things **outdoors** include noticing and speaking about the sky, clouds, the moon and stars, water, frost and snow; street lights, headlights, reflections, and shadows; trees, plants, animals, birds and insects; the effect of distance or height on perception. **Indoors**, children can look at reflections in mirrors and polished surfaces, the colours in prisms and light catchers, pictures, photographs, plants, fruits, stones, artefacts, fabrics, projected light, flickering lights, changing lights and bubble tubes. They can use kaleidoscopes; light boxes and overhead projectors to experiment with shadows and the superimposition and blending of coloured transparencies; microscopes and magnifying glasses. There will be traditional small world toys, ranges of spoons of various sizes and button boxes, and increasingly digital cameras will be available.

Hearing

Music speaks to every one, of all ages and cultures. Don Campbell (2002) argues that hearing the patterns in music has an effect on the firing of the neurons. Music, he believes, especially strengthens our ability to balance and regulate muscle movements. It also nourishes the creative right-brain processes connected with spatial and temporal reasoning.

Musical ability shows early, so adults must be on the lookout for children who are very interested in sound and rhythm.

FOCUS

From their earliest days all children need opportunities to experience rhythm by being dandled in time to songs and nursery rhymes. As they gain more control over their bodies they need to make music, both by singing and by using a range of instruments, commercial and home-made.

Young children need opportunities to listen to birds, rain, wind, hail, traffic (cars, lorries, motor bikes, tractors, trains, police cars, ambulances, fire engines, planes, helicopters), to the sound of footsteps, to distant sounds, to note the sounds of large quantities of water moving outside (the sea, streams, fountains), and the smaller sounds of water inside (water dripping, splashing, squirting, gushing, being poured out, gurgling as it is draining away, coming to the boil).

They need opportunities to listen to a good range of music from several cultures, and various ways of making music, from the human voice to solo instruments or bands and orchestras or synthesisers. It is also important for them to have opportunities to be without noise, to be able to pay attention to the tiny sounds we often ignore.

Toddlers enjoy experimenting with musical instruments

CASE STUDY:

WORKING WITH CHILDREN AT SURESTART

Alison writes:

I work with a group of children aged between two and three, attending SureStart provision. Each child has been diagnosed with some special need. I had read that it was important to get the regions of the brain to work together and that musical activities would help to link the auditory, visual and motor areas. So we planned a daily music session.

We played Mozart's variations on *Twinkle, twinkle little star* (K265) as the children entered. The children then shook hands with each other and joined in a welcome song. Then they sang together five songs, for example:

- *Twinkle, twinkle little star*
- *If you're happy and you know it*
- *Put your finger in the air*
- *Polly put the kettle on*
- *London Bridge.*

Then each child was given a musical instrument, and the songs were sung through again.

This was followed by five action songs, for example:

- *I'm a little tea pot*
- *Heads and shoulders, knees and toes*
- *Row, row, row your boat*
- *There were 10 in the bed*
- *Ring-o'-roses.*

At the end of the session we sang the welcome song again and played the Mozart as the children departed. The children enjoyed the sessions, especially the social aspect. Buoyed up by the music they all seemed to grow in confidence – even the most timid child began to join in – and they all improved in language development and physical co-ordination.

We shared what we were doing with the children's parents. The parents followed up what we were doing at home. One began to use music successfully to calm her child.

KEY TERM: SureStart

A government programme to deliver the best start in the UK for every child. It brings together early education, childcare, health and family support.

Physical skills

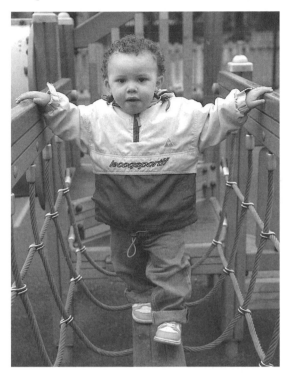

Developing a sense of balance

The years before four are important for the development of physical skills. Opportunities to move in various ways include having the space indoors for crawling, walking, dancing and balancing. Outside, children need space for running, climbing, jumping, hopping and skipping. Ball skills, including kicking, throwing, catching and striking should be introduced from toddlerhood. The development of muscles in the arms from using climbing frames has to precede the development of fine motor movement in the fingers needed for writing.

REFLECT ON YOUR PRACTICE

It is a skill to encourage children's physical skills.

How physically active are the toddlers, twos and threes who attend the setting encouraged to be? Have you ever checked the level of a child's activity by using a pedometer? Are there opportunities indoors to move at various levels and to dance to a range of rhythms and sounds, to lift, to push and to pull? Are there opportunities outside to run and develop stamina? To climb and balance, to develop ball skills beyond attempting to be footballers? What use could be made of public provision of resources such as parks, soft play and ball pools?

Opportunities to touch include the chance to examine smooth, rough or prickly surfaces, to feel fragile fabrics and feathers, to work with malleable clay and play dough, to feel ice-cold and warm surfaces, to handle lighter and heavier objects.

There should be opportunities outside to smell plants and grass, wet earth and rubbish, and inside the scents of fruits, foods in preparation, herbs and spices, clean linen, disinfectants, perfumes, scented candles.

CASE STUDY:

FOREST SCHOOLS IN DENMARK

Yasmin describes how the Scandinavian countries encourage young children to spend a large amount of time in the open air.

In the 1950s, Denmark responded to the move of women into the workforce by encouraging the existing kindergartens to supplement their indoor provision with outdoor provision. This outdoor provision was given the name of the forest school.

The children are outside for the whole day and they have suitable clothing to cope with all kinds of weather. In some forest schools the staff will pack everything they need onto a trolley and they go into the woods, build shelters and cook their own food over an open fire. Children are able to join in these activities as soon as they are mobile.

Forest schools give young children opportunities to develop a wide range of skills, particularly independence and problem-solving skills. They learn to take risks and develop a sense of their own limitations. Young children enjoy being outside and become very absorbed in their work and explorations. Forest schools give children the opportunity to discover their environment, to face challenges and to gain a wide range of skills.

Outdoor fun is an important learning experience

CASE STUDY:
OUT OF DOORS IN FINLAND

Sharon writes:

Unless the temperature falls below -10 degrees centigrade, toddlers in nursery settings in Finland are outside for two 2½-hour sessions each day. To prepare for work with young children in Finland you have to be ready for any weather.

Children are encouraged to be independent in getting dressed / undressed into their outdoor kit, but all the physical contacts are used as opportunities for conversation. Before lunch there is an extended period of outdoor activity in the sand area where even the youngest will move, carry, pull, push, dig, move around.

Lunch is eaten together in the class and there is a snooze afterwards before another outdoor session, this time spent in the forest setting where the children experience boulders, logs, sticks, grass and mud. Here they walk, climb, jump, sit, make dens, shuffle, collect. The adult's role is not to intervene but to stand back. If the children step too far or climb too high and get stuck they ask for help. The adult also encourages the children to explore. She uses the resources of telling stories and legends and improvised drama to enhance each child's own story.

Maryam writes:

When I visited Finland to look at early years settings there were several ways in which they differed from settings in the UK. Because of working patterns in Finland, many young children spend a long time in daycare settings. Several of the settings I visited had opted to create an atmosphere that was as like home as possible. They tried to follow the routines that would exist at home; there was a very relaxed atmosphere that followed the needs of the child. The rooms had sofas and armchairs and looked more like a sitting room than a school room. Staff did not wear uniforms and the routines were flexible enough to meet the changing needs of the children. Each child was allocated a key worker who stayed as their key person for the whole time the child attended the setting. Great care was taken to communicate with parents and carers at the end of each day.

My overwhelming impression of the daycare settings in Finland was of a relaxed and friendly atmosphere that enabled each child to develop at a pace that suited his or her needs. Childhood and individuality were greatly valued and there was a strong emphasis on social and emotional development.

FIND OUT MORE

Campbell, D (2002) *The Mozart Effect*, Hodder and Stoughton

Goldschmeid, E and Jackson, S (1994) *People Under Three: Young Children in Day Care*, Routledge

REFLECT ON YOUR PRACTICE

It is a skill to see the opportunities for extending children's understanding in the home, in the childcare setting and in the wider environment.

The weather plays a large part in our environment.

◆ What experiences do the children you work with have of rain, wind, frost, snow, mist, sunshine, thunder and lightning?

◆ What experiences could you plan for children below 18 months?

◆ What could you tell them about the elements? List the words you could use to describe the various sensory aspects of the experience of rain, snow, frost or sunshine.

Temperature and light are important factors – what opportunities could there be in the childcare setting for the baby or toddler to experience the difference between light and darkness? Or for the older child to control light sources (such as torches)? Or for the child to notice shadows? Or for the child to notice variations in temperature – or see temperature being measured?

It is a skill to use the features of the children's environment to maximise their opportunities to develop understanding of the world they live in.

There are **living creatures** in the child's world – plants, birds, worms, beetles, fish, pets.

◆ What opportunities exist at the setting for the children to see and talk about these?

◆ How could you provide opportunities for the children to experience them?

◆ How could you support and extend a child's interest?

Water, sand, mud and clay are the stuff of the world.

◆ What access do the children have to these materials in the setting? What access could you plan to ensure that all the children have opportunities to explore them, indoors and out?

◆ What arrangements for progression in their experiences could you make?

◆ What words would you use to talk about the attributes of these natural materials to the children?

We have many **machines** in our world.

Can you list at least ten machines a child will be familiar with at home? What do these machines do for us? What do we do to make the machines at home work? Which ones will a child be able to operate?

◆ Which machines will the child see being used in the setting?

◆ Which machines will the child see being used in the wider environment beyond the home or setting? Which ones could be drawn to the child's attention?

◆ How could you support the child's interest?

Chapter 2 How babies and young children learn

It is a skill to refresh our own vocabulary.

◆ What are the words you as an adult would use to describe (not just label) each object in your treasure basket?

◆ What words would you use to describe the sound of rain or wind or a car passing?

◆ How would you comment on the effect of sunlight on water or gathering twilight?

Barriers to learning

All children develop in their own way and at different rates. For some, development may be delayed for physical reasons. For some otherwise normal children, there may be other barriers to successful learning.

A child's brain uses more glucose than an adult's, so a sick or malnourished child may not have the energy to think.

A child may be deprived of opportunities to learn for several reasons. An adult may be unaware of how important it is for a child to have sufficient experiences to strengthen the neural pathways in his or her brain. An adult may not know what the appropriate provision is for a child at a particular stage. An adult may be unaware of schemas and so a child's explorative activities may be interpreted as naughtiness and punished. An adult might have prejudices that lead to low expectations for a particular child. In some cases, an adult's own problem of depression or addiction may make it impossible to pay attention to a child's mental or emotional needs.

Children may fail to learn because they have had their belief in themselves as learners damaged. This can happen if no approval is given to the child's attempts to explore the environment or if the child is actively prevented from exploring the environment by an adult's fixation on routines or on maintaining standards of tidiness or hygiene.

REFLECT ON YOUR PRACTICE

It is a skill to nurture each child's drive to learn.

◆ How do you gain information about each child's progress?

◆ How do you show interest in what a child is doing? How do you show approval of a child's efforts?

◆ How do you encourage a child to try a new experience? How do you select that new experience?

◆ Keep an audit of yourself for a session. Note how often you stopped an activity. Reflect on your reasons for doing so.

It is a skill to meet each child's individual learning needs.

◆ How often is each child observed? What happens to your observations when they are written?

◆ How and when are decisions made about what to provide for a child?

◆ How do you prepare to introduce new materials to a child? How do you decide what to say about them?

It is a skill to provide appropriate materials.

◆ How often are new materials or resources introduced?

◆ How is equipment stored?

◆ How aware are you of any materials that might be relevant to a child's interests which are currently being kept in another staff member's area or out of the child's reach?

◆ How do you decide what to provide?

Conclusion

This chapter has discussed how children's minds develop.

◆ Babies and young children have a drive to learn. Their mental activity as they process their experiences builds their brain.

◆ With the brain it is a case of 'use it or lose it'. The years from birth to three are vital for brain development.

◆ It is the adult's responsibility to provide children with appropriate, interesting experiences to give them opportunities to learn.

◆ People who work with babies and young children must pass on to each child's parents their knowledge of how energetic and single-minded babies and young children are in their pursuit of understanding the world around them.

The following skills have been highlighted.

◆ It is a skill to encourage the process of accommodation.

◆ It is a skill to provide a full range of opportunities for babies to develop their brains through sensory experiences in the childcare setting.

◆ It is a skill to support the child in his or her learning by providing a treasure basket.

◆ It is a skill to encourage a toddler's sense of self.

◆ It is a skill to support a toddler's sense of mastery.

◆ It is a skill to foster a toddler's awareness of others.

◆ It is a skill to share your knowledge of schemas with the parents of the children in your care.

◆ It is a skill to support a child's current schema.

- It is a skill to encourage children's physical skills.
- It is a skill to see the opportunities for extending children's understanding in the home, in the childcare setting and in the wider environment.
- It is a skill to use the features of the children's environment to maximise their opportunities to develop understanding of the world they live in.
- It is a skill to refresh our own vocabulary.
- It is a skill to nurture each child's drive to learn.
- It is a skill to meet each child's individual learning needs.
- It is a skill to provide appropriate materials.

Why communicate?

All humans have a very strong drive to communicate. We need others to acknowledge our existence. We feel incomplete if we cannot share our experiences, feelings and ideas with others. When we are successful in making contact with others, we grow as people. Feedback from our attempts at communication is evidence that we are recognised and are affirmed as a person.

This need for recognition and affirmation fills our consciousness from birth to old age. Even a newborn child has an instinctive drive to make contact with others – babies need help to survive, and affirmation to thrive.

Communication means making contact with another person, and we do it for several reasons. We greet people because we want to be friendly and also because getting a response to our greeting means that our existence is recognised.

We tell others what we need to be more comfortable. We communicate to organise help for ourselves: 'It's so hot in here – can you help me to open the window?' We share personal feelings: 'I love it when…' or 'I feel awful after that news' or 'I can't stand that!' Again, this is to gain affirmation and sympathy. We ask others to help us find a solution to a problem: 'Should we try phoning to see if they're open?' or 'What do you think she meant by that?' or 'What shall we try next?' At times we pass on factual information: 'You turn right at the roundabout.'

Expressed in this way, communication seems an easy matter. It's not, because there could be problems with either the teller or the responder. The teller may not encode the message effectively and the hearer might not receive it properly.

For any communication to succeed, both sides must be active. On the one hand the teller has to ensure that the message is effectively encoded, and on the other hand the responder has to decode the message efficiently so that the teller's emotion, need or information can be understood. In order to manage this, each partner in the conversation has to be sensitive to the other person.

For communication to happen and for the message to be transferred from one person to another, the hearer may need to ask for further clarification and the teller may have to adjust the message until it is understood. At times the teller has to adapt the style of the message according to the recipient. 'I want…' may be better expressed as 'Wouldn't it be lovely if…' or 'Look, there's an ice cream shop over there, Grandma!'

FOCUS

There are patterns in communication, as the partners respond to each other.

◆ A stakes a claim; B may accept the situation or make a counter claim.

◆ A states a fact; B may agree and draw on his or her own experience to make a comment or B may have a query about the fact.

◆ A describes a feeling; B may draw on an example in his or her own experience or accept and sympathise with how A is feeling.

◆ A asks a question; B answers it.

◆ A suggests a theory; B accepts and expands on what A said, or analyses the implications of A's idea, or proposes another theory.

Here are some examples of the above patterns.

A 'That's mine.' **B** 'Oh no, it isn't.'

A 'It's raining hard.' **B** 'Oh is it? I'm going to get my umbrella, then.'

A 'I feel so sad to be leaving.' **B** 'I hated leaving too, but I enjoyed my next job.'

A 'Where's today's paper?' **B** 'Over there.'

A 'Do you think they've missed the train?' **B** 'Perhaps. Or there could be a hold-up on the line somewhere.'

Sometimes no reply is expected, as in a warning such as 'Watch out' or when an order is given, such as 'Sit down.' There are ways of giving orders, some better than others: there is often aggression or disrespect when the last word is heavily accented, such as 'Do it *now*.' Sometimes the consequences of an action are spelled out: 'If you push too hard, the wall will fall down.' Sometimes there is a threat: 'Do that once more and I'll….'

As adults we are able to communicate with language, but we also use **non-verbal** ways of communicating, sometimes consciously (a loving hug, a warning glance) but most of the time, unconsciously. A high proportion of anyone's interpretation of a verbal message is based on information from non-verbal sources. In the sections that follow, both verbal and non-verbal means of communication are described, as the ways that babies, toddlers and 2- and 3-year-olds send and receive messages are discussed.

> **KEY TERM: Non-verbal communication**
>
> *Communication that does not rely on words. It includes facial expressions, gestures and body language.*

Babies as tellers

Using sounds

Babies have no words but they communicate very well by using sound. Many of the messages babies convey are about their own urgent needs. As tellers, babies cry to inform someone that they are uncomfortable or hungry. Carers can interpret their cries and they usually know whether the message is that the infant is hungry, thirsty, uncomfortable, tired, lonely or in pain. A young baby's passionate expression of a felt need is spontaneous and automatic. They do not cry merely to gain attention, but to have a need fulfilled. As we saw in Chapter 1, babies urgently need outside help to calm down after being stressed by fear or anger at discomfort.

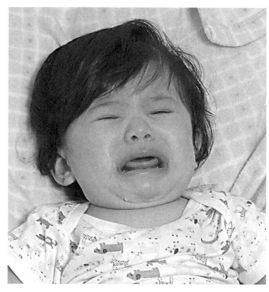

Is he angry or uncomfortable?

Babies express their happiness by coos and babbling. The babbling begins quite early. Babies of about 4 weeks old can be seen pushing their tongues out through partly opened lips. The baby then brings the lips together and a little bubble of saliva emerges from the mouth. There is no sound at this stage, but the baby is taking the first step in learning to speak. Speech depends on co-ordinating the breathing with the movement of the tongue and lips. By about the age of 3 months, sounds can be heard. At first they are mostly splutters, but as the weeks go on the **vowels** (the variations on A, E, I, O and U) are practised. Vowels are made when the air from the lungs is breathed out. They vary in sound according to where the tongue is placed. The tongue may be moved up and down or front to back.

Notice where your tongue is when you say the vowel sound in *cooed* and then in *beat*.

The **consonants,** the sounds represented by all the other letters of the alphabet, are added next. Sounding consonants is harder. The sounds are made by using the lips and tongue. As a baby's lips and tongue become more co-ordinated, he or she begins to make consonants.

Some consonants are easier to manage than others. For a sound like *pa* or *bo* the stream of sound is shaped by vigorous lip movements. The sounds *k* and *g* are made with the back of the tongue against the soft **palate**. A sound like *ma* is made by letting the air flow through the nasal cavity. (This explains why it is easier for a baby to say *dada* than *mama*.) Hissing sounds (*s* and *z*) are made by putting the tip of the tongue on the ridge just behind the upper front teeth.

The arched bony structure in the roof of the mouth, divided into the hard palate and the soft palate. The soft palate is nearer to the back of the mouth.

FOCUS

Make these sounds and notice what is happening in your mouth as you say them: *maa*, *po*, *ka*, *ta*, *tee*. Sometimes it is mainly the lips that are active. Sometimes the tongue is being used in various parts of the mouth. Note where you put your tongue as you slowly say 'That trog went slowly up the path.'

Sometimes we vibrate our **vocal cords** to change the sound. Put the first finger and thumb of one hand on each side of the front of your throat. First make the sound *f* and then the sound *v*. Did you feel a difference? Now feel the difference between the two sounds *s* and *z*. The vibration you feel in your throat when you sound the second of each of these pairs is called **voicing**.

If you heard the sound of a young infant babbling, you would not be able to distinguish between an English, a Japanese or an African infant. Babies are born with the ability to produce the sounds of every language. However, by about 7 months they have focused on the sounds of their mother tongue.

Japanese speakers do not use the distinction between *r* and *l*. Japanese babies can distinguish between these sounds at 7 months, but at 11 months they have lost the ability to do so. They have got used to the sounds of their own language. Babies babble with the intonation (tunes) of the language they will speak.

Using non-verbal means

Babies mostly use non-verbal means to communicate. They use their whole body to convey their emotions: they wriggle with pleasure or squirm with annoyance or stiffen in resistance. They are born with the ability to use facial expressions to tell us about their feelings. From their earliest days they are able to show disgust to indicate their desire to avoid an unpleasant taste or smell.

Facial expressions showing sadness and anger begin to be used at 3 or 4 months, although in one experiment the researchers tied a string to the arms of babies who were just 2 months old. Each arm pull had the effect of turning on a short burst of music. The infants showed every sign of joy and pleasure at this – mouths open, eyes wide, broad smiles. When the experimenters switched off the music and the arm pulling had no effect, the babies showed every sign of anger – clenched jaws or bared gums, square mouths, frowns.

When babies find something interesting they stare at it. They show surprise with widened eyes and raised eyebrows. A baby responding to a situation he or she finds pleasant has an alert, open gaze or a soft, relaxed contentment.

What are these babies trying to say to us?

Smiles

From very early on babies show they also want to use communication to be sociable and to share enjoyment. Smiles mean friendship and pleasure. The smile, a pulling up of the corners of the mouth, is a universal greeting signal. Desmond Morris describes a similar phenomenon in animals and says it is a way of showing a willingness to appease, to be friendly, non-violent and non-censorious. The adults in a baby's life cannot help smiling as they look at the child and the baby associates smiles with safety and love.

In a baby there is a development in smiling. First there is the **reflex** smile of the first 4 weeks of life. This smile happens as a response to the mother's voice, or to tickling, or perhaps to wind. A **general** smile begins to be used when the baby is about a month old. This smile lasts longer; it is broader, and the baby's eyes twinkle. The stimulus for this response is seeing an adult's face at close quarters. Any smiling adult's face will do.

A truly **specific** smile is first seen when the baby is between 4 and 7 months old (usually when the infant is at 5–6 months). This particular smile is now a highly personal response to communicate a pleasurable emotion, for example when the baby recognises his or her parents.

The smile is the beginning of social communication

Using the smile is the beginning of social communication. The first intentional smile is in response to another person's smile, but soon babies begin to use smiles and coos on their own initiative to greet people and engage in communication with them. From 2 to 7 months, babies begin to acquire the basic rules of communicating with another person. At first the adults who are caring for the baby take the lead and develop a social exchange by responding to the baby's signals and fitting their interjections into the pauses in the baby's vocalisations. When the baby experiences this loving exchange, he or she takes an important step forward in learning about communication.

First, babies learn that for communication they need to be aware of another person and to focus on him or her. Second, they learn that communication needs co-operation – the teller and the responder have to take turns to maintain the flow of communication. These skills of shared focus and turn-taking are the basis of all conversations. The American educationalist Jerome Bruner pointed out the importance of playing the game of Peekaboo (or Peep-o) for learning the skill of turn-taking in conversations.

Laughter

Laughing is an important way of sharing a pleasant experience. The baby learns to laugh in the fourth or fifth month of life. Laughing begins as a cross between a wail and a contented chortle. When a baby has a shock he or she starts to wail. If a parent

says 'Boo', or lifts the child high in the air, or swings the child round, or comes close to the child and blows a raspberry, the child instinctively senses danger, but then sees that the person who is behaving in this strange way is a person who can be trusted. The infant realises that this shock has been lovingly administered, and the person can mean no possible harm. This unusual action must be harmless because the person who's doing it is a protector and this person is smiling. So the wail combines with a contented chortle sound, and the baby laughs. As babies laugh they realise that laughing makes one feel good, and so laughing becomes adopted as a useful, happy response. The infant also discovers that laughter evokes a

A baby's laughter evokes a warm response in adults   warm response in adults.

Gestures

Gestures are also an important part of non-verbal communication. Even a young baby looks away from an interaction that is too much for him or her. Babies make it clear when they have had enough food by pushing the food or the nipple away. They twist away their heads to the right or the left. (This movement evolves into the shake of the head that nearly all cultures use to indicate refusal.) When babies dislike the food they are offered they will push the spoon out of their mouths with their tongues. This indicates that they want the person feeding them to stop. This gesture of rejection can persist in later life; sticking out a tongue is used by older children to tell someone to leave them alone.

Babies have habitual gestures that show they are tired. At around 6 months, when babies have more control over their limbs, they begin to learn to use certain gestures for specific events, such as to clap hands or wave goodbye. They will follow adults' head movements to see where they are looking. At 12 months, some children can sway and clap their hands and move their heads in time to the beat of music, communicating their pleasure in this social activity.

The unmistakeable gestures for 'That's enough!'

From around 8 to 10 months babies begin to use gestures to ask others for help. A baby who wants a toy may reach towards it and then look back and forth between the toy and the adult nearby to show the adult that it is wanted. Sometimes these gestures are accompanied by crying, which stops when the request is met. Babies of this age also use the gesture of pointing to indicate something interesting in the environment. At 11 to12 months, babies hold up an object to share their interest in it with someone else. Babies may pass the object to an adult as if to elicit some comment about it. Babies will show interest in other children and will sometimes show them a toy to share their interest.

Social referencing

The most sophisticated use of non-verbal communication is when the baby looks to adults for advice and refers to them to see how they judge an activity. A baby who is at the crawling stage will set off towards a new cupboard and will then glance back to check whether the adult is happy to let him or her proceed. If the adult appears worried the explorer will hesitate. If the adult nods in approval, the baby will proceed.

'Can I carry on?'

If something alarms the child during the exploration he or she will check back again, and sometimes will even return after his or her own appraisal of the situation for a further check

'Do you like this?'

with the adult. This sort of behaviour is called **social referencing** and it is very important because it shows that the baby has an awareness of boundaries. There seems to be a gender difference in this behaviour. Generally girls are more aware of their carer's concerns than boys. For boys, a more emphatic negative warning response may be needed.

> **KEY TERM: Social referencing**
>
> *The action of a baby who is crawling about and exploring but looks back at an adult for approval or permission to continue. Doing this shows that the child is aware that there are boundaries to be observed.*

FOCUS ✓

The implication of this information about a baby's drive to communicate long before he or she can talk is that as adults we have a double responsibility. We have to work to understand what babies are urgently trying to convey so that their needs (for survival and affirmation) are met. We must also help babies to develop the understanding that communication means an interchange between tellers and responders, and that awareness of others and a responsiveness to them is a very important aspect of successful communication.

It is a skill to interpret a baby's non-verbal messages.

How does each baby in your care show that he or she:

◆ is pleased

◆ is excited

◆ needs something

◆ rejects something

◆ is tired

◆ is bored

◆ is afraid?

It is a skill to help a baby to learn the skills of conversation even before he or she can talk.

How does each baby in your care show he or she wants to attract another person's attention?

How does the child show he or she is ready to share an exchange with another person?

It is a skill to hear the sounds the baby is making in various situations.

Do you take note of the actual sounds the babies in your care can make? Watch a baby or a toddler communicating by voice. Try to identify the purpose of the communication – to greet, to get help, to share feelings.

Babies as understanders

As understanders, babies are well equipped to be able to pick up non-verbal messages.

Babies respond to how they are touched. Being lovingly held is important. A tense baby's heart rate has been found to synchronise with the parent's heart rate. If the parent can be calm and relaxed, the baby's heart rate steadies, as he or she is soothed by being held and rocked.

As we saw in Chapter 2, babies are interested from birth in looking at faces. The psychologist Allan Schore believes that being surrounded by smiling faces helps the baby's brain to develop, because the pleasurable feelings in response to a smile make the body produce substances that enable the orbitofrontal and prefrontal parts of the brain to grow new tissue.

FOCUS

The implication of this is obvious! There should be no glum or expressionless faces around babies.

Even the tiniest babies are able to interpret the basics of **body language** that are used in every culture. From about 6 weeks they can read and understand a range of facial expressions. These include a person showing **disgust**, where the lips are pursed and turned down; **surprise**, when the eyes widen and the mouth opens; **anger**, when the face stiffens and the lips tighten to show the teeth. The baby's response to a **shock** is a startled glare, an intake of breath and often a scream. Sudden fear is very catching and the emotion of startled fear is perhaps the hardest one for an adult to hide from a baby. It passes instantly from adult to child (or from child to adult and back).

> **KEY TERM: Body language**
>
> *Facial expressions, eye contact, body posture, the distance people maintain between each other and gestures used by people for telling or responding in a face-to-face situation.*

Babies are attuned to the sound of the human voice. Young babies interpret the underlying emotion that is expressed in the tone of voice, rather than the words that are said. They respond to the emotional state of the adult who is with them.

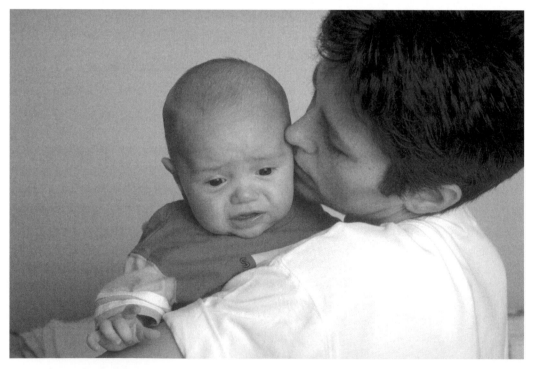

Babies demand a lot of care

CASE STUDY:

GOLEMAN'S RESEARCH

Daniel Goleman (1996 page 194) reported two scenarios taken from a report by the American National Center for Clinical Infant Programs to illustrate this point.

Say a 2-month-old baby wakes up at 3 a.m. and starts crying. Her mother comes in and for the next half hour the baby contentedly nurses in her mother's arms while her mother gazes at her affectionately, telling her that she's happy to see her, even in the middle of the night. The baby, content in her mother's love, drifts back to sleep.

Now say another 2-month-old baby, who also awakes crying in the wee small hours, is met by a mother who is tense and miserable, having fallen asleep just an hour before after a fight with her husband. The baby starts to tense up the moment his mother picks him up, telling him 'Just be quiet – I can't stand one more thing! Come on, let's get it over with.' As the baby nurses the mother stares stonily ahead, not looking at him, reviewing her fight with his father, getting more agitated with herself as she mulls it over. The baby sensing her tension, squirms, stiffens and stops nursing. 'That's all you want?' his mother says 'Then don't eat.' With the same abruptness she puts him back in his crib and stalks out, letting him cry until he falls back to sleep exhausted.

Goleman comments that the first baby is learning that her communication is effective. She is finding that people can be counted on to notice her needs and help her. In addition she takes in the information that the person who is taking care of her loves her. The other child is learning that no one cares about him, and that any of his attempts at communication are liable to meet with failure. The second of the two scenarios is an extreme example of a distressed mother, but it is not unusual for adults not to be at their most patient with an infant after many sleepless nights, or if they are stressed or depressed for some reason.

What is happening in this pre-verbal stage is that babies are building up a store of sensory images connected with emotions, which can affect an infant's future outlook on life. One person brilliantly described these impressions as 'unforgettable but unrememberable'. They are pre-verbal emotional schema that have a lifelong impact, particularly on patterns of relationships.

Babies listen to the language they hear around them. One mother wanted her child to be exposed to the sound of the poetry of someone she considers to be one of the greatest English poets.

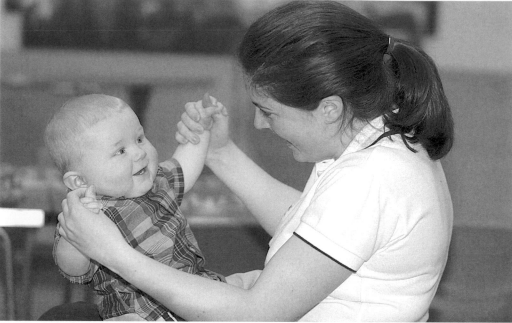

Having a good time together

CASE STUDY:
READING POETRY

Catherine writes:

I read poetry to my gorgeous 9-month-old baby, Julia. Let me tell you my reasons and beliefs about how we expose Julia to language. I do not pretend to be an expert, but I have simply followed my instincts and passions in an attempt to allow Julia to experience the beauty of words from the earliest possible age. I believe this has played a massive part in making her so well socialised, very content and interactive and empathetic.

The fall and death of Satan may well seem an odd bedtime story for a 2-month-old baby, yet Julia nightly fell asleep to the poetry of Milton's *Paradise Lost* read in hushed, steady tones, combined with the warmth and closeness of breast feeding. I was keen to replicate the experience of the womb and to me Milton seemed an obvious choice, because his sonorous language and steady rhythm created wonderful sounds and exposed Julia to many combinations of syllables.

CASE STUDY:
PHOEBE

Another mother read to her child to keep her happy:

Phoebe was just over 3 weeks old when I started reading to her. Her Dad had gone back to work after paternity leave and suddenly I was left alone. At this time Phoebe cried every time she was put down. I started talking to her as I put her down, but I wouldn't know what to say (there are only so many times you can tell her how beautiful she is) and the crying would start again.

I knew it was my voice that kept her happy. If we had visitors, Phoebe was a very contented baby because people were talking. She was forming a definite pattern – when visitors came she would sleep through the visits, and the second they left she would wake up crying because it was quiet.

Various people told me that they had spoken to their baby non-stop, but I just couldn't do this. I found singing helped, and she would watch intently while I did this and stay content. But there were only so many nursery rhymes and songs that I knew and I would get very bored and feel slightly silly.

Then one day I read her a short baby book, which had come free with a magazine. I made sure she could see the pictures and I explained what was in them. Phoebe's focus on the book would not last long, but the fact that I was talking would keep her listening and happy, so I continued to read other children's books. Most of these were Beatrix Potter books that had been mine as a child. It was nice to feel I was sharing something I had loved with my baby, and the bonus was she was lying in her bouncer or Moses basket. Therefore if she fell asleep I could move, because she wasn't on top of me.

In early July the latest Harry Potter novel came out. I have been a huge fan of this series and felt sad that I would miss out, but there was no time for reading a book for my own entertainment. I bought a copy to put aside for the future. I had this in the back of my mind when I was reading the children's books to Phoebe, and then in a selfish way I decided to read the Harry Potter. It hit me that she was just over a month old and she wouldn't mind if it was Harry Potter I was reading as long as she could hear my voice. So I put her in her bouncer and started to read aloud. I looked at her at the end of every couple of lines so that she knew my words were directed at her. We spent a good few hours a day for a whole month on that book, and both Phoebe and I were happy. We were doing an activity that entertained us both.

Phoebe is now 6 months old and I still read to her regularly. I read my book to her for an hour or two during the day. She continually tries to grab it. If she won't go down at night I read a child's book to her.

Reading to Phoebe appears to have given her a huge interest in books, and I hope this has given her a chance to love reading throughout her childhood. I am hoping it could make her willing to learn how to read. It could also make her aware of how grammar and diction work and give her a wider vocabulary.

Reading to Phoebe has given us a good bond, one we can always share, because even when she is too old to read to any more we can still discuss books.

While I have been writing the last few paragraphs, Phoebe has woken and I have read aloud as I've been writing, which again has kept her occupied. I think that a mother reading to her baby has so many positive outcomes that I will continue to do this with any future children. It also gives a new mother a bit of entertainment aside from the baby, which we all need.

FOCUS

Because they have been listening, babies begin to remember groups of sounds they often hear, such as *Up you come*. They hear the group of sounds as a whole, and only begin to be aware that sentences are made up of separate words later.

Between 6 and 9 months some babies may recognise one or two words, such *Clap hands,* or *Bye bye*. They may be able to recognise objects that are being referred to without a gesture from an adult.

FOCUS

The implication of knowing about babies' sensitivity to the feelings and voices around them is that adults must be careful to avoid distressing them by speaking in an agitated way. Childcare workers should be on the lookout for evidence of the child's responses and be able to extend each baby's growing understanding of the world.

REFLECT ON YOUR PRACTICE

It is a skill to watch out for evidence of how much a baby understands.

How do you note a baby's growing understanding? How do you share your observations with the parent? What information do you ask for from the parent?

It is a skill to foster a baby's growing understanding of the patterns of sound in the language.

Do you give the babies you care for the opportunity to listen to you reading aloud to them? There is no need to read Milton to them, but there are plenty of accessible rhymes or stories with strong repetitions for a baby to enjoy. How do you organise your time to ensure that every baby in your care is read to as an individual at least twice a week?

FIND OUT MORE

Goleman, D (1996) *Emotional Intelligence*, Bloomsbury

Morris, D (1991) *Babywatching*, Jonathan Cape

Murray, L and Edwards, L (2000) *The Social Baby*, CP Publishing

Toddlers as understanders

Toddlers take in much more of the world around them as they become mobile. They build up an understanding of sequences of events, and learn the names of the objects in the environment.

They may begin to realise there are scripts or conventional sayings for greetings and departures. There are also scripts for beginning and ending phone conversations, for use on public transport, in the post office or in shops.

Toddlers learn about prohibitions and adopt the use of the negative ('No!') themselves. They begin to realise that words can be used to postpone an event, or anticipate it. They may begin to hear words being used to build up their personal history when words are used to fix and capture memories, for example, 'This is when you were a baby' or 'This is when the snow came.'

Toddlers as non-verbal tellers

Toddlers continue to use non-verbal means of communication. Even when they have learned to talk they may deliberately use crying to attract help. Now they can calculate that the further away the adult is, the louder the crying has to be.

Throughout early childhood, children's emotions continue to be reflected in their body language. In these months they have a greater control of their limbs than of language. Toddlers will pull at an adult's clothes to get attention, will follow an adult and cling on to him or her if they fear they are about to be abandoned. The body language of a 2-year-old in a tantrum is unmistakeable. Toddlers jump about when they are excited, and point at something they are interested in. They stamp and run in exhilaration. They interact with other children, often copying another child's actions.

Besides intentionally using facial expressions, gestures and movements to communicate their needs and to share their enjoyment of life with the adults who care for them, the actions of toddlers who are now able to get about under their own steam can also indirectly reveal the state of their interests, knowledge and feelings as they handle the objects in their environment (indoors or outside) and the toys that adults have provided. Look back at Chapter 2 to remind yourself about schematic behaviour.

Some children find they need the reassurance of a familiar object. In the second half of the first year a child may grow attached to what Donald Winnicott called a **transitional object**, that is a tangible link with a place he or she finds secure. Some toddlers will therefore not be parted from a particular blanket or soft toy. Other children adopt an imaginary companion. Some toddlers express sibling jealousy safely in the way they treat a doll.

Toddlers may grow attached to a transitional object

REFLECT ON YOUR PRACTICE

It is a skill to respond to a child's non-verbal communication.

How do you deal with the transitional objects a child brings into the setting? If a child wanted to take something home from the setting, what would you do?

Are there limits to the toleration of transitional objects? How would you react if the child is nearly four and is still seeking the comfort of a dummy?

Beginning to talk

Language has been called the human race's greatest invention. Spoken language can do all the things that facial expressions, gestures and body language can do: it is used to greet people and acknowledge them, to ask others to do something to ensure one's needs are met, and to share feelings and facts.

It can do more. It connects mind to mind; it can hurt and heal; it can empower or disenfranchise. It can fix impressions, recreate the past and consider the future. It can also bring into the mind things that could never be but are only imagined. It underpins the whole of human endeavour. It makes it possible to share plans, inventions and skills.

Once we learn to use language, it becomes difficult to imagine life without it because language fixes ideas, and once we have done this we can begin to reflect on our impressions and analyse them. Used internally, language connects a person to his or her innermost self. We cannot remember being a baby because at that stage we had no command of language.

Babies are very receptive towards speech. As was mentioned in Chapter 2, 2-day-old infants already show a preference for hearing their native language – they started paying attention to it before they were born. Shortly after birth they show that they know the sound of their mother's voice, and perhaps their father's too.

> **CASE STUDY:**
>
> **JOHN**
>
> John says:
>
> It was amazing. The moment I spoke to Jo just after the baby was born, the baby turned her head and looked at me. The midwife said 'She knows your voice.' That's because I used to lean on Jo and talk to our baby when she was in the womb.

Intonation

There are two aspects to language, its tunes and the words that the tunes carry. Both the intonation and the words contribute to the meaning. Let's take intonation first.

The first thing one has to learn about a language is the tunes or **intonation** it has. Different accents and languages have their own tunes. We recognise an Irish person by a lilt in the voice. We recognise that an American from the deep South has a different way of speech. Even if you haven't learned the language, you will have an idea of how an Italian speaks Italian, or the tunes of German or Urdu.

> **KEY TERM: Intonation**
>
> *A distinct pattern of pitch in a sentence, which is used grammatically to indicate meaning or context.*

> **FOCUS**
>
> Babies learn the tunes of the language first. They babble with the tunes of English if that's the language they hear. They do this without knowing any of the words we use. They practise the range of sounds and intonation they hear.

Different types of sentences have characteristic tunes.

◆ There are patterns for **statements**: 'The weather is clear today.'

◆ There are patterns for **questions**, especially when a question word (such as *what* or *when*) is not used. We say: 'You're going now?' with a rise at the end.

◆ There are patterns for **commands**. One is the statement pattern, but with greater stress. An actor may declaim 'Go now!' The other command pattern has a more pronounced stress at the end of the sentence: 'I told you to go *now*!'

◆ There is a pattern for **refusing**: 'Certainly not.'

◆ There is a pattern for expressing **hesitation** and **uncertainty**: 'Oh, I don't really know….'

◆ There are patterns for **tentative requests**: 'I'm so sorry, but would you mind….'

◆ There is a pattern for **pleading** and another sharper one for **warning**.

Words

The tunes are the vehicles that carry the words. The majority of words are made up of two or more parts or **syllables**, each syllable containing a vowel.

> **KEY TERM:** Syllable
>
> *One of the units that combine to make up a word, acting as a unit of rhythm. It contains a vowel, either alone, as in the first syllable of a/bout, or within consonants, as in seg/ment. In a word of several syllables some are given greater stress than others.*

English works by having lighter and heavier stresses on the syllables that make up a word. We rarely use words with even stresses one after the other, though we do use an even stress for marching: 'Left, right, left, right.' Using an even stress instead of the expected tune in other situations indicates anger or exasperation.

Many English words have the stress on the first syllable, for example *baby, open, kitchen*. We keep the stress pattern when we turn a **noun** stem into an **adjective** or an **adverb**, such as *hope, hopeful* (one heavy, one light stress), *hopefully* (one heavy, two light stresses). When a **verb** is changed to indicate a change of tense the stress is still on the first syllable, for example *eat* can become *eaten* or *eating*.

> ## FOCUS
>
> To hear how stress makes a difference, say the sentence 'I will not go' four times, putting the stress on each word in turn:
>
> '*I* will not go, I *will* not go, I will *not* go, I will not *go* (but I will phone).'

Playing with sounds is an early attempt at talking

CASE STUDY:
MARK HALLIDAY

Mark Halliday, an expert in linguistics, listened to the sounds his 10-month-old baby made. He had the skill of being able to capture the sounds precisely in written form using the **International Phonetic Alphabet**.

He realised that his son was very organised in his use of sounds and intonation for conveying meaning. The child had one sound for greeting people, another to show interest, one for making a request and another sound for pulling out of an interaction. There was one sound that was used when the child wanted something and another when he was displeased. Halliday was convinced the baby had noticed that there were specific tunes for specific intentions. The baby had done this by listening to the tunes that were used in different circumstances as adults spoke to him, and also to the conversations happening around him.

KEY TERM: International Phonetic Alphabet

A system first devised in 1888, which has a symbol to identify and describe every sound of every language, e.g. for the nasal sound -ing.

'Bye bye'

'Allgone'

Up to the age of 9 or 10 months, babies use sounds to communicate, but it is in their own private language. No two babies, not even twins, use the same sound for identical purposes. But the adults who converse with the baby learn to decode the child's meaning from non-verbal behaviour and gestures, and they use their language to respond. They are able to articulate the baby's feelings in the situation they are sharing, 'Oh – that's nice, isn't it?' As a result the baby begins to associate the word or phrase the adult uses with the situation. Babies may also begin to realise that it is a more efficient way of getting the things they want if they use the sounds that adults use.

As we talk to babies we naturally stress the important words. So children pick up on the important words such as *hello* or *up* or *there* and begin to use them in appropriate contexts. The baby is beginning to communicate by using the language the rest of us use.

To make the words, the child has to master the sounds that make up the word. There is a definite pattern in the order in which sounds are mastered.

Under 3 Years   3½–4½ Years   5–8½ Years

Learning sounds

Toddlers talking

When children begin to speak, generally some time around their first birthday, at first they communicate verbally by using only one word at a time – these are known as **single-word utterances**. But with only a few words they can express a variety of meanings. They can communicate emotion, e.g. *Ehyee* (meaning 'That's nice') or get someone to do something, e.g. *Ahh-dah* (meaning 'Show me, that's interesting'). They can give a command or make a comment: *Down* may mean 'I've dropped it' or 'Put me down').

> **KEY TERM: Single-word utterances**
>
> *The first stage of using words to communicate, most noticeable between 12 and 18 months. One word, or a phrase used as one word e.g. all-fall-down, carries meaning. Most words used at this stage are the names of people, food, clothing or household items.*

Toddlers begin to use words to name things. The words they use first are connected with the important aspects of their experience: parents, siblings, toys, pets, cars, food. Words are used to make social contact, to draw another person's attention or to share information (e.g. *dindin*, or *tar* for 'car'). They start to use some negative words, e.g. *no* or *gone*. They use *more* to bring attention to quantity or to ask for or describe a recurrence of an item or an event. They have some action words, e.g. *run* or *eat*, and can refer to location, e.g. *there*.

FOCUS

Keep a diary of a baby's first words. Identify the baby's purpose in using them. Is he or she naming a person or thing, or requesting something – and is this person or thing in sight? Is he or she telling someone to do something, or expressing affection or another feeling?

After the stage of one-word utterances, toddlers move to a stage of **two-word sentences**. At this stage children seem to sort the words they know into two groups. For many of their sentences young children use combinations of two words, one from each group. One group contains useful words, such as *allgone, no, that, more*. This is called the **pivot group**.

> **KEY TERM: Pivot group**
>
> *The closed group of useful words that can combine with any word in the child's open group at the stage of two-word utterances, e.g. no, more, allgone, that.*

The other group (the **open group**) contains all the names that the children are learning for the people and objects in their environment.

> **KEY TERM: Open group**
>
> *That part of the young child's vocabulary that is continually expanding when the child is at the stage of two-word utterances.*

> **KEY TERM: Two-word utterances**
>
> *A way of speaking that begins to be used about the age of 18 months. The child has two classes of word, pivot or closed class and open class. Pivot words are only used with open words. Two open-class words can be used together.*

By combining a word from each group, therefore, children can announce (and be understood) *Daddy allgone* or *dinner allgone* or *birdie allgone*. It is remarkable that they can do this, because it is not at all what they would have heard an adult say. Toddlers may have heard an adult say 'Well now, that's good – your dinner's all gone', but toddlers use the key meaning-carrying words in their own way, using their own categorisation. This is a primitive **grammar** that toddlers work out for themselves. Sometimes they might combine two words from their open group, such as *Daddy coat*, but they never put two pivot-group words together.

Children order words carefully. If they want to tell their brother he is naughty they will say *naughty Jack*. If they want to tell their mother that their brother has been naughty they will say *Jack naughty*.

> **FOCUS**
>
> Note down examples of a toddler's early two-word sentences. What are the words in the child's pivot group?

Developing grammar

The next stage is for the young child to adopt the grammar that the rest of us use. Grammar is the way we pattern words into sentences, making meaning through being aware of their underlying structure. We have learned to organise words into sentences and that they fit into particular slots. Because we know what to expect, we know that a sentence such as 'The car a drive the left man in' does not make sense. We have learned to expect particular categories of words in particular places, and because of the order in which the words come we can decode the different meaning in two sentences such as 'The dog bit the man' and 'The man bit the dog.'

Adults take care to name things for young children. More importantly, they are also unwittingly teaching the child what to do with the words – how to use them and how to arrange them to get shades of meaning across. Children derive most of their knowledge of grammar not by being formally instructed but by listening to and copying how people express meanings.

Consider how a few changes in words make a difference in what we understand by the statements:

◆ I'm going out now

◆ He's going out

◆ I went out

◆ I'm going tomorrow.

The child begins to learn the rules of grammar by listening. One rule that is learned early is to put an *s* on the end of a word to indicate a plural. Children will also begin to use the suffix *-ing*. Between two and three, children will begin to use a wider range of location words (**prepositions**) such as *in, on* and *under*. They will begin to use **pronouns** such as *I, me, you* and *it*.

Grammar differentiates between various types of words. There are naming words (**nouns**) such as *house* and action words (**verbs** such as *to paint*). We say 'He painted the house.' We can tell from the pattern of the words in that sentence that *paint* is an action word or verb, and *house* is a noun.

Not everyone has been taught the names of the groups of words in a language, but everyone using the language knows how to use these categories. In English, some words have multiple uses and we can only tell whether they're a verb or a noun by knowing where they appear in a sentence. *Paint* is one of these words. *Paint* functions as a noun in the sentence 'I chose blue paint for the door.' The position of the word as it occurs in this sentence tells us that *paint* is referring to the stuff in the tin. If we mention a *paint brush, paint* is being used to describe the specific type of brush, and so it's functioning as an **adjective**.

FOCUS

Take the word *work*. We can use it as a **verb**, an action word: 'I *work* at the setting.'

By changing the word a little we can say: 'I *worked* at the setting last year' or 'I *will work* late on Tuesdays.'

We can use the word as a **noun**: 'My *work* is pleasant.'

We can use the word (or a variant) as an **adjective:** 'I'm a *working* person' or 'in my *work* place'.

Can you think of some more hard-working words?

The following table shows the development of the child's skill in making the sounds and sentence patterns we use in English.

Approximate age	Consonants used	Description of speech	Examples
9 months	*m, n* *p, b, t, d* *w*	Babbling progresses to use intonation patterns Babbled sounds are combined Favourite babbled sounds may function as words Parts of word are repeated End sounds are missed off	*Da-doo* *Dah* *Baba* *Bibi* (for biscuit) *Ba* (for ball)
12 months	*k* and *g* may be added to the above	Words that are more recognisable Ends of words missed off One-word utterances Two-word utterances	Cat may be *ca* or *tat* *Down* (several meanings) *Mummy sock* (could mean 'Mummy's sock', 'Mummy this is your sock', 'Mummy I want my sock')
2 years	*ng* now added as well as *m* and *n* *k, g* *f, s* *w, h*	*k* and *g* now used in words *f* and *s* used in some words End sounds can still be left off Basic sentences, but without pronouns or auxiliary verbs	*Going nana tar* *Go tee tie* (seaside) *Where man?*
3 years	*l* is added *f* and *s* are now used but not *sh*, *th*, *ch* or *j*	Recognisable sentence patterns are now used including questions and negatives Most words now have a sound at the end, but it's not always the adult sound Some confusion with irregular plurals and past tenses	*Where's teddy?* *I don't know where he's going* *We caught a big fiss* *Foots/feets, mouses* *I eated, I goed, I bringed*

Two-year-olds as tellers

It is more useful to note a young child's mastery of grammar and the sounds he or she can command rather than to attempt to estimate the number of words he or she uses. We all know more words than we tend to use. However, young children can be clever in getting their meaning across by using equivalent words.

Judy Dunn and her co-workers noted that 2-year-olds begin to be able to talk about emotions, their own and other people's: 'Me 'fraid', 'Me glad', 'Lucy sad'. The researchers found that the frequency of references to emotions in conversations between mothers and their children more than doubles between the ages of two and two-and-a-half. Mother and daughter conversations are characterised by more references to feelings than mother–son conversations.

CASE STUDY:

ELLIE

At two, Ellie was a competent talker. However, sometimes she became frustrated when her vocabulary didn't have the words she needed. One such occasion was when she was on one of her early visits to the beach. She became very cross with her Mum and Grandma when they couldn't understand her request for a *bag and boon*. After much arm waving and foot stamping she finally made them understand that she wanted a

bucket and spade. She didn't have those words in her vocabulary so she chose words that best described what she wanted. A *bag* has a handle and is carried in the way she carried a bucket, and a *boon* (spoon) was the nearest word she could think of to describe a spade.

Young children don't necessarily have the vocabulary to name desired objects

Since conversations about emotions enable children to understand their own emotions and other people's behaviour, the implication is that carers must acknowledge, identify and respond to children's feelings, especially those of boys.

It is a skill to help children to identify and talk about emotions.

What are the emotions (positive and negative) that children have words for? When do they speak about emotions? When do they need help to identify an emotion?

Two-year-olds as listeners

At two, children have built up a wide range of experience of the patterns of intonation as people have spoken to them. Questions have been asked of the crying baby, comfort has been given, warnings have been uttered, jokes have been overheard. As stories are told with expressive adaptations for a mouse speaking or a giant growling or the three bears asking 'Who's been sitting in my chair?', each in their own way, the child's familiarity with the range of the tunes of the language is expanded.

Nursery rhymes are invaluable for learning the stress patterns of English. In nursery rhymes the patterns of the syllables of English words are varied and repeated. The following nursery rhymes are shown with the symbol / above a stressed syllable, and ˘ above an unstressed syllable:

Hickory Dickory Dock

The mouse ran up the clock

The clock struck one

The mouse ran down

Hickory Dickory Dock

Little Miss Muffet

Sat on a tuffet

Eating her curds and whey

Along came a spider

And sat down beside her

And frightened Miss Muffet away

FOCUS

Can you write out the beat of the following two rhymes, identifying where the stresses come? It might help to clap out the beat as you say the rhyme aloud.

Little Jack Horner
Sat in the corner
Eating his Christmas pie
He put in his thumb
And pulled out a plum
And said 'What a good boy am I!'

This little piggy went to market
This little piggy stayed at home
This little piggy had roast beef
This little piggy had none.

Nursery rhymes also model grammar, such as:

◆ how to make statements – *Little Miss Muffet sat on a tuffet*

◆ how to ask questions – *Where are you going to my pretty maid?*

◆ how to report speech – *'I'm going a-milking, sir,' she said.*

Some rhymes link shorter sentences together into a longer one by using *and*: *The little dog laughed to see such fun and the dish ran away with the spoon.*

Others model the device of linking sentences by using **subordinate clauses**: *As I was going to St Ives, I met a man with seven wives.*

KEY TERM: Subordinate clause

A clause that contains a verb, but cannot stand alone; it needs to be associated with a main verb in a sentence to make complete sense, e.g. The baby, who had just woken up, *began to cry.*

FOCUS

Children need to become familiar with nursery rhymes to help their language development. Some rhymes soothe, such as *Rock-a-bye baby*. Others energise, such as *The grand old Duke of York* or *Ride a cock horse*. Some are nonsensical, such as *Hey diddle, diddle*, and others tell a simple story, such as *Little Miss Muffet* or *Jack and Jill*.

All rhymes introduce the very important idea that words can be used to convey experiences beyond the here and now. Repetition of rhymes not only teaches language patterns, but also helps children to develop a memory for sequences of words.

REFLECT ON YOUR PRACTICE

It is a skill to know and use a wide range of nursery rhymes in your work with children.

How many rhymes do you know? Which rhymes fit which routines? Do you know which are the favourite rhymes of each child you work with? What do you tell the parents about how and when you use rhymes with their child? How could you help parents to use rhymes with their children?

FIND OUT MORE

Opie, P and Opie, M (1963) *The Puffin Book of Nursery Rhymes*, Puffin Books

Opie, P and Opie, M (1951) *The Oxford Dictionary of Nursery Rhymes*, Oxford University Press

Children of three as understanders

Children of three make connections. They begin to ask for and give explanations for objects or events: 'That's to show how fast we're going', 'They're waiting here because the taxi hasn't come yet.'

They hear people linking phrases to give information – 'This is the boy who lives next door to Granny' – or to express a condition: 'We will go out when it stops raining.' They hear people specifying the order in which events occurred: 'Before we lived here we lived in...', 'After we got to the station we...' The ability to report a connection you have made depends on your ability to link phrases, or to link smaller sentences to make longer ones.

When we speak we do this linking of ideas all the time. Stories are also full of these links, and this is another reason why hearing stories is an important experience for children.

The 3-year-old enjoys stories, and they are considerably more complex than nursery rhymes. At its simplest, a story links two events, as in the Miss Muffet nursery rhyme, or 'It was raining so we stayed at home.' A more developed story gives an introduction to the setting where the events take place. It specifies the characters, and these characters meet a problem. There is an explanation of how the problem is resolved, and very often a reflection at the end.

FOCUS

Build these pairs of short sentences into one longer one. Use words such as *so*, *if*, *because*, *when*, *after*, *before*, *although*, *then*, *now*, *but*. Combine each pair in three ways, using a different linking word each time.

◆ We wanted to get there fast. We took a taxi.

◆ We had no cash. We went to the post office.

◆ We were late. We waited for her.

◆ It was sunny. We went to the beach.

◆ It is easy. Make up some more.

You will notice that one verb in your new sentence carries the more important piece of information, and the other is the less important or subordinate idea.

The importance of stories doesn't go away as we grow up. We all make sense of our lives through stories; we cut a sequence out of our waves of experience, mark a start and an end and parcel it into a story for ourselves and others. We do this all the time, every day. At night our dreams take story form.

FOCUS

Fill in the gaps in this story.

When I was at the supermarket checkout	*Setting*
I saw these two…	*Characters*
Their trolley was laden. They had…	
Well the girl rang it through and…	*Problem*
They looked in their pockets…	
Finally they had to…	*Outcome*
I'd hate that to happen to me.	*Reflection*

Some stories are written down, but the majority of the stories we hear are about the lives of people around us. The stories we construct for ourselves underpin how we approach people. We make judgements according to what we have decided happened.

Stories in books often have a formula for the beginning (*Once upon a time*) and ending (*And they all lived happily ever after*). In between, we hear about the forest or the palace (the setting), the people who lived there (the characters), their problem and their solution. The story often has a message. The youngest and least

regarded often comes off best in traditional stories, and there is often a warning not to trust strangers or to be proud or greedy. The characters in traditional stories are strong and memorable, with clear motives.

The value of stories is that they are little segments of experience. Gordon Wells, in a longitudinal study in Bristol, found that the children who had had most stories told to them did better throughout primary school. This was thought to be due to the fact that they had learned to rely on language to gain access to events beyond their immediate experience, and much schoolwork requires this ability.

Enjoying books at an early age is a valuable experience

FOCUS

Hearing stories being told and having stories read aloud is vital for a child's development. Stories can be read to children from when they are very young. Stories are a way of sharing experience, and they can also be a way for a child to ensure he or she takes part in the heady delight of communicating with friends.

CASE STUDY:
JOSH

Josh was a sociable 2-year-old who liked to feel involved in adult conversation. At the time he was also very interested in Thomas the Tank Engine and all his friends. If there were times when he wasn't able to follow the conversation, or he didn't feel involved, he would demand that the adults should 'Talk Thomas'. This was his way of joining in and making sure that he could contribute to what was being said.

It is a skill to be able to tell stories to children informally using events from everyday life.

How often do you tell the children about events in your own life? How often do you use events at the childcare setting to make up a story? How would you encourage a child to tell a story?

It is a skill to be able to bring stories to life as you read them to children.

Group story sessions are not appropriate for young children. And television programmes are not a replacement for stories.

To make sure the child understands a story, adults must use all their observational and vocal skills. How can you arrange for children to experience stories one-to-one? How do you record which stories a particular child has heard being read? Which stories appeal to each child in your care?

Children of three mastering communication through speech

Children aged three are particularly skilled at non-verbal communication. They are able to imitate the movement of an elephant or a rabbit or a galloping horse. They can jump like a monkey, be a giant, a pirate or a shopkeeper. They also reveal the more complex emotions of pride and shame with their whole body.

By observing children in situations with games or puzzles where they are likely to encounter either success or failure, researchers have been able to see that pride in a task successfully completed makes the body expand: the child stands with the head up and shoulders back. The arms are often raised and the eyes raised. There is often a smile and words such as 'I did it.'

On the other hand, where there is a sense of failure and shame the body seems to deflate: hands are down, or sometimes they cover the face; the eyes and the corners of the mouth are down. They child may say 'I'm no good at this.'

A study led by M. Lewis in 1992 in which children of three were given a selection of easy and more difficult tasks found that the children rated themselves correctly. No child showed pride on failing and no child showed shame on succeeding. Boys and girls did not differ in their manifestation of pride. However in situations of failure, especially on easy tasks, girls showed significantly more shame than boys.

At around three, children are more aware of others' non-verbal expressions. They can identify the event that triggered a dispute: 'He's angry because she took his bike.' They may also talk about the inner state that underlies behaviour: 'She is sad because she misses her mum.'

They develop strategies for joining a group. These range from playing alongside, to joining in with a suggestion, to touching, laughing, vocalising, to connected speech. They begin to negotiate: 'Why don't we…?', 'If you… then….'

At three children are mastering most of the rules of grammar. They can turn a statement into the question form or into a **negative**. An example is the way a statement such as 'The door is open' turns into the question – 'Is the door open?' – or the negative: 'The door is not open.' The same words could be rearranged to make a command: 'Open the door.'

> **KEY TERM: Negative**
>
> *Ways of expressing 'No'. For example, the positive statement* I like it *is changed in the negative to* I do not like it. *Young children often take time to learn to use the negative form correctly. They'll often say, 'I no like it.'*

> **FOCUS**
>
> Can you make two sentences using the word *house*; one with *house* as a noun and the second with it as a verb? Think of at least three other words that can have two lives. Are they pronounced in exactly the same way? There is often a subtle difference. Can you hear it? Does it happen every time?

Between the ages of three and four the child's sentences become longer. The child starts to use *the* and *a* in sentences, and uses **possessives** such as *Mummy's bag*. The word *is* is used to give emphasis: *It **is** big.* Children begin to use more pronouns, adding *we, he, she*.

> **KEY TERM: Possessives**
>
> *Words that indicate ownership, e.g.* mine, hers, his. *Possessives are also formed by adding an apostrophe and* s, *e.g.* Tom's house.

Another step taken at this time is to add the suffix -*ed* on the end of a verb to indicate the past tense. The -*ed* ending works with most verbs, but there are a few **irregular verbs** that don't follow this pattern. A child may say *I bringed it* or *You taked it*. These mistakes are called **virtuous errors**, because the child has learned the way in which the past tense is generally formed and is applying that rule.

Again, no one will have explained this rule – children work it out for themselves. It is counterproductive to correct the child continually: concentrate on the child's message.

KEY TERM: Irregular verb

A verb that does not behave as the vast majority of verbs do, for example by adding -ed to indicate the past tense. Instead, in some verbs the vowel changes in the past tense, e.g. ring becomes rang. Other verbs change their shape entirely to indicate different persons or tenses, e.g. I am, she is.

FOCUS

Can you think of some more examples of verbs that are irregular in the past tense?

REFLECT ON YOUR PRACTICE

It is a skill to be able to analyse the command a child has of language.

Tape record and then transcribe a 2- or 3-year-old child's speech and comment on how much the child knows about the rules of grammar.

There is an example of a transcribed and analysed dialogue in Appendix 3 to show you a useful layout.

REFLECT ON YOUR PRACTICE

It is a skill to analyse the range of purposes a child has for talking.

Listen to some 3-year-olds at play. What do they use their utterances for? Are they self-maintaining, directing, reporting, predicting, reasoning something out, or projecting?

Hint: listen to the sentence structure, and especially the verbs. Is the child issuing commands or threats (self-maintaining), using the future tense (predicting), using the present or past tense (reporting), using words such as *if*, *because* or *when* (logical reasoning) or *might be*, *would be* or *must be* (projecting)?

CASE STUDY: LEEDS NURSERIES

A 3-year-old becomes very proficient with his or her mother tongue. Joan Tough listened to children of three and four in nurseries in Leeds as they played and talked to each other, and she identified several uses of language.

The children were using talk for the purpose of influencing others. She called this **self-maintaining**, for example: 'That's mine', 'Get off'. When the child used words to get someone to do something, Tough called that use of language **directing**, for example: 'Put it there', 'You push it'.

A child might also be heard telling himself or herself what to do, such as 'This goes here and now that piece goes there.' Lev Vygotsky believed that this thinking aloud became the voice in the head that we hear when we are planning what to do next.

The children often **reported** what they were doing ('I'm eating it all up') or seeing ('It's raining') or what they had done ('We went to the beach'). Tough also heard children **predicting** what would happen: 'I'm going to Gran's this weekend.'

Children also used language to reason, using words such as *because* and *if*: 'It's stuck because the hole's too small.' If the child uses words such as *if* or *because* it is an indication that he or she is linking events together and seeking a reason for them, in other words using **logical reasoning**.

Tough heard some children using language to **project** into the feelings of others when they said things such as 'She would be sad' or 'They would be frightened' or 'She must have been glad.'

The implication of this is that all children need one-to-one exchanges with adults about what is happening or will happen, or describing what is in an illustration or a story, in order to have these uses of language modelled.

Adults helping children to talk

Children are born communicators but they need help if they are to develop speech.

Adults talking to babies instinctively speak clearly, emphasising the intonation patterns and putting stress on the important words in their sentences. Their sentences are shorter, with few subordinate clauses. There are more directives and more questions. This way of speaking used to be called **motherese,** but observations have shown that it is not only used by mothers.

KEY TERM: Motherese

The name given to the way people talk to very young children. Outside the UK it is sometimes known as caretaker speech *or* baby talk. *Many adults use it instinctively and even children as young as four use it to younger children.*

Toddlers using one-word utterances are helped by having their word extended by hearing it repeated by the adult with an additional piece of information: 'Yes, it's a flower, a *red* flower.' The adult can interpret a child's gesture and put into words what the child means, for example: 'Oh, a hole – a great big hole in your sock.'

Toddlers learn the meanings of words by hearing them over and over in different circumstances, so we talk about *new shoes*, *dirty shoes*, *Daddy's shoes*, *the shoes under the bed*. It is important to give a running commentary to toddlers when you are caring for them: 'Now off with your shoes, first this one and now the next one'. It is important to talk about things that are physically present so the toddler can see them as well as hearing the word. This is quite unlike much of what we do in adult talk. It is good practice to use the names of the objects spoken about, and not use pronouns for them. For example, say 'Where's that shoe?' rather than merely 'Where is it?'

David Wood listened to childcare workers talking to children aged three and over in nurseries in the Oxford area. He identified five approaches that were used in all the childcare settings. These were:

◆ management – telling the children what to do

◆ instruction – giving information, decided by the giver

◆ conversation

◆ play

◆ rapport – being sociable, oiling the wheels: 'How nice', 'That's lovely'.

He discovered that the children always spoke less when all of a practitioner's talk was in the first two categories. The focus on the adult's own agenda meant there was an imbalance of power, with the children being made to feel that the adults were unapproachable and liable to be disapproving.

There was far more language from the children when the majority of the adult's talk was in the third and fourth categories. Here the relationship was more evenly balanced, and the child's contribution was respected. The five categories were mixed in different ratios by different members of staff. If the recipe was made up of a good measure of genuine conversation and a readiness to follow the children's interest, the children flourished. Otherwise they did not.

FOCUS

You are using management mode when you:

◆ tell the child what to do next – 'Tidy up time' or 'Go and get your coat on'

◆ stop the child doing something – 'That game's too noisy in here'

◆ delay the child – 'Wait till Ben has finished, then you can'

◆ tell the child what you're going to do next – 'I'll be back in a minute'

◆ help the child to get ready for an activity – 'Let me put that apron on you before you paint.'

You are instructing when you:

◆ describe or highlight something in the environment – 'Look at that cat over there'

◆ ask the child to name or comment on events or objects in the immediate environment – 'What's the colour of your jumper today?'

◆ demonstrate or tell the child how to do something – 'Look, hold it this way'

◆ assist the child in what he or she is trying to do – 'Let me help you to balance it'

◆ evaluate what the child has done – 'That's lovely.'

In play mode you go along with the game and:

◆ elaborate the play – 'Oh, so you're the wolf. Come and eat me up'

◆ allocate roles – 'You be the mummy.'

In conversation mode you:

◆ ask for information about things you do not already know – 'So where did you go on Saturday?'

◆ tell the child about something not ongoing – 'We had the men in to mend the climbing frame'

◆ ask for an explanation or give one – 'Why do you think…' or 'We're waiting because the bus is late'

◆ talk about reasons for others' actions – 'She's crying because….'

Using the rapport mode you:

◆ agree with the child – 'Yes, it's like the one we saw yesterday.'

Monitor yourself to find out how much language you get from children when you use the management or instruction modes when you are talking to them. Listen to find out whether you get more language from them as you try the conversation or play modes. Can you think why there is a difference?

Children with problems

Some children have difficulties with developing language.

Sometimes there is a problem with **hearing**. In her useful text published in the 1970s, Mary Sheridan said it was advisable to check a child's hearing if he or she was:

◆ not responding to everyday sounds by 6–8 weeks

◆ not showing an ordinary interest in people or playthings by 3–4 months

◆ not babbling by 10 months

◆ not speaking single words by 21 months (the average is 13–15 months)

◆ not putting two or three words together by 27 months (the average is 18–22 months)

◆ not using intelligible speech by 4 years (the average is 3–3½)

◆ not using conventional grammar by 5 years (the average is 4–4½).

Sometimes there is a problem with making the sounds (**articulation**). The child might find it hard to say some of the more difficult sounds such as *k* or *r*, saying *tat* for *cat* and *wabbit* for *rabbit*.

> **KEY TERM: Articulation**
>
> *Production of the sounds of speech by movement of the jaw, lips, tongue, and vocal cords.*

Sometimes there is a difficulty with **phonology**, that is not being able to distinguish between similar sounds (*p* and *b* or *tr* and *ch*), or put the sounds together in words. These children may overuse one sound, as in 'I wan go geep but egun maging goig' (I want to go to sleep but everyone is making a noise). Note that this child is also missing out some of the words a mature speaker would have used.

> **KEY TERM: Phonology**
>
> *The study of the sound system of a language: the sounds the language uses, and the way syllables are stressed.*

Sometimes the child does not seem to have developed the **vocabulary** that is needed to have a conversation, such as this child approaching four looking at a book with an adult:

Adult 'Oh look, there's a car'

Child 'That'

Adult 'Yes, it's a car'

Child 'Car'

Adult 'They're going on the road'

Child 'That'

Sometimes the child has problems with **grammar** and the words are in the wrong order, such as 'Mummy where bus is?'

Sometimes the child has a problem with turn-taking in the conversation, and his or her comments are not related to the other speaker's, or the child may have difficulty in attracting a listener's attention before saying something. The technical term for this skill is **pragmatics**, that is knowing how to hold a conversation.

> **KEY TERM: Pragmatics**
>
> *The study of the range of language uses available for various types of interaction, e.g. in social interactions remembering to say* please *and* thank you.

Normal speech	A child with a difficulty
Child 'I got new shoes'	**Child** 'I got new shoes'
Adult 'How nice'	**Adult** 'How nice'
Child 'Yes, they're red'	**Child** 'I got new shoes'
Adult 'How lovely'	**Adult** 'How lovely'
	Child 'I'm going out now'

Speech therapists work with children whose speech is causing concern

CASE STUDY:
DANIEL AND SUSAN

Olga writes:

I am a mother of two children – Daniel aged three and Susan aged 11. I work full time while my husband looks after our children and the running of the house.

Daniel is a happy, sociable boy. The only thing holding him back is his speech. I first worried about Daniel when he was about 22 months old. I know I shouldn't have compared him with other children, but at a SureStart-run toddler group the difference was obvious. When I raised my concerns with my family they told me not to worry, that all children were different. But I still worried.

When it came to his next check-up I raised my concerns. The nurse spent a little time with him and listened to his speech. She agreed with me and noticed that his word endings were missing and simple words that he uses every day were very unclear. For example, for milk he would say *ba*. This was consistent for milk. He would say *bo* for bottle, *mu* for mum and *da* for dad, and so on.

He was referred to the multidisciplinary team in October. I received an appointment for a speech assessment for Daniel in February, which I was pleased with as I had heard you could wait a long time for your first appointment. Daniel was seen by the speech therapist who said at this age, 2½, not to worry as his speech could come without intervention. His speech was reviewed in April, with a small improvement, and again in June, when it was decided he would benefit from a speech therapist who would visit him in school and do sessional work with him. To get this he needs to be assessed by an educational psychologist with whom we are awaiting an appointment.

I also raised my concerns with the local SureStart programme, who referred him to their speech and language development worker. Her programme consisted of an 8-week home visit package, which I was very pleased with. It was great because she would discuss things with my husband and give him tips on how to promote speech through play. Since the programme there has been improvement in Daniel's vocabulary but still many of his words are unintelligible and we have problems understanding him, which results in screams of frustration from him. I find this very upsetting.

In the last 3 months Daniel has attended a nursery run by the SureStart speech and language development worker. He attends three afternoons per week and has benefited from this experience. He has come away with heaps of confidence to communicate. Daniel loves his new nursery, but the nursery will close during the summer holidays. I am truly grateful for this help, as on his last review his report said that he had 'severely delayed expressive language as well as extremely unintelligible speech'. Although I am so grateful that he is on the waiting list for speech therapy, I feel it is a very slow process, which proves to be frustrating.

From about the age of four, the amazing ability to acquire language described in this chapter begins to wane. This is why it is so important that children under three are talked to, one to one. Having the radio or the television on in the background will not do. The child needs to get the idea that language is an effective method of communication by learning at first hand how good a tool language is for welcoming, for giving comfort, for sharing ideas and needs, and for opening a window into another's mind and spirit.

Instant feedback as to whether their message has been received and understood is the key to developing children's competence and confidence in themselves as communicators (as both tellers and understanders). The art of conversing is very important and children learn this from the adults who talk to them as babies about what is happening as if they knew exactly what was being said, and who open up to toddlers' needs and foster young children's confidence.

FOCUS

Adults working with children must expend considerable energy in one-to-one situations to develop the child's competence in using language. Group work or watching television does not help because there is no instant feedback, which is what face-to-face communication requires.

REFLECT ON YOUR PRACTICE

It is a skill to share your understanding about a child's language with parents.

What would you say to a parent who said to you 'Oh, he's too young to talk yet', or to the adult who constantly corrected a child's attempts at talking?

Conclusion

This chapter has discussed how children communicate as tellers and understanders, non-verbally and using the spoken word.

There are two sides to communication – being a teller and being an understander.

Language learning begins at birth. The child has an urge to communicate, to bind to and to share with others. While babies use non-verbal ways to communicate, they also listen to and learn the tunes and individual sounds used in language. The child learns the importance and flexibility of language through experiencing many loving face-to-face interactions. As adults talk to children they work out how language is used and construct their own idea of what the rules are.

Toddlers use tunes and words to communicate their intentions.

At three, children have most of the sentence patterns they need and they show that they are aware of the way talk varies in different situations, for example when it is used by a shopkeeper, a waiter, a doctor or a childcare worker.

Young children have to be respected as communicators using language if they are to master it. Constant corrections can sap a child's confidence. It is for the adult to work hard as an understander and to construct the child's meaning, to give the child feedback to show that he or she has been understood and, most of all, to develop strategies that encourage the child to extend his or her competence through encouraging talk.

We must listen to what children say and how they say it. We must talk to them and slip in comments and questions that encourage them to spread their wings as tellers.

The following skills which are vital for anyone working in childcare have been highlighted:

- It is a skill to interpret a baby's non-verbal messages.
- It is a skill to help a baby to learn the skills of conversation even before he or she can talk.
- It is a skill to hear the sounds the baby is making in various situations.
- It is a skill to watch out for evidence of how much a baby understands.
- It is a skill to foster a baby's growing understanding of the patterns of sound in the language.
- It is a skill to respond to a child's non-verbal communication.
- It is a skill to vary your voice to help babies' understanding.
- It is a skill to help children to identify and talk about emotions.
- It is a skill to know and use a wide range of nursery rhymes in your work with children.
- It is a skill to be able to tell stories to children informally using events from everyday life.
- It is a skill to be able to bring stories to life as you read them to children.
- It is a skill to be able to analyse the command a child has of language.
- It is a skill to analyse the range of purposes a child has for talking.
- It is a skill to share your understanding about a child's language with parents.

Chapter 4

How babies and young children communicate through symbol systems

This chapter considers the way children begin to send and respond to messages which do not require the teller and the understander to be in each other's presence for the communication to take place. It is a very important step for the child to move on from using only the resources of his or her body – gestures, voice and speech – for sending and receiving messages. Children have to begin to understand that there are messages to be interpreted out on the street, or in squiggles on a piece of paper, and that people are able to communicate by entrusting messages to something external to themselves.

This chapter is divided into the following sections:

◆ Signs and symbols in the environment

◆ Children using marks to communicate

◆ Children communicating through play

◆ Children communicating through stories

◆ Children and literacy and numeracy

Communicating through symbol systems means moving beyond the here and now

Signs and symbols in the environment

One way of thinking about the many ways of conveying information is to group them according to their distance from physical methods. The **enactive** mode uses the body and includes gestures, role play and sociodramatic play, dance, drama, music and sound. The **iconic** mode includes artwork – pictures and statues. The **symbolic** mode is the most abstract and includes letters and numbers, musical notation, maps and other signs and symbols.

The baby comes into a world that has many ways of exchanging messages at a distance. Babies see adults using telephones, and slowly begin to realise that people can store information on video or in written form – anything from the last text message to the *Encyclopedia Brittanica*. Babies are particularly ready to accept that messages also exist in visual form. There are 'No smoking' signs; there are signs to toilets and emergency exits indoors, and road signs outside. There are logos to identify firms and products. Colour is used in traffic signals and road markings. Numbers are used to identify buses and houses. Sound is used by the police and emergency services – and the ice-cream van. Police officers, fire fighters, soldiers, medical staff and others wear distinctive uniforms that identify them. The child gets used to the idea that a plethora of messages are continually being received and sent. These messages may identify a person, place or product; may provide information, issue a warning or make a prohibition. The child needs help to notice them and to pick them out.

FOCUS

We should draw children's attention to the many signs and logos that surround them, so that they notice them, look for them and get used to the idea that information and messages do not rely on only face-to-face communication.

REFLECT ON YOUR PRACTICE

It is a skill to make children aware of the messages that are in use in the society that they live in.

One way is to point out signs and logos as you take the children for a walk. You could make an album of photographs of signs in the area that the children know, so that you can talk about them with the children. Do you have relevant examples of notices and signs for identifying, informing, warning, etc. in your setting? You might encourage the children who are about three to make their own notices and see which categories they choose. Note which logos a child can 'read' – anything from products in supermarkets to McDonald's, from road signs to television stations.

Children using marks to communicate

Early mark making

Becoming aware of non-verbal or non-physical ways of communicating encourages children to draw.

Drawing begins when the child makes the marvellous discovery that a movement can leave a mark. This might happen with movements of the fingers on a plate of food, or wet feet on a floor, or footprints in mud, damp sand or snow. These marks happen by accident, but finger painting or 'painting' with water outside on a sunny day helps to fix the idea, as does applying chalk, charcoal or crayons to paper. At first the impact is in the power of making a mark, but sooner or later a mark stirs a memory and the drawing can be labelled. This is a great breakthrough, because the way is now open for a child to communicate a chosen meaning in a way that relies on abstract symbols.

At first, even before the age of two, the child begins drawing with vertical or horizontal lines or circular scribbles, placed at random on the page. These drawings are a form of sensorimotor exploration. The hand moves about on surfaces in horizontal, vertical and circular movements. Each movement has a different effect. Gradually these basic marks are given meaning by the child, but often the same scribble can be given several different meanings in quick succession.

Between the ages of three and four the child begins to give explicit meanings to specific collections of marks. Often children at this age do not start off with a clear intention of what they want to produce, but halfway through a subject presents itself and the child will pursue this. At this stage they are using marks as tellers.

FOCUS

Chris Athey (1990) collected and analysed hundreds of children's drawings. She found the children all used two different groups of marks: lines and curves. She noticed that children arrange these marks in different ways. Are they placed above, below or beside each other? Do they intersect? Does a circular enclosure contain other marks? Do lines project from the edges of a circular enclosure?

Lines included:

- vertical scribble
- horizontal scribble
- continuous horizontal or vertical scribble
- differentiated horizontal and vertical scribbles
- open continuous triangles (zigzags and diagonals)
- horizontal lines
- vertical lines
- straight parallel lines
- grids.

(At four and five, children could produce triangles, squares and rectangles.)

Curves included:

- circular scribble
- circular enclosure
- core and radial
- oval
- enclosed curve
- closed semi-circle
- open semi-circle.

(Older children could make loops, spirals and concentric circles.)

Using these lines and curves, children can represent their ideas. Grids, for example, allow them to draw ladders or railway lines; circular enclosures allow them to draw animals and people; using core and radial allows them to draw leaves, flowers and spiders. Zigzags make it possible to create stairs or a crocodile's teeth.

Athey says the ability to construct these lines and curves and to decide where they go in relation to each other depends upon the child's experiences with the three-dimensional world; for example, rotational experiences provide the understanding needed for drawing circles, and experiences on the slide contribute to the ability to make a diagonal mark.

FOCUS

Look at the children's drawings reproduced below.

A The first example shows a few dabs on the page. This child is literally making marks, and is finding out about the fact that pens and pencils leave a trace.

B The second example shows a circular scribble. It is a trace of the hand's movement.

C Here, two colours of circular scribbles are superimposed.

D Here there are wandering lines and some lines go in the opposite direction making intersections.

E More control is required to produce these straight lines.

F The marks at the top show letter-like forms, an example of early literacy rather than drawing.

G and H The last two are the first real drawings – attempts at representing the human figure. The earlier one has a head and legs, the next has arms as well.

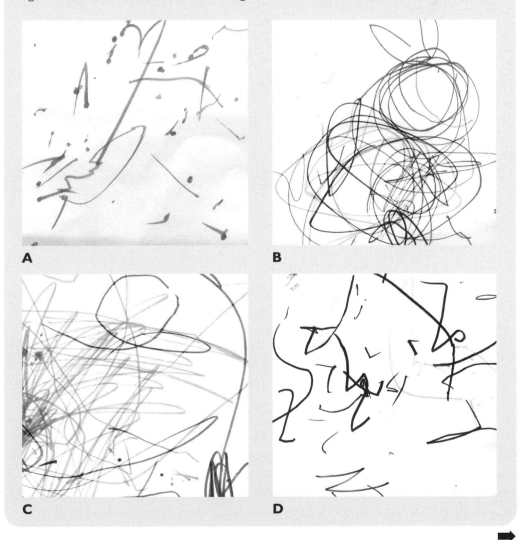

A

B

C

D

E

F

G

H

It is important to realise that the child is *not* attempting a realistic drawing. The child has made the great discovery that one thing can be represented by another. Young children are to be respected as discoverers in their exploration of the marks they can make. If they give meanings to their marks, this shows they have understood that there are many marks in their environment that contain messages. In their representations of the human figure, they select the most important features of a human being – the head and the means of locomotion.

REFLECT ON YOUR PRACTICE

It is a skill to respond appropriately to young children's drawings.

An appropriate response is not a perfunctory 'That's lovely – now put it over there to dry.' In discussing a child's drawing do not make remarks such as 'Where are Mummy's fingers?' If you do that, you fail to support the child and you induce a feeling of failure and disappointment instead of a celebration of effort.

By the same token, amending a child's work, or worse still giving a child something to copy, closes down the child's willingness to attempt to understand that representing three-dimensional reality using two dimensions is an intellectual struggle.

It is better to comment in terms of the marks themselves. For example, 'I see you've put those circles in a line, and there's one over there by itself.' Do not assume that the child was intending to produce a realistic representation of something seen. It is enough to be exploring the idea of conveying a message using marks on paper. Monitor yourself for a session and see how the children respond to the types of comment that are recommended here.

Children communicating through play

Mark making becomes more sophisticated

Play is a method children use to help them to understand what they see happening around them.

Caroline Hutt says that play takes two forms. The earliest form of play is a way of learning about the properties of objects. This is the **exploratory play** that babies and toddlers engage in when they have a treasure basket or a session of heuristic play. This type of play also happens wherever a baby gets hold of something that intrigues him or her. The questions answered by this type of play are questions such as 'What is this?', 'What does this do?'

> **KEY TERM: Play**
>
> *A child's self-chosen activity, whether it is exploratory, or involves pretending. Children may be seen playing by themselves, playing alongside others but without interacting with them (parallel play) or jointly pretending with all involved in taking a specific role (sociodramatic play).*

> *The type of play in which the child's chief purpose is to discover the characteristics and potential of something, such as water, sand, clay, paint, sound, a new toy, etc.*

Ludic play

The other type of play is what Hutt called **ludic play**. This is when the child proceeds to ask 'What can I do with this?', 'How can I use this?' A leaf will be used as a stand-in for a fish, or an acorn for a cup. It begins to happen around the age of two, when a child has achieved the concept of object permanence. It indicates that the child has definitely reached the understanding that objects have an existence of their own, even when they are not seen, touched or heard.

KEY TERM: Ludic play

> *The type of play in which children are exploiting what they have learned through exploratory play and feel confident enough to be able to make fanciful adjustments to what they know is reality.*

This milestone means that children's view of the world can expand. They are no longer tied to the here and now. They no longer rely solely on the information coming in through their senses – they move out of the sensorimotor stage. They begin to realise that they can pretend; a doll can be said to be a baby, a wooden block a car. Their imagination is liberated because they now realise they can manipulate reality and create a pretend world of their own. They begin to realise that symbols can carry any meaning they like.

The challenge to the mind when selecting a symbol to carry a message is that the mind has to keep two things in focus at the same time. One is the message you wish to send and the other is the suitability of the symbol or message carrier you have chosen. Choosing a useful symbol to carry a meaning means that we know its attributes or characteristics and have decided that they will be effective.

For example, if a child is playing with a daisy and says that it is a fried egg, he or she is focusing on the fact that a fried egg and a daisy both have a yellow centre and a white surround. Nothing else is the same, but the symbol serves its purpose.

Musicians, painters and sculptors are recognised as being creative, but it is a mistake to think that creativity belongs only to them. **Creativity** means linking items or ideas together. We are all being creative as we put a meal together or select an outfit or write a letter. Children are being creative as they consciously link a toy to a situation they know in real life. They are not hallucinating as they call the doll a baby or say they are making a dinner while they stir an empty pan. They are aware of both the reality and what they intend it to be. They are using their memories alongside the current input from their senses of touch, sight and hearing.

Pretend play

From an early age, children are helped to learn to pretend. Judy Dunn and Carol Wooding (1981) looked at children aged between 18 and 30 months and watched for pretend play – that is, when an inanimate object is treated as though it were alive (such as a doll being 'fed'); when one object is substituted for another (for example, a block is used as a mobile phone); or when everyday actions take place without the object being present (such as pretending to drink from a pretend cup).

The researchers found that these episodes were very brief at 18 months, but they lasted considerably longer with 2-year-olds. The majority of these bouts of pretend play were initiated by the child, but not many were completed if the child was playing alone. The children needed the support of the carer if the play was to be continued.

Howes (1992) watched parents pretending with their children.

◆ When the children were between 12 and 15 months, she noticed that typically the adult coached the children in how to pretend by suggesting and demonstrating.

◆ Between 16 and 20 months, the adult tended to correct the child when pretend acts violated the rules of the real world, for example by saying 'Aeroplanes can't swim.'

◆ Between 21 and 24 months, adults stepped back and became interested spectators.

◆ Between 25 and 30 months, the child offered a story line and the adult provided prompts for a more detailed or realistic enactment of the child's idea: 'Oh, it's a shop. What has the man come in for?'

◆ At 31 to 36 months the adult praised the child's pretending and encouraged independence in pretending.

FOCUS

Adults encourage children to pretend. They provide children with toys to help them into a realisation that pretending is possible. They give children miniature versions of items in the adult world – cars, cups, dolls – and dressing-up clothes. These props encourage **role play**, that is play in which the child adopts a role of a powerful person he or she has observed, a mother or father, or a fire fighter, lorry driver, shopkeeper or doctor. Dressing-up clothes also give children the opportunity to pretend about work situations (construction workers, medical staff, shopkeepers) or fantasy play (story characters) or leisure (such as camping) or domestic pursuits (such as cooking).

> **KEY TERM: Role play**
>
> *The type of play where a child plays out a role, e.g. a mother, a builder. The purpose is to have an opportunity to think about what it must feel like to be this person. In that sense role play is a version of exploratory play.*

REFLECT ON YOUR PRACTICE

It is a skill to help children to learn to pretend.

This needs to be done in a one-to-one situation by an adult whom the child knows and trusts, when the child is ready to take this step. How can you ensure there is time for this? How can you arrange for continuity in the child's experience?

It is a skill to provide appropriate props to help children pretend.

What type of props do you provide? Do they allow for a range of situations or characters? Dressing-up clothes that are based on adult-created fantasy figures (for example, fairy princess outfits or full pirate rigouts) inhibit the child's imagination. A piece of cloth for a cloak or a collection of various types of headgear is better.

The same applies to the objects that are available for play. Plastic pans are less effective than a small version of the real thing. A rag doll demands more of the child's imagination than a Barbie doll. Finally, are you encouraging gender stereotyping by your choice of equipment?

Sharing play

At first play is **solitary**; the child is intent on his or her own concerns. At times, **parallel play** may be observed. This is when two or more children play alongside each other, perhaps watching and copying each other and perhaps sharing resources, but not interacting with each other.

Solitary play

Parallel play

It is an important step to move on from playing alone to playing jointly with another child or other children (this is called **sociodramatic play**), because this step presupposes a discussion of intentions. It makes demands on the child's ability to communicate, either as teller or responder, by using language.

> **KEY TERM:** Sociodramatic play
>
> *Play in which children assume roles and agree on a storyline to develop with other children. This type of play usually begins when a child is over three. It requires language skills and the ability to negotiate.*

Sociodramatic play

Howes (1992) watched to see how children learn to share their pretending.

◆ Between 12 and 15 months, isolated pretend acts do not bring a response from other babies.

◆ Between 16 and 20 months, children may be seen copying each other.

◆ Between 21 and 24 months, simultaneous pretending is seen, plus some social exchanges.

◆ Between 25 and 30 months children can be seen playing to the same scripts (for example, domestic play) but without any integration. One child will tell the other what to do or comment on his or her own actions.

◆ Between 32 and 36 months, Howes began to see joint pretend play, with children in complementary roles – for example, one being mother and the other the child. At this stage, children show they are able to break off from speaking in the role they have taken for the play, to talk out of role about what should happen next. At this stage children assign roles to each other ('You be the witch') and negotiate the theme ('And I'll hide and I'll catch you').

Themes in play

When children are playing they are thinking hard. Lev Vygotsky said: 'In play a child is above his average age, above his daily behaviour; in play it is as though he were a head taller than himself.' Unlike adults, who often use play to relax, children use play to make up their minds about the choices and challenges life presents. They sense a dilemma and create a situation in order to be able to think about what it means by acting it out.

Certain recurring themes can be seen in many play situations. These include what it feels like to be **powerful** – in contrast with how powerless children often feel. A lot of role play (giving out food, being the captain of a ship) is concerned with this.

Attachment is another topic that is particularly relevant to young children. They often jointly consider affiliation and acceptance as opposed to separation or rejection. They examine their fear of being rejected through considering characters in stories who have been rejected, but who have coped (for example Hansel and Gretel).

Children need to think about escaping from **threats and danger**: 'Look, a lion's coming. We'll hide in this tree.' Children use play to think about **losing and finding** things. They may play about going on a **quest**.

When children are playing **goodies and baddies** they are examining the pros and cons of social regulation, contrasting the effects of complying with the rules or flouting them. There are many marvellous examples of this in Vivian Paley's book *Bad Guys Don't Have Birthdays*. The children in her class were collaborating in considering what it is to be powerful, and they were also looking to see how far power could go.

Many traditional stories are about these same themes. These stories can encourage children by showing that the weak have power within them (for example *The Three Little Pigs* or *The Three Billy Goats Gruff*). They illustrate that there can be happy endings. Knowing the story, the children are able to relate themselves to the framework of the story. They think simultaneously about the story and about themselves and their concerns. They are thinking as if the story was real, and as if they were there. They know their game isn't reality, but the situation in the story gives them a way to think and to respond without the exercise becoming too hard or too abstract. As adults, we do the same when we read a novel or watch a film.

In order to find events and characters for their play, children freely use fragments of all the stories and television programmes they know. Jack (of *Jack and the Beanstalk*) can mingle with Superman and pirates. Together, they provide characters whose interactions can be scripted at will in order for an emotion to be tried on for size.

FOCUS

The implication of this is that children need to know lots of stories – some read to them, many times if they like them, and many told to them, in a one-to-one situation if possible. Group story times are for older children only, but even the very youngest children need to have plenty of stories on a one-to-one basis.

FIND OUT MORE

Bettelheim, B (1976) *The Uses of Enchantment*, Thames and Hudson
Paley, V G (1988) *Bad Guys Don't Have Birthdays*, University of Chicago Press

REFLECT ON YOUR PRACTICE

It is a skill to discern the themes that underlie the topics of children's play.

Even when the play seems to be about cooking a meal, there may well be an underlying theme – it may be about the exercise of power or about the reassurance of having an affiliation. The idea may only be examined briefly, but it is interesting to note it if you see it.

Look at the themes of the stories you have available. Go beneath the surface events and try to identify what the underlying theme is. Once you have done that you may be able to read a story that has the same underlying theme as the play.

FIND OUT MORE

The Centre for the Children's Book gives advice on books for children: www.sevenstories.org.uk, telephone 0191 276 4289.

Imaginary friends

Sometimes a child produces an imaginary friend, who is used as an individual source of support.

CASE STUDY:

RAFIK

Shaheen writes:

Rafik, one of the little boys who has been using the crèche, has an imaginary friend. His friend is a dog called Jack. Jack has to be included in all of the children's activities, and most importantly he has to take part in snack time. Rafik uses Jack to voice his likes and dislikes, and gets very upset if Jack is given food he doesn't like. Jack prefers grapes to apples and would rather have juice than the water he is offered in crèche.

Although Jack is used to tell the staff about Rafik and his needs, the staff are also able to talk to Rafik through Jack. They are able to tell Rafik that dogs like water more than juice and that Jack is quite happy to have water at snack time.

Rafik is very close to Jack. At the moment they are quite inseparable. Jack seems to help Rafik to work through his emotions and cope with new situations.

Even an imaginary dog can be a valued friend

When they are playing, children are in control. They can decide when to begin and end the play, and how far to go along one line of thought. These ways of exploring fears or feeling of weakness are very much child-led. The child makes up or adopts an interesting situation and plays it through in order to think about it safely.

Children communicating through stories

Children use the same way of thinking when they make stories, except that if they make up a story they are creating situations that they can think through by using words only and not actions. Making stories is about creating possible worlds and possible courses of action. It is a very normal activity. We all make stories to explain to ourselves the events that we are involved in, such as 'It's all because…' or 'If I can only…'. Whether we are contented or paranoid, we link events together to make some sense of our lives.

Children learn to do this by working out the schema of a story, that is it has a beginning, an end, a setting and characters with a problem to resolve in between. This happens if they hear plenty of stories.

CASE STUDY:
NURSERY STORIES

Joan encouraged the 3-year-olds in her nursery to capture sequences of events in the form of spoken language. She sat at the word processor and the children were welcome to dictate their stories to her if they wished. Joan found that the children (and their parents) valued the print out. Usually the children used the opportunity to recount some important event in their lives. Joan recorded hundreds of stories in her nursery.

Jane seemed haunted by a sad event.

I had some bees but they died.
We just left them in the bee house.
We've still got the bee house.

Other children retold stories they knew. Laura told the same story twice, the second time 4 months after the first.

The sad old fox and the big hen. Two sly old foxes. The sly old fox came to the hen's house and he tried to get in. He said 'You can't get me.' 'Yes I can get you' and he twirled round and round. The chicken fell down in the bag. The sly old fox had him for tea.

The second version, below, is more coherent, providing not only a title but giving the setting in greater detail than in her earlier version. This version has more echoes of the language of the original and it is neatly concluded. You will also notice that there are many more of the words that link shorter sentences together, which we were looking at in the last chapter.

The sly old fox. He went for a walk. He saw a little house that the hen lived in. He wanted to eat the hen so he went in the house. He went home to get a bag and he went back again and the hen said 'You can't catch me for a bumble bee.' The fox twirled round and round and said 'I can catch you.' The big hen made him tired and he twirled round and fell in to the bag. The fox went home to eat him.

Paley (1986) tells how she asked the 3-year-olds in her class to tell stories. At first the stories were very short, capturing a fleeting action. William's story was: 'The gorilla gets out of the cage.' Barney gave a little more information: 'Batman goes whoosh. In the Batmobile.'

But some stories reflected the child's worries. Mollie's first story was about the fears she had of the older children in the school: 'About a bad guy and a horse. The robbers and the horse. He takes things away from the girl.'

CASE STUDY:
MARGARET

Paley (1986 page 62) found that it helped if she encouraged the children to act the stories out. Now the story telling became a co-operative venture as the children worked together to construct a satisfying plot. They not only made up a story but re-entered it as the characters they had invented.

Margaret makes her doll the heroine but then watches the audience reaction so closely that certain children feel compelled to help.

'Cabbage Patch comes. Then a wolf comes. Then she is scared. She runs away.' The wolf, who is Margaret, howls modestly and looks around.

'No Margaret,' Adam blurts out. 'The wolf howls like this. ROARRR. Let me be the wolf because I really know how they howl.'

'Let me be the mother that picks her up,' Libby offers.

'No, I'm the mother that hasta pick her up,' Margaret whispers, hugging Cabbage Patch. 'You be the sister that picks her up. And then it's summer and she goes out to play.' Again Margaret peers about, waiting.

'But doesn't she meet the wolf again?' Erik asks. 'Before you went out didn't the wolf hided by the other side of your house and he came out and scared you again?'

'Yes.'

My turn. 'Does Cabbage Patch run away or does she do something different this time?'

Margaret hesitates only a moment. 'She scares the wolf away. Then she goes out to play.'

'With me,' Mollie suggests, rising hopefully from her seat.

'Yes.'

Children act out stories and construct a plot together

FIND OUT MORE

Paley, V G (1986) *Mollie is Three*, University of Chicago Press

One widespread source of stories is television, where the child is at the receiving end of very emphatic messages carried by light, colour and sound. Children of the age we are considering need an adult to be with them while they are watching television because television gives no opportunity for the child to respond and comment, or ask for more information. An adult watching with a child provides the child with a link to reality. The adult can respond to the child's responses and queries about the magnified, pounding, incessant communication that flickers from the screen.

Many programmes intended for children are produced by adults who unthinkingly use the techniques that adults enjoy – short bursts of quickly changing images, frenzied presenters, tricky camera angles and busy, distracting backgrounds. These features are not appropriate for young children, who need time to look closely, to reflect and to take things in at their own pace, using all their senses. Television does not allow this.

Children and literacy and numeracy

Children take time to come to terms with the abstract and formal systems of organising and saving information. The two chief ones are **literacy**, which encodes speech in books and writing, and **numeracy**, which is a standardised way of talking about quantity. Numeracy also identifies the way that items are placed in relation to each other (*beside*, *in the middle*) and specifies other ways in which to describe how items relate to each other (*bigger than*, *earlier than*, *heavier than*).

Because these systems enable a person to have access to other people's ideas and to share ideas with people who are not physically present, they do not lend themselves to improvisation. These systems, whether of words or numbers, encode ideas in specific marks on paper. When you use them there are rules to be followed and expectations to be met. In numeracy, the expectations include accuracy and logic, and in literacy, precision and clarity of expression are expected.

The underpinning ideas of literacy and numeracy are gained by the child as a result of many experiences in an environment where the child sees them being used in an everyday, informal and stress-free manner. It is **not appropriate** to begin formal teaching of these skills for children of the ages covered in this book.

Literacy

Understanding that messages can be encoded in marks on paper comes gradually if the adults in a child's life give him or her opportunities to be involved with the use of reading, writing and counting. The child's own skill in mastering the full potential of these systems will come later.

Introducing a child to books as early as possible is a very important start; it helps the baby to gain an insight into the fact that information can be acquired in a way that is not quite like the usual sensory exploration. A child loves the close contact and the emotional rapport with an adult that sessions with a book involve. In the case study below, one parent describes how she began to share her own love of books with her child.

CASE STUDY:

JULIA'S BOOKS

Catherine writes:

The desire to ensure that Julia grew up with a love of words was important to me. Before she was born her bookshelf was already established, while the toy pile was rather pitiful. By the age of 2 months, we would daily sit together and read book after book. I encouraged Julia to touch and help me turn the pages, so that by 3 months she would sit and turn the pages of a cloth book by herself. It was delightful to see her face light up at familiar pictures. She began to recognise the picture sequence and the repeated phrases.

Now at 10 months Julia has favourite books and happily points out the sun, stars, animals and also different colours on the pages. We carry books with us wherever we go. The many interactive books particularly enthral her and she eagerly lifts and closes flaps, revelling in the discovery of hidden pictures.

Reading together affords us both closeness and enjoyment, along with the advantage of the exposure to different sounds, colours and images. It is astounding to observe her wait till the end of the text of a page before she turns to the next page, showing a deeper understanding than one may expect.

Catherine's baby's first understanding that books can interest and amuse grows out of happy emotional experiences. At 10 months, books for Julia mean a close interaction with a loving adult. They are sources of interest and amusement.

Some parents may need encouragement to read with their child, finding it hard to believe that a very young child could understand a book.

Once researchers in the 1980s had begun to notice that it was the children who had had contact with books and stories from an early age who succeeded better in school, even up to the age of ten, there have been several initiatives to encourage parents and carers to share books with their babies.

It is now being realised that there is even more to books than enjoying them for their link with loved adults and the pleasure of the book itself. The extra bonus is that through being accustomed to books, the child finds out that there is more to explore and learn about the world he or she inhabits than just the here and now. Books open the door to a wider world. Being familiar with, and unafraid of, books leads to the child being ready to expect to find meaning in the media of words and pictures. The child pays attention to the words of the story and examines the pictures in the books, thus learning to pay attention to words and the nuances of language. Books become an enjoyable and motivating source for conversation and learning with a loving adult.

It's never too early to begin sharing books

CASE STUDY:

BOOKSTART INITIATIVE

The initiatives to encourage parents to share books with their babies began in Birmingham, and they have now spread to many parts of the UK. Birmingham's Bookstart began in 1992 and there is now, under Book Trust (a national, independent charity), a national scheme based on the simple principle of encouraging parents to share books with babies from a young age.

The schemes set up in each area vary in detail, but they usually involve the provision of a free book, often with a poetry card, an invitation to join the local library, booklists and a poster as well as information about local bookshops and other book-related organisations. This is usually given when the children have their 9-months health check.

The Birmingham pilot project has been monitored over time. It was found that receiving the pack encouraged parents or carers to read to children, to use the library and to buy books for children. When the first group of children were between 30 and 36 months old, some were compared to children of the same age who had not been part of the project. The children who had been involved in the project concentrated more and showed more interest in books than the other children. They pointed to the text more and tried to turn pages. They joined in more with the reading and asked and answered more questions. They made more predictions about what might happen next in the story.

The original group of 300 children were followed until they were in school. When they were compared to a carefully matched **control group**, it was found that the project children fared better on **baseline assessments** on each of the nine areas examined when they started school. They were frequently well ahead on the speaking and listening and reading and writing measures and, interestingly, they also performed better on assessments of using and applying mathematics, number and shape, and space and measures.

When the **Key Stage 1 SATs** results of the group were checked, the Bookstart children were still ahead of their peers in maths and science as well as in English.

Although we as adults may be more conscious of the differences between literacy and numeracy, there are important similarities between them. Both of them use a symbol system to store meaning, and both require attention to sequence and detail for understanding to be unlocked. This is what children learn from early exposure to books. As the Birmingham researchers reported, 'It is likely that the attention and concentration we have noticed in early book sharing is in itself a key learning achievement which children later can transfer to other subject areas' (Wade and Moore, 2002 page 44).

Experiments investigating people are generally measured by having two matched groups. One group receives the special treatment, whether it's a medication or an opportunity to use extra resources. The other, the control group, is similar in all respects to the experimental group but does not receive the treatment. The two groups are measured at the beginning of the experiment and at the end to see whether the treatment has had the effect of making a difference between the experimental group and the control group.

FOCUS

Parents and carers can make an important contribution to young children's success in school. This success is unrelated to socioeconomic factors; it comes from the early enjoyment of books in a close and loving context. The Bookstart project shows that enjoying books with an adult is not only an occasion for a warm emotional experience. The contact with books also improves a young child's ability to pay attention to and think about information received in an indirect way. A book read through again and again from front to back embodies an unvarying sequence, just as familiar rhymes and oral stories do as they are repeated word for word on every telling. As a result of many such experiences the child becomes attuned to seeking out patterns and sequences in events, or explanations.

It is important to ensure that reading a book to a child gives the child a stress-free emotional experience as you interact with him or her. You should be enthusiastic about the book yourself. The book should be attractive in format. There are plastic books that babies can have in the bath, there are board books and cloth books. Babies can handle and gnaw these books without destroying them.

Slightly older children are intrigued when there are flaps to lift or holes to peep through as the pages of the book are turned. Many attractively illustrated books, by artists with a variety of styles, are available today. At an early stage the child might use the book to learn to recognise drawings or photgraphs of farmyard animals or fruits, toys or vehicles. However, books link ideas for consideration in the imagination and should provide starting points for a conversation with the child. The type of book that merely labels one object on each page is rather limiting in this respect.

Becoming familiar with the type of books that rely on words to link ideas helps a child to become familiar with written language, which is not quite the same as spoken language.

CASE STUDY:
MIKE ROBINSON

Mike Robinson (1989) described how his son first began to use quotations from his favourite books for situations in his own life, and then later began to imitate book language. At 22 months, his son was fascinated by the *Thomas the Tank Engine* series. He was especially taken with the authority figure, the Fat Controller.

The child began to use the words '"Silence," said the Fat Controller' to reprimand his noisy younger brother. On other occasions he would declare '"I cannot allow it," said the Fat Controller.' By two and a half he no longer quoted directly from the book but copied the book's style. Called into the kitchen, he would arrive with an exaggerated dash, saying '"I'm coming, Mummy, I'm coming," exclaimed Joseph, running as fast as he could.'

As books do, he quoted speech as it was spoken. And as books do he also took the role of a story teller, indicating who was the speaker and what the speaker's actions were. Robinson calls this phase of knowing about some literacy conventions before being able to read or write **proto-literacy**. It is evidence of how an understanding of literacy grows in the child long before the child can read or write, through encountering books and stories.

KEY TERM: Proto-literacy

The stage before the complete understanding of reading and writing, when children have realised that print carries meaning and that there are literary conventions, e.g. that stories often have a formal beginning and ending.

REFLECT ON YOUR PRACTICE

It is a skill to select a book to read to a child.

Take two books from your book box, one you are fond of and one you like rather less. When you examine them think of the criteria necessary for a story, which were mentioned in Chapter 3. What about the setting of the story, the characters involved, the problem they face and the way they resolve it? Is the tone of the book appealing? Share with a colleague the reasons you like the particular book you have chosen. Why is it one of your favourites? What would you say to a parent who wanted your advice on buying a book for a child?

FIND OUT MORE

Book Trust, The Book House, 45 East Hill, London SW18 2QZ. Telephone: 0208 516 2984

Wade, B and Moore, M (2002) 'A Sure Start with Books' in *Early Years* Volume 20 Number 2, Spring 2000, pp 39–46

An early start with books introduces the child to literacy, which is a way of representing speech with squiggles on paper. Literacy is everywhere in our environment. The word **literate** means the ability to deal with written language, by either reading or writing. After the development of language, literacy is possibly the human race's greatest invention. By having a system of capturing language in writing, we are able to preserve and store our thoughts. Having done this we can communicate with others without having to speak to them face to face. Literacy surmounts the barriers of space (we can read a letter sent from Australia) and time (we can access the thoughts of a person who lived hundreds, or even thousands, of years ago, or we can leave a letter to be opened after our death).

FOCUS

Some of our literacy skills are vital for basic functioning in everyday life. We read the directions on medicine bottles or packaged foods, we read signs and notices, posters and notices, bills and reminders.

Another type of reading helps us to function more effectively, by enabling us to make choices from menus or TV listings, or to access news through cards or letters, newspapers and magazines. We read to help our personal development when we read to study. We may also read for pure pleasure and relaxation.

It is very hard to function in our society if you are not able to read. You may have realised this for yourself if you have visited a country such as Greece, Russia or China, or the Middle East and Far East, where they do not use the Roman alphabet.

The written word is everywhere and young children see literacy all around them in the environment. There are signs on shops and on packets of sweets. Young children may recognise the M for McDonalds, or the box of Smarties, soap powder or cornflakes, or the TV logo. These signs are meaningful for them because they relate to their lives. Children may receive cards on their birthdays, or help to select a card to send. In responding to the message they are showing that they are beginning to understand that messages can be sent and received using the hands and eyes rather than the mouth and ears.

Young children may be partially aware of the power of the written word, but their real interest in it begins when they find that the adults around them like it and put a value on books. When this is so, their early experiences with books are happy and warm, and the child interacts with the experience, pointing things out and asking and answering questions. Learning that you have to interact with a text is as important as learning to interact in a conversation. Through watching the adult paying attention to the page, commenting on what is on the page, turning over to the next page and guessing what might come next, a baby begins to realise it is important to attend to the illustrations and the written word.

An interest in books can develop in the first years of a child's life

CASE STUDY:

DYLAN

Marion Whitehead (2002) documented one child's contact with books in his first three years.

The records began when the child, Dylan, was 8 weeks old. At this stage he was held while an adult was comfortably reading a book or a newspaper or magazine. At 11 weeks he was seen gurgling at a TV listings magazine and reaching out to grasp and pull at the pages. At 13 weeks he enjoyed a book being read to him. His pleasure grew, and by 8 months he showed an excited reaction to two of his favourite books. Book sessions at this time included, as Whitehead writes, 'a whole performance of wild lunges at the books, high-pitched squeals, hand waving and energetic banging on the pages'.

At 9 months she noted that 'a quieter and more private response to magazines and books began to emerge'. Dylan would lie alone on his stomach on the floor with a catalogue or magazine, gazing at the pages, turning the pages with skill and care, sometimes banging on the page with his hand, at other times gently scrabbling at the pages with the fingertips of one hand. At 12 months he focused on the physical business of turning the pages without help, or lifting the flap and making appropriate animal noises.

Dylan's emotional responses grew. At 13½ months he was spending considerable amounts of time looking at his favourite books. At 18 months he could identify the books that had a special meaning for him and he was fascinated by naming objects and characters in the books. By the time of his second birthday, books were very important comforters at bedtime and in new situations, and a huge amount of learning about the outside world was occurring as Dylan became an 'expert' on tractors, sharks and elephants.

FIND OUT MORE

Whitehead, M (2002) 'Dylan's routes to literacy: The first three years with picture books', *Journal of Early Childhood Literacy*, Volume 2, Number 3, 269–289

We can see from such accounts that very young children are able to derive pleasure from books and that practitioners should be ready to share the enjoyment of books with even the youngest children.

REFLECT ON YOUR PRACTICE

It is a skill to provide books for children and to encourage them to enjoy them.

How many books are there in each room of your setting? How easy is it for the children to get at the books? Do you share at least one book each day with each child in your care? Do the children have favourite books? How do the books for babies differ from the books for the twos and threes?

Literacy means the ability to use the system not only for reading (being an understander) but also for writing (being a teller).

We have the same range of purposes, from the mundane to the self-fulfilling, when we write. We can write reminders for ourselves or others, we can write to clear our thoughts (anything from deciding what to pack for the holiday to what we'd like to say if we are called for an interview). We can write to 'fix' what we are learning, or we can write to express our feelings (anything from letters of complaint to love letters, a novel or a poem).

Children see so much writing activity in everyday life that they want to use this power themselves. They may see adults writing a shopping list or filling in the lottery coupon, the pools or a catalogue order form. It is easy to see what adults are doing when they make marks on a piece of paper so young children like to try out making marks.

FOCUS

The implication of this is that children should see us writing and that we should explain to them what we are doing. Children also need the chance to have a go themselves. They do **not** have to be coached in forming letters or writing their names. The important thing is for them to realise that a message can exist in marks on paper.

It is a skill to make sure that children have the opportunity to make marks (write).

What opportunities exist for the children at the centre to make marks freely? It is inappropriate to use tracing or over-writing for children of the ages we are concerned with. List the resources for mark-making you could provide for a) toddlers and b) 2- and 3-year-olds. What progression have you provided as you do so? What happens to the marks the children produce?

An interest in literacy depends on seeing adults enjoying reading and writing.

CASE STUDY:
ROBIN'S GRANDDAUGHTER

Robin Campbell (1998) noted the number of experiences with early literacy his 3-year-old granddaughter had in one day. These were in addition to all her other activities – talking, playing, constructing.

At the start of the day she joined her grandmother and sister in bed and asked to play *I Spy*. She then collected the book *Where's Wally?* and looked for Wally on each page. At breakfast she looked closely at the print on her table mat. She asked about the letters on it. Still at the table she burst into song: *One two three four five*. She asked about what her grandfather was doing when he was writing. Seeing her older sister making a card for their father's birthday, she made one too.

They went to the library. At the library she looked at an information book as well as choosing story books. She examined and talked about one of the library books to herself in the back of the car on the way home. (She asked to have this book read to her four times during the course of the afternoon.) At lunch she spontaneously burst into song again. On the way to the park she looked at the numbers on the houses they passed. On a trip to the supermarket she was able to find and pick out a large bottle of cola and a box of cornflakes. At the end of the day there was another story. She knew this one well and joined in reciting the text as the adult read it to her. There was a final story at bedtime.

During the day she had looked at favourite books and at new ones. Her contact with books was happy and an important and easy part of family life. She had recited nursery rhymes, she had asked about writing, and had done some. She played with the initial sounds of words and showed that she understood that a book's text was unchanging. The point that Campbell stresses is that she was the initiator of all of these activities.

Early literacy can mean
fun at the library

FOCUS

The implication of the fact that children learn about literacy as they live their daily lives is that the childcare setting must provide an experience of easy, immediate and personal access to books.

REFLECT ON YOUR PRACTICE

It is a skill to provide children with opportunities for learning about literacy in an informal and emotionally secure way.

How can we provide similar opportunities for literacy learning experiences in the setting from babyhood to three? Are books always available? Do the children hear rhymes? Are there informal opportunities to notice labels and captions in the environment of the setting?

It is a skill for adults to let children see them reading or writing in order to further children's understanding of some of the purposes of reading and writing.

A child fortunate enough to have plenty of good experiences with books and writing learns a lot about literacy in an informal way. What opportunities do the children at each stage (babies, toddlers, 2-year-olds, 3-year-olds) have for seeing adults using literacy, that is reading and writing for purposes that are explained to the children? What further opportunities could we provide? Be specific.

Numeracy

Learning about **numeracy** begins in the same informal way.

Babies have an early idea of quantity, and can distinguish between a single item and more than one. They become accustomed to pairs – the people they see have two eyes, two hands, two legs. The child becomes aware that he or she has two hands and two feet. Two can be recognised immediately. The process of being able to recognise a quantity at a glance is called **subitising**. Most adults have the ability to see that there are four objects in a group without having to count each item individually.

> **KEY TERM: Subitising**
>
> *Correctly recognising the number of units in a group without having to count them one by one.*

One pan for each hand!

FOCUS

We use numbers a lot in our environment. Sometimes the numbers are used as a label.

How many numbers label *you*? Can you think of ten numbers (such as your telephone number) that identify you? How many number labels might a 3-year-old be aware of?

However, the major use of numbers is to know quantities – or to count. Using the number system allows us to keep track of things – anything from coins to temperatures to time. People have always found it necessary to know things such as how many cattle they owned or to be able to describe the size of their buildings or to calculate time. Recording quantities or measures preceded writing.

Rochel Gelman and Charles Gallistel described the steps we take before we reach an understanding of counting. Counting successfully depends on several steps.

1 We must learn the **number sentence** – *one, two, three, four,* etc.

2 We must get the sentence right every time. Some young children go through a phase of using their own sentence, such as one, two, five, six. If they use it consistently it shows they have understood step one, which is the realisation that the sentence always has to be the same. Always using the same list is called the **stable order principle**.

3 We must give one number word to each item that we intend to count. This is known as the **one-to-one principle**. We must include all the items to be counted and not count anything twice. People adopt various strategies to achieve this. Some touch each item with their fingers. Others point at each item. Some move the items one by one as they count them.

4 It can be quite hard to realise that it doesn't matter in which order you count the items so long as all are counted. This is called the **order irrelevance principle**.

5 The hardest thing of all to realise is that the last number you say is the total of all the things you are counting. The technical name for this is the **cardinality principle**. We show that we are aware of this by putting a stress on the last number word we say.

REFLECT ON YOUR PRACTICE

It is a skill to help children to begin to understand counting.

Apart from the use of numbers for labels, what do *you* mostly use numbers for? What do children tend to use numbers for? When could you use the number sentence with the children you work with?

What steps can we take to ensure that the growth in children's understanding of the number system is supported? Make a list of all the stories and rhymes you know that involve numbers. Which numbers frequently recur?

There are many rhymes that help a child to get the number sentence right. List and recall the exact words of at least three. Then look for two rhymes that are new to you.

Which methods of keeping count do you find yourself using? In which circumstances? How could you make it obvious to the children in your care what you are doing as you are counting?

What could you say to a parent who says that his or her child of three can count up to 20?

FIND OUT MORE

Gelman, R and Gallistel, C (1978) *The Child's Understanding of Number*, Harvard University Press

Maclellan, E 'The importance of counting' in Thompson, I (1997) *Teaching and Learning Early Number*, Open University Press

Numbers are the language of mathematics, but are not its substance. The substance of mathematics is the discussion of how things relate to each other. So when a child says 'She's got more', 'That's the baby bear', 'Look up there', 'I'm going inside', 'That's heavy' or 'That's the same', the child is thinking mathematically. He or she is making comparisons, describing positions or size, or making measurements.

It has, however, been noted that although young children are mathematically aware in the sense that they regularly make comparisons and refer to size and location, they do not necessarily use numbers to count precisely. They work at using number words but see this largely as a fun and social thing. The following case study discusses this.

Numeracy can be explored in many ways

CASE STUDY: FRANCES

Karen gives this account of her daughter's mathematical development.

Frances began being a mathematician when she was 14 months old, or at least this was the time that I first realised her spontaneous play was mathematically oriented. It was Christmas time and Frances was sitting on the floor playing with the contents of a large box of Quality Street chocolates. At first her selection of one chocolate after the other appeared to be quite random, but once there were 20 or so chocolates on the floor in front of her it became apparent that she was in fact *sorting* the contents of the tin. There on the carpet were little piles of chocolates that were the *same*. I was quite surprised at this. At first I wondered whether this could have happened by chance. But clearly it had not. Each of the piles contained between four and eight sweets – there were no 'mistakes'. Frances had worked on this task for about 10 minutes.

A number of mathematical terms spring to mind: *the same as*, *sorting*, *classifying* and *grouping into sets*. This had been a complex task, involving decision-making about *colour*, *shape* and *space*. For example, the toffee buttons were in a separate pile from the toffee sticks. Both have golden wrappers, so clearly Frances was applying more than one criterion to her sorting.

I began to look out for other examples of this behaviour as she played with plastic food, farm animals, bricks, tea sets and other toys. I began to use simple mathematical language with her, both to describe what she had done and to encourage classifying behaviour in other situations. Frances enjoyed these activities and was soon classifying on a regular basis. The cows in her farm were generally sorted into three groups or *sub-sets*: *standy up*, *liey down* and *eating grass*. Although she could not articulate it, there was clearly much early mathematics going on here.

Frances learned the number sentence one to ten at around the age of 18 months. It was for a time her party piece, but I was fully aware she had no understanding of the concepts involved in the counting process. Within her use of the counting words there was no intention to count anything at all; she simply learned the sequence of words.

By the time she was about 22 months she was beginning to develop a sense of number and was making generalisations about quantity. We live in a fairly rural area with many fields of animals close at hand. At the bottom of our street is a field with three horses, and every day as we passed we talked about the horses and what they were doing. At around this time Frances's interest changed to considering how many horses there were in the field. She consistently referred to the horses as *two and three*: 'There are two and three horse today, Mummy.' Similarly, people walking their dogs always had *two and three dogs*. Frances had developed her own labelling system for groups of things that contained less than five. Fairly soon after the emergence of *two and three*, she began to use *eight nine ten* for a lot. All the fields now contained *eight nine ten* sheep or cows.

It was clear that Frances was not yet counting accurately. However, it is apparent that there was an understanding that number words have something to do with *how many?*. Her use of *two and three* for groupings of less than five and *eight nine ten* for larger groups shows she had a developing understanding of how the number words relate to the increasing numbers in a group, and that the first numbers in the count refer to small quantities and the end numbers to larger quantities.

Frances began recognising numbers at around the age of two and a half. Number eight was the first one she recognised – you've probably already guessed it is the video channel on our television. Once she made the connection between the counting we did, the number words she knew and the number symbol for eight, she began to ask what numbers were wherever she saw them. She had many number books and these were often chosen as her bedtime reading, and we bought some numbered dice so she could choose to use numbers or spots when we played board games.

At around the age of three, Frances began to demonstrate further development in her ability to count and to handle quantities. She began to be able to sense the number of small groups of objects without physically counting them out (subitising). It first began in dice games, and at first we assumed that Frances had memorised the patterns and recognised them without counting them. But this ability was not restricted to the game-playing situation. For example, when we were out for a walk one day, we passed three girls in the street. Frances looked at them and said 'What are them three girls doing – they're just like the three little pigs.' Unfortunately the girls heard and were far less impressed than I was. This ability to subitise was also interesting in that it occurred at a time when her ability to count objects accurately was still not consistent with groups of four or more.

There are two important elements in this account.

1 The way the child has taken the lead and the understanding of numbers has emerged.
2 The way the adult followed, respected and supported as the child busily responded to her environment. The adult used everyday objects and events to help this knowledge to emerge.

FOCUS

The implication is that children must be allowed to take the lead in exploring numeracy, as with literacy, and that adults must be able to provide a facilitating environment and respond to the child's needs for support and explanation where necessary. It is also important to be able to make use of all opportunities that present themselves.

CASE STUDY: KARLI

Joanne writes:

The children (3-years-olds) were sitting on the mat at the beginning of the session on Tuesday morning when Karli burst through the door. She was late but she stood by the door and proudly announced to everyone, 'Look at this lovely cardi my Gran has made for me. It's got a yellow stripe, a blue stripe and a pink stripe.' She had obviously talked about the pattern at home and she came across and sat on my chair. 'Look, my Grandma made this lovely pattern – yellow wool, blue wool and pink wool.' She pointed to the colours and demonstrated how the stripes went from top to bottom. Afterwards she painted a picture of the stripes, and other children copied her. They all started to talk about patterns. When we went outside they noticed that the nursery fence palings were painted blue, then yellow, then green.

The next day we went out for a pattern walk – all of us, for about 20 minutes, just up the road. I pointed out a fence that had a paling with a pointed top alternating with one with a horizontal top. The children noticed the roundabout had black and white stripes, they saw the zebra crossing, there were herringbone patterns in driveways, and interlocking patterns in the paving stones.

The whole nursery was involved in looking for patterns. Children were bringing in stuff from home. One boy brought in the place mat he used. It had horizontal stripes. Three days later he had turned from horizontal stripes to zigzags. 'Look, it's jaggedy like the pointed fence.'

The children saw Karli talk about the pattern on her cardigan as important because she was very excited as she burst in the door. She sat in the teacher's seat and started a frenzy.

The important points of this account are:

1 The sensitive response to the children's interest.

2 The use of everyday reality in a familiar environment.

3 The way the enthusiasm spread as the children became excited by the connections in the various aspects of their experience.

To open up their minds, young children need access to the systems we use for storing information and experience. At the same time, children need to develop their confidence in their own power of reaching out to others by using those carriers of information that are universally understood, or those that are personally attractive to each child. There are many open-ended systems such as painting, drama or exploiting sounds for music making. For children to flourish and reach their full potential they have to become familiar with both the formal and the open-ended systems of communicating, using each type as a teller and an understander.

REFLECT ON YOUR PRACTICE

It is a skill to be aware of the need to support the growth of numeracy.

Make notes of the stages through which the understanding of counting develops. Where is each child you work with?

Do a number-use audit in the room you work in for one session. When are numbers mentioned? Where and by whom? Evaluate your findings. How could you increase number references when you are working and playing with the children in your care? What opportunities and resources could you provide to develop mathematical awareness in the children you care for by using their experiences and fostering the language of position (under, behind) and comparison (bigger, nearer)?

It is a skill to help children to use words that express the positions of things, or to make comparisons between items.

What steps can we take to ensure that we support children's use of words to express mathematical ideas? List the words you will model and then listen out for them being used.

These beads are long!

It is a skill to provide an environment in which the child's emergent understanding of these symbol systems can grow.

How often are the children in contact with books, stories and rhymes? How often do adults notice how much understanding each child is showing? How do practitioners help parents to exploit the many opportunities for fostering understanding of literacy and numeracy that there are in daily life?

Children can learn many concepts while playing in the sand

Our role as practitioners is two-fold. We must help children to notice all aspects of their environment so that they have experiences to select from. Then we must be on the look-out for and recognise the child's growing communicative powers. Loris Malaguzzi, who was behind the development of the under-six system in Reggio Emilia, wrote that unless we notice each way in which children put across a communication they will stop trying to use that channel, and ultimately if we do not respond to their attempts to communicate they will become frustrated, lonely and unhappy individuals, always on the outside looking in. He wrote the following poem.

No way. The hundred *is* there

The child
is made
of one hundred.
The child has
100 languages
100 hands
100 thoughts
100 ways of thinking
of playing, of speaking.
100, always 100
ways of listening
of marvelling, of loving

100 joys
for singing and understanding
100 worlds
to discover
100 worlds
to invent
100 worlds

to dream.
The child has
100 languages
(and 100,100 more)
but they steal 99.
The school and the culture
separate the head from the body.
They tell the child:
to think without hands
to do without head
to listen and not to speak
to understand without joy
to love and to marvel
only at Easter and Christmas.
They tell the child:
to discover the world already there
and of the 100
they steal 99.
They tell the child:
that work and play
reality and fantasy
science and imagination
sky and earth
reason and dream
are things
that do not belong together.

And thus they tell the child
that the 100 is not there.
The child says:
No way. The 100 is there.

Source: Edwards, C, Gandina, L and Forman, G (eds) (1994) *The Hundred Languages of Children: The Reggio Emilia approach to early childhood education*, Ablex Publishing Corporation, reproduced with permission of Greenwood Publishing Inc., Westport, CT, USA

Conclusion

This chapter has looked at the ways babies and young children communicate through symbol systems. These include making marks or drawing, different types of play, stories, and the beginnings of literacy and numeracy.

Once children have begun to see that meaning can be stored and transmitted by using symbols, they are freed from communicating only in the here and now. They can make whatever connections they wish if they decide to use the open systems of drawing, play and story making. If they decide to adopt the formal systems of literacy and the number system, they are rewarded with access to the wisdom of the ages and they too can make their contribution to others' understanding across time and space.

The following skills have been highlighted:

- It is a skill to make children aware of the messages that are in use in the society that they live in.
- It is a skill to respond appropriately to young children's drawings.
- It is a skill to help children to learn to pretend.
- It is a skill to provide appropriate props to help children pretend.
- It is a skill to discern the themes that underlie the topics of children's play.
- It is a skill to select a book to read to a child.
- It is a skill to provide books for children and to encourage them to enjoy them.
- It is a skill to make sure that children have the opportunity to make marks (write).
- It is a skill to provide children with opportunities for learning about literacy in an informal and emotionally secure way.
- It is a skill for adults to let children see them reading or writing in order to further children's understanding of some of the purposes of reading and writing.
- It is a skill to help children to begin to understand counting.
- It is a skill to be aware of the need to support the growth of numeracy.
- It is a skill to help children to use words that express the positions of things, or to make comparisons between items.
- It is a skill to provide an environment in which the child's emergent understanding of these symbol systems can grow.

Working collaboratively to care for babies and young children

Childcare workers have seen their role gradually widen to include the needs of the parent as well as those of the young child. Now their horizons are widening still further to include communities as well as families and to work alongside other services with different histories and traditions.

This chapter is divided into the following sections:

◆ Working in childcare
◆ How childcare workers help children and families
◆ How childcare workers help local communities
◆ How childcare workers focus special care
◆ Childcare workers alongside other services

Childcare is about caring and collaborating

Working in childcare

Very few **nuclear families** have ever been self-sufficient. In the past parents have always been able to call on the help of other family members, or if they could afford to, employed nannies. For at least a century in the UK, help has been available outside the home in nurseries.

> **KEY TERM: Nuclear family**
>
> *The smallest family unit – parents and children.*

> **KEY TERM: Extended family**
>
> *The wider family including grandparents, aunts, uncles and cousins, etc.*

There have been two main strands of childcare provision in the UK. One strand traditionally focused on caring for children whose home circumstances had been deemed to be inadequate. The emphasis in these nurseries was on meeting the child's physical and emotional needs. The other strand was more piecemeal and tended to focus on the child's cognitive development – in these nurseries a philosophy has grown about appropriate activities for young children when they are at nursery.

These two strands can no longer easily meet the demands of a modern British society. We now realise that there can be no care without education – every interaction where an adult is looking after a child will result in that child forming an idea of whether he or she is respected. At the same time there can be no education without care – a child who is not cared for cannot learn effectively.

Urie Bronfenbrenner produced a diagram (illustrated opposite) that placed the child at the centre of a series of concentric circles, all of which have an impact on the opportunities available to the child.

Bronfenbrenner begins with the child's relationship with the primary care-giver – together they form a **dyad**. In the next circle come the people in the child's immediate family and childcare workers, then the **extended family** and neighbours. These have been called the **polyad**. These people are part of the local community. In their turn these neighbourhoods and the people who live in them are at the mercy of economic and social factors in the country as a whole. In some areas there are plenty of opportunities for employment, in others there may be less work.

> **KEY TERM: Dyad**
>
> *A close pair.*

> **KEY TERM: Polyad**
>
> *A small, closely connected group.*

Bronfenbrenner's diagram of the influences on a child's well-being

Childcare workers, depending on the circumstances of an individual child, may be included on any of Bronfenbrenner's layers. A practitioner may be part of the innermost circle as the child's primary significant care-giver, for example as a foster carer. The childcare worker may have cause to work with the immediate family, including grandparents. Working outwards, the practitioner may have to work with other service providers in the community to help the child's family. The childcare worker may live in the same area as the child and so will be a part of the local community. As a member of a democracy, the childcare worker may cast a vote in an election that might have an effect on how a government spends its resources or plans an input into childcare services. The purpose of this chapter is to reflect on what these varying roles mean for the childcare worker today.

How childcare workers help children and families

More families than ever before are seeking childcare. A parent's relationship with a child is moulded by many pressures. There are pressures from the government, which expects adults to play an active part in the economy. There are pressures in the workplace, where career breaks – or even maternity and paternity leave – are not particularly encouraged. There are financial commitments to be met. For people with young children the childcare setting and the childcare workers are the first line of defence. However, sometimes leaving the baby in the care of others is difficult.

Helping parents cope with leaving their babies

The staff at one setting received this letter:

Dear nursery staff

Please look after my precious Molly. I've got to go back to work now; I've really enjoyed maternity leave but the mortgage (and the nursery fees) have to be paid.

She loves to go to sleep on my knee, listening to her favourite music; she likes eating brown food, and is not very interested in veg, although I try. She loves looking at light through the leaves on the tree in our garden and she loves digging for worms.

Please take care of her – I'll have my mobile switched on so send me a text if you have any questions – or just text me and tell me how she's getting on.

Thanks – I'll be thinking of you

Sarah (Molly's mum)

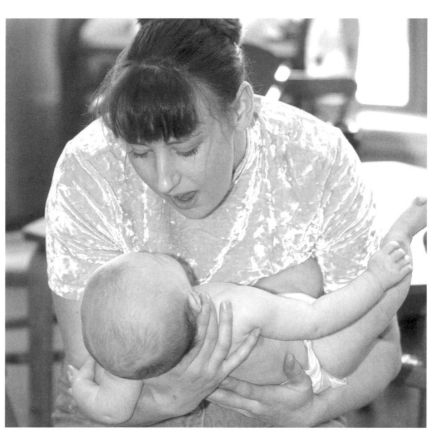

It's a hard decision to leave your baby and go back to work

CASE STUDY:

SORYA

Sorya was another new mum who found she was reluctant to go back to work. She wrote:

My baby is now 6 months old and I have to make some decisions about going back to work. When I left work to have Mia I wanted to get back to my work as quickly as possible, and I even looked at nurseries before she was born. I am surprised to find that I have enjoyed being at home with my daughter and I don't want to go back to work yet, but I can't afford to stay at home all the time. I want to negotiate working part-time until Mia is a bit older, maybe 15 or 16 months. I am beginning to look again at the different childcare options. Now that I know my baby and she's a real little person I'm not sure whether I want to put her in a nursery or send her to a childminder.

Inside I am very sad that it could be someone else who will see her take her first steps and do lots of other things for the first time. I don't think that it will feel so bad when she's three and she can go to school nursery and wraparound care, but at the moment she seems very little to leave. No one told me that being a parent could be so hard.

Other parents are relieved that the setting is so pleasant and that the child has settled in well. They see their child is happy and they trust the childcare worker as a partner and friend.

CASE STUDY:
HAYLEY

My Hayley goes to nursery full-time. She is only 23 months old so I found it quite hard to leave her at first, but the staff were so lovely I just knew she would be fine.

The thing I love is that she runs into nursery. The environment is beautiful and the staff are so welcoming. Every morning they all smile and are genuinely happy to see the children. They say 'Good morning, Hayley' with really bright happy faces. That's so important to me. Haley runs to Cathy and grabs her hand. I feel I can go to work and do my job because my precious child is also precious to others. They do a wonderful job.

CASE STUDY:
CHEN

Chen, who is three, loves his nursery, which is a blessing for me. He has language problems so making himself understood worried me. He has been at nursery since he was two and a half and his language is improving. He talks a lot about one of the staff. He has obviously bonded with Mandy. 'Mandy took me outside', 'I see Mandy today', 'Mandy laughs hard.' In my eyes Mandy is an angel. In Chen's she is his hero, friend and carer.

REFLECT ON YOUR PRACTICE

It is a skill to reassure parents about your role working alongside them in caring for their child.

How do you cope with a mother's understandable feelings about sharing her child with you? How does your setting meet the needs of a parent leaving a child for the first time? How do you meet the parents' ongoing needs? What information do you give them about their child? How often is the information given? Who gives it, where and when? What form does it take? What are the pros and cons of webcams and other similar devices?

What information do you ask for from the parent? How is it recorded? Who has access to it? Who needs to have access to it?

How do you ensure that the child's home experience and experience at your setting merge in a meaningful way a) for babies, b) for toddlers, c) for children over two?

Many parents value the opportunity to be able to fulfil themselves at work as well as at home. The relationship of the childcare worker with this group of parents raises other issues.

CASE STUDY:

JO

Jo explains:

It's a lovely feeling dropping the kids off at nursery and then coming to work. I need to work at least part-time for my own self-esteem and sanity. I love the children so much. However, I've found in the past that when I stayed at home full-time I became slightly depressed and felt isolated, and that the children didn't receive much 'quality' time with me. It's funny, but now I'm working part-time the children receive more quality time from me and I enjoy their company to the full. I look forward to going to work and I look forward to seeing the children. Our time together is so much more precious and enjoyable. This is a poem I wrote.

A day in the life of Jo

Three little faces smile up at me
With tousled hair and bright eyes
They're beautiful to see

Three little angels aged 5, 3 and 1
I've got no time to stand and stare
There's bums to be done

We comb our hair, we brush our teeth, we play
One seems out of sorts
It's another busy day

We're nearly there, there's little left to do
Oh no! What's that smell?
Someone's done a poo

At last we're off, not much stress
We won't be late for school
Anyway who cares if the house is in a mess

First stop infant school, I am in a rush
What's for tea, will I be late
This twin pram's hard to push

We're off again, up the hill and I am in a state
We have to catch a special bus
I hope it isn't late

At last the little one's in nursery, another day of play
I'm on my own, I'm off to work
My goodness, is it still Monday

Sanctuary, normality, adults and me
I'll do my work, I'll earn my pay
But first, a cup of tea!

It is a skill to be aware of the range of feelings in the parents you work with.

What are the pressures on the parents who work? Do they have different needs, such as travelling to the setting, perhaps feelings of guilt that while they feel fulfilled in a demanding job they also miss the child's first words or steps?

How do you communicate with busy parents? Are there any other ways that you might try besides the usual home / setting diary, for example, texting, emailing, digital images and consultations?

Parents under pressure

There are many types of family. Besides conventional families, there are reconstituted families, such as Jane's. Jane is a working mother with two children aged eight and four, and she separated from their father when the younger child was one. She married Mark, who has two children aged seven and 18 months. These children live with their mother, but spend most weekends and holidays with Jane and Mark. The children have had to adjust to two sets of rules. Bedtime for Mark's children when they are with their mother means falling asleep on the sofa and being carried to bed. In Jane's house there is a fixed bedtime.

There are families where children are cared for by grandparents. One mother cares for her daughter, who is 22 and has mental health problems, and the daughter's 5-month-old baby. There are issues about the father's access to the baby. The household is overcrowded and the grandparents suffer from stress and lack of financial support. The outlook looks bleak, as there will come a time when the grandparents will not be able to continue this level of support.

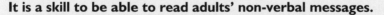

It is a skill to be able to read adults' non-verbal messages.

To do this effectively we have to have an awareness of our own prejudices (positive or negative) about class, appearance and presentation (including dress, accent, accessories, smell) as well as unexamined feelings about gender, ethnicity, age and health, all of which could distort our response to a person.

What are the signs of stress you notice in an adult? Do you hear indications in the voice? Do you pick up on the use of particular mannerisms? Do you notice bodily changes (high colour, perspiration or lethargy)? Do you notice expressions in the face or certain patterns of behaviour? How do you respond to stress in other adults? What staff training would help you?

There are newly arrived families, families in transition or families who have moved to find jobs, who all have to manage without the support of the extended family. There are lone parents, male and female, teenage parents and those who have come late to parenthood. Many of these may be under considerable stress. In addition, in some families both parents must be in employment to meet their financial commitments.

Some adults under extreme pressure may appear discourteous to staff. Defusing confrontation is a useful skill and worth practising. The main things are to avoid showing a tense or angry reaction or to tell the person to calm down. Doing this makes matters worse. Don't laugh or smile – things you may tend to do if you are nervous. Look sympathetic and nod a lot. The first words you say should be in agreement. End by saying, 'and I'm sure we can…' This shows you are responding to what the person has been saying and that you will both put in effort to resolve the difficulty.

Childcare workers may also be under their own stresses. Stress not only results from major life events (such as moving house or job, the break-up of a relationship, a change in family circumstances or bereavement) but it also builds up from an accumulation of the minor problems of everyday life. It may be work-related or may come from a noisy or polluted environment. It has an emotional impact (depression, anxiety, anger, fear). It can result in poor concentration and impaired memory. You may feel always tired or have sleep problems as a result of it.

REFLECT ON YOUR PRACTICE

It is a skill to recognise the signs of stress in yourself and to have strategies for dealing with it.

Once stress is recognised, there are ways of dealing with it. The first step is to decide whether there is really a threat and then to ask whether it really matters. It helps to focus on the emotions you feel and to try to reduce negative emotions by seeking help, or turning your attention elsewhere, or finding a safe way to release the emotions.

Secondly, it is useful to clarify the problem. Eliminate the notion that nothing can be done and consider alternative courses of action. Decide on an action and take it.

Finally, many people find that it helps to learn relaxation techniques and take regular exercise.

In your setting, have there been examples of families under stress? How is stress dealt with in your setting, a) on the personal level, b) on a whole-setting level? In what ways can babies and young children be shielded from the effects of stress on the adults in their lives?

Childcare workers see it as part of their remit to help to ease some of the pressures on families. This can range from arranging transport to help a mother to attend an early morning hospital appointment for her child, to giving understanding to a woman at the end of her tether. One children's centre supported a parent in crisis in a very practical way, by filling a gap.

CASE STUDY:
FRED

It's essential for Fred (aged two and a half) to get a brain scan. His appointment is at 8 o'clock in the morning at the hospital. For us in nursery it's meant lots of planning – ringing Fred's mum to wake her up, having two staff ready to greet Fred's little sister (aged one) at 7.30 a.m., making toast and having a cup of tea before the nursery opens at 8 a.m. It's worth it. It'll make a difference to Fred.

Another parent needed a different and more professional on-going kind of support.

CASE STUDY:
TESIA

Tesia wrote:

I am a single mother with four kids. I have one aged two, one aged six, one aged eight and one who has just gone to secondary school. There are times when I really feel that I'm struggling with the kids. Their Dad isn't there when they need him.

Some days I get so angry I just want to hit out at them. I've had a bad life myself. My Mum died when I was eight and I was looked after by my aunt, who was like the Wicked Witch of the West. My Dad tried really hard but he had to go to work so Aunty Alina had to help out. I was so unhappy, I hated it and I used to get angry with my Mum for leaving me, and my Dad for sending me away. I know that I had bad tantrums until I was quite old. Even though I'm a mother, I still feel that I need a Mum myself and some days I want to leave them like my Mum left me.

REFLECT ON YOUR PRACTICE

It is a skill to know where to send parents for the help they need.

How does your staff training programme help you to help parents? Do you know about the Credit Unions in your area? Do you know the sources of other help for parents in your locality? Have you practised developing your listening skills?

Childcare workers in some areas face many families with problems. Besides personal relationship problems, a common source of stress is money.

Chapter 5 Working collaboratively to care for babies and young children

CASE STUDY:
JENNY

Debbie, who is 2 years and 9 months, and her sister Julie, who is 10 months old, live with Jenny, their mother, aged 22. Jenny has been separated from her partner on and off for the past 2 years.

When home visits were made at 10 a.m. by the outreach worker, she would find Jenny and the children still in bed. According to Jenny the children didn't eat breakfast. The house was a complete mess and looked as if it hadn't been cleaned in weeks. Later, Jenny confessed she had no money to go shopping. Jenny was also in debt and was in the process of having her electricity cut off. She had not even made contact with the suppliers to ensure this would not happen.

Jenny's despondency and debt problems were the result of spending a lot of money on alcohol. She said that once the children fell asleep, she drank to blot out her life. The impact of this on her children's lives has been devastating. They are under-nourished, have no language and are not able to crawl or walk. They have spent their lives in buggies and cots, with no stimulation.

But of course not all parents with money problems are in such dire straits. Most people have their own strategies for coping.

CASE STUDY:
WORKING IN A SUPERMARKET

I'm working all the shifts I can so I can pay off money for the holiday we had, and get sorted for Christmas. I'm keeping the car even though I've not paid the tax yet, because it's the only way I can get the kids to nursery and then me to work in the evenings while my Mum babysits.

CASE STUDY:
THE PAWNBROKERS

I use the pawnbrokers for my banking. I save up and buy any gold jewellery that I can and then when I need some cash – like for a wedding or a funeral or the kids' birthdays – I can go and put my jewellery in the pawnbrokers. You can tell when I'm stuck – look, no bracelets.

Listening skills are often rated less than fluency in speaking, but in fact they are essential for getting on with others because by using them you are showing that you respect the other person. Listening skills ensure that communication happens.

The techniques include giving your full attention to the person you are talking to – not having half of your attention somewhere else. Give non-verbal clues that you are listening; lean forward, use eye contact, acknowledge what you have heard by making reassuring sounds and nodding. Don't fidget or move about. Restrain yourself from bursting in with an anecdote from your own experience. Give the person space – don't try to fill every silence.

When you do speak, use your words to bring out the other person's point of view. Ask open questions (those that need a fuller answer than closed questions, which only need the answer *yes* or *no*). At appropriate points rephrase what the person has said to check whether you have understood correctly. Practise these skills in your everyday life until they become second nature. They will be very useful in your work.

Supporting parents' development

A further part of the childcare worker's task is now seen as supporting parents' own development. With the support of childcare workers, parents can be helped to gain the confidence and experience that will help them towards getting a job.

CASE STUDY:

JAN

I'm Jan. I lived in a residential home all my teenage years. I used to be in charge of lots of the new kids and tried to settle them in. I ran a girls' netball team and used to play all over the region.

That stopped when I left at 16 and had two kids. They were taken off me and I don't see them now. I've settled down now with Hal, and we have four kids aged five, four, three and the baby. I'm doing an access course at the moment and going on to university to do sports science; I love studying and I'm still under 30, so when I graduate I'll get a good job. I couldn't have done it without the childcare support.

In one area parents are empowered by taking responsibility for making suggestions for activities at the local centre. The minutes of a recent meeting at the centre included suggestions for publicising childcare provision in schools, hospitals and surgeries, producing age-specific welcome packs for new parents coming to the centre, establishing a Mum's club along the lines of the existing Dad's club, arranging outings, evaluating the response to centre activities, and extending the centre's programme by arranging activities for older children. They were also planning to lobby local councillors and the MP and to have a suggestions box. These activities in voluntary work help parents to develop skills which can lead to employment.

A 'Dads and Lads' group can be highly successful

In the case study below, Elisha describes how she is benefiting from having been involved in such a programme.

CASE STUDY:

ELISHA

I'm Elisha and I have a son called Joshua, who's four. Now he's in full-time school I'm doing voluntary work in my children's centre to help with the administration and start up the Mum's club. At the moment I'm organising a trip to see the Blackpool lights. I am studying sign language and child psychology. I want a job as an administrator and I am building up my skills.

Developing parents' belief in themselves has been an important aspect of the work of SureStart and of the children's centres that are developing from it. Children's centres will allow access to many services under one roof. They will provide a variety of health-related courses, such as baby massage, weaning groups, baby yoga and healthy eating for children. Parents will come to courses such as these for their child's sake, not because they are interested in formal learning. Children's centres will have activities and courses targeted at parents of toddlers and

Story sacks provide a stimulus

nursery-age children. These will include language development groups, play and learn groups, story sacks (that is a bag containing a book and some toys related to the story to take away to read at home), and other enjoyable activities designed to help parents or carers and children to learn together.

In addition to 'child-based' learning, many parents will be involved in 'first step' courses such as first aid, alternative therapies, cooking and flower arranging. Enjoying these short courses can give many parents the learning habit, and they can become a springboard for accessing more formal educational opportunities. Some parents may be able to move on to employment through the confidence they gain from 'first step' opportunities, while others will want to further their education through more traditional routes and go onto an access course leading them to higher education. The government's *Every Child Matters* framework (2004) expects children's centres to show evidence that parents are being helped to achieve economic well-being.

Some children's centres will be able to provide parents with formal opportunities to study through outreach provision from local adult education providers such as further education colleges, training agencies and the local education authorities. Course provision will depend on local needs, but it will often include English as an Additional Language (EAL), IT courses, basic skills opportunities, and relevant vocational opportunities such as childcare and health-related opportunities. Liaison with local advice and guidance agencies and job centres will be offered by the children's centre, and this should enable parents or carers to follow the educational pathways that will help them to discover and then achieve their long-term goals.

It is a skill to arrange opportunities that will support parents' own development.

Do you know what the needs of parents are in your area? Do you know where they will be given help e.g for personal development, childcare arrangements, transport, advice about health issues, counselling and welfare rights?

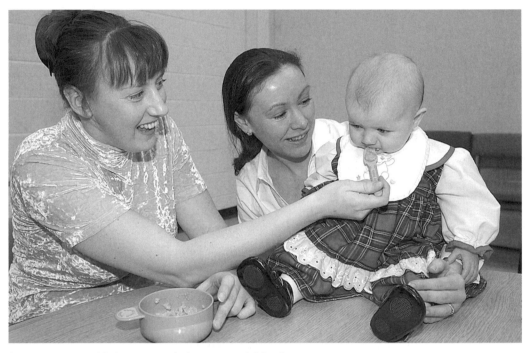

Parents may need help weaning babies onto solid food

How childcare workers help local communities

Neighbourhoods vary considerably in what they can offer to young children and their parents. Fill in the chart on page 180, considering what facilities might be available in each of the different types of location.

REVIEW OF LOCAL FACILITIES

Opportunities available for	Locations					
	City centre	Inner city	Privately owned housing	Rented accommodation	Small town	Village
Employment						
Shopping						
Transport – local						
Transport – national						
Education – schools						
Education – post-school						
Health care						
Childcare						
Play spaces for young children						
Places for adolescents						
Cross cultural experience						
Leisure and entertainment						
Worship and interest groups						

REFLECT ON YOUR PRACTICE

It is a skill to empower parents to use their local environment for the benefit of their children.

When you have filled in the chart consider the particular strengths and needs of your area. Analyse your local area in terms of its strengths. How can it compensate for the gaps? How do you help families to make the most of what is available in the area?

Childcare workers can help to give families opportunities to enjoy themselves together, thus having an impact on the well-being of the whole community.

CASE STUDY:

KARL

Karl writes:

Each year our centre takes part in family learning week. The local family learning team organises fun activities for the whole family. Last year we had a drumming workshop, an art afternoon, and an Indian dance. Every activity was well attended and we all had fun together.

One of the centres in Liverpool recently launched a Baby Book Crawl. The aim of this was to encourage parents to see that their young children could become active members of their local library from a very young age.

The SureStart staff invited parents and their children aged between 6 weeks and 3 years to a series of events at the local library. The events included story tellers, puppets and song and drama sessions. The children were given a free book for attending the first session and they were also encouraged to take a library book home. At each weekly session there was time set aside for the children to change their library books, and they were given a special Baby Book Crawl stamp on their card.

Never too young to join the local library

At the end of 6 weeks everyone was invited back to a special celebration party with certificates for all who had taken part. The parents and children enjoyed the events and many of them developed the habit of taking their children to the library each week.

One nursery took on an allotment to help involve parents and the community with children in the nursery.

CASE STUDY: ALLOTMENTS

Our nursery has an allotment plot. The aim was to build on our healthy eating projects and to support the learning of our children in partnership with parents. What was outstanding was the range of individuals involved in the project and the commitment from parents, grandparents, young people and community members in the area.

Following a meeting with parents and the community to discuss the project, it was agreed that a team of adults would work on the allotment on a Tuesday, and children and parents or carers on a Thursday. The outcome of this was that quite different adults and children attended the allotment virtually every day, including the weekends, to prepare the ground for planting and the all-important garden shed.

Once the shed was put in place the gardening tools were bought in adult and child sizes – gloves, wheelbarrows, hoes, trowels, rakes and buckets – to enable the children and families to prepare the soil for planting potatoes, cabbages, cauliflowers, carrots, runner beans, radishes, spinach, strawberries, rhubarb, lettuce, tomatoes and onions.

The nature of work on an allotment means that all those involved can contribute as much or as little as they are able. Young children were given a section of land that they could dig over and over again until

Fun at the allotment

they were ready to plant. Liam said: 'I'm digging real deep, in the dirt.' The children were involved in all aspects of the process and have been interested in watering and weeding, observing growth and change, harvesting the produce and cooking with the vegetables. Patrick said: 'It's a big lettuce, I've just picked it from the ground.' His mother said later: 'I love coming to the allotment, as Patrick has grown so much in his speech and confidence.'

The language opportunities were endless, with opportunities for the children to ask questions, and to describe observations ('The wind is blowing the windmill around') and to talk about what they were doing ('I'm watering the flowers and plants for you'). The activity provided the opportunity for shared fun and learning, with parents supporting their children's social and emotional development. Natalie, a parent, commented: 'I never thought I would enjoy working on an allotment.'

Parents clearly enjoyed learning alongside their children and each other. One father who uses a wheelchair contributed by planting seeds in pots at the patio table, engaging with the children in the process. Mature community members played a mentoring role to the younger parents, guiding them and encouraging them through the planting process to the cooking of the produce.

The production of the vegetables encourages healthy eating and saves parents money. We recorded the project through photographs and these were recently exhibited to the wider community. The putting together of the exhibition, and writing anecdotes to support the photographs, also created many opportunities for shared learning between parents and children. Everyone is keen to continue with this, and we are now preparing the ground for winter planting.

The results of some community building can show quickly, but strengthening a community can take much longer before it becomes apparent.

REFLECT ON YOUR PRACTICE

It is a skill to arrange opportunities to build a community feeling.

Make as long a list as you can of the positive outcomes of the allotment project – not just the vegetables! – and the Baby Book Crawl. Why do you think they were successful? What could you arrange to help the parents of the children who attend your setting feel more part of the community? Remember that each location will have its own characteristics. What other provision in the area could you link with? Do you contribute to an exhibition in the area? Is the local community aware of your existence?

CASE STUDY:

SPECIAL DAYS

A celebration can be shared with everyone

Sandra writes:

In our nursery we encourage everybody to see birthdays as a celebration. The Family Link worker asks parents to be involved. Many of the parents bring in food and birthday cake. If the parents cannot afford a cake, our cook bakes a special cake for the occasion. We hope this will be part of the special memories children will have of the nursery. We see this as part of the social and emotional development of our children.

Tapati writes:

In the nursery we celebrate Diwali, the festival of light. The nursery becomes a sea of shimmering, sparkling light. Members of the Hindu community come to our nursery and prepare activities (dance and music) and special food, and dress up in traditional clothes.

Dowrinda writes:

Carnival is in the summer. Our nursery is in an inner city area and we have lots of AfroCaribbean families. The first year was quite a small affair in the nursery garden. Each year it has grown, to what it is today. We now have several community groups involved. Food, music and dance contribute to the carnival atmosphere. Families enter into the spirit of it and contribute food. Next year we are hoping to have a local poet working with the musicians to create a carnival rap.

Lucy writes:

Christmas is my favourite time of year in the nursery. We have parties, a grotto and the staff all dress up. There is a lovely atmosphere. We always try to organise something for the parents to share with us, usually arranged on a shoestring. Many of the parents have financial worries at this time of year so we organise our activities to cost as little as possible. Ellen, one of the parents, blames the Three Kings. If only they hadn't brought gifts…

It is a skill to ensure the childcare setting makes a contribution to the community in general.

Make a list of all the community-building activities that have happened in your area over the past 12 months. What is your setting planning next?

What resources can you offer as a childcare setting? Think of the talents, ideas and enthusiasm you have as a staff group. Think of the resources of the parents you work with. Have fun.

Time management

It is becoming obvious that childcare workers' responsibilities are becoming very wide. Time-management skills are helpful. One commonly recommended tool is this matrix, which not only looks at how *urgent* activities are, but also how *important* they are.

	Urgent	**Not urgent**
Important	**I** Crises Pressing problems Deadline-driven projects	**II** Prevention, looking ahead Building relationships Recognising new opportunities Planning
Not important	**III** Interruptions, some calls Some messages, some meetings Pressing matters	**IV** Trivia Some meetings, some calls Time-wasters

Focusing only on the activities in square I leads to stress and burnout; focusing only on squares III and IV leads to feeling out of control and being dependent on others. But time spent focusing on square II is time well spent. It leads to a development of a sense of purpose, a vision and perspective. It produces self-discipline and control, and consequently fewer crises arise. Square II activities, while not urgent, make a positive difference to the way you work, in whatever capacity.

FOCUS

Begin to reallocate time you currently spend on activities in squares III and IV to square II. Doing so will help you to focus on what is important and basic as well as urgent. It involves you in identifying your roles and selecting goals.

How childcare workers focus special care

Some children need extra help; slow development in language, for example, is not unusual.

'Chatterbox' is a course developed in one SureStart programme. It encourages language development through play. Through paired play activities, parents and toddlers are able to focus on areas of learning, and parents gain valuable information about how their child learns.

CASE STUDY:

JAQUI

I have two sons, Tom who is seven and Sam who is two. Last year Sam was not doing well. He found it hard to play on his own, and his speech wasn't there. He used to get very frustrated.

What we used to do in Chatterbox was to get him to interact with other children his age who had the same problem. We would also play with play dough.

One time the childcare workers brought bubbles into the group. I said 'Why are we doing this?' Lucy said that when they blow bubbles it helps to develop the muscles around the mouth, which I found interesting.

What I enjoyed the most was meeting all the other mums and knowing I wasn't on my own. I think what Sam enjoyed the most was mixing with other children his own age.

Chatterbox has made a big impact on Sam as he really came out of his shell. It also helped me and Tom understand him a lot more, and we can support his needs.

We still do things with Sam from Chatterbox. I attend a lot of courses at SureStart, so some of the time he goes to the crèche, where again he is learning a lot.

Chatterbox has brought me and Sam a lot closer on the communication side. Not only has it benefited Sam, but the rest of the family too. We can all understand and talk to Sam now. Thanks to Chatterbox, Sam is learning new words every day. Both Sam and I have gained a lot of confidence.

Sometimes a parent needs help to manage a child's behaviour, for example if there is a problem with potty training or sleeping. In these cases the parent can be introduced to a structured programme like the Portage method to use at home. With this behaviourist approach, the task is broken down into manageable, small steps and consistent rewards are agreed. This is usually used to bring about more complex behaviour change, for example in behaviour connected with sleeping or eating which is causing concern.

Parents can attend behaviour management courses at their local family centre

In one SureStart programme, where the childcare professionals see slow emotional or social development, their 'Nurture Base' responds by providing small-group full-day care once a week for 3-year-olds. There is a calm atmosphere here. Lunch is served with a table cloth, china plates and metal cutlery. Healthy options are prepared and presented, favourite meals are noted and encouragement is given to the children to try new foods. There is a consistently positive approach, rewarding good behaviour and ignoring the behaviours that are to be discouraged. This has helped children, for example those who do not speak well. In Nurture Base a team of professionals work together. The educational psychologist, health visitors and the nursery staff provide an integrated service.

REFLECT ON YOUR PRACTICE

It is a skill to be aware of what childcare work now involves.

Reading these accounts, what do you think are the extra qualities now required in a childcare worker?

Childcare workers alongside other services

Childcare workers are only one of many services involved with families. Collaboration with other services is far from easy, not because of personality problems with the people involved, but because services are not all the same. Each service has its own history and set of values. This variation in approach applies even within the childcare field itself.

The tradition in working with young children, which has come from the education service, has a different feel from the one that has grown from a group of volunteers working together for their own children in a playgroup. There is another strand in early years work that has traditionally had welfare as its focus, and now there is yet another strand which is driven by the economics of business considerations and pleasing the customer.

Each service for families has its own priorities and focus. The medical service looks at the child's health from before birth, and will be concerned with the person's health until death. The librarian is concerned about the number of books borrowed; the teacher is interested in the good effect that early familiarity with books has on the child's success in school. The child must go to school and at a certain age will leave teachers behind, but the librarian will always be available if the person wishes to use the service.

Each service has its own procedures for **assessment**. The doctor or speech therapist will assess a case by careful diagnosis, and will usually know exactly what to do next. The educator and childcare worker will both use formative assessment to decide which among several options might be the best to follow next – perhaps using this activity instead of the other, this story instead of that. Using another sort of assessment, a summative (summing up) assessment at the end of a course or a stage, a teacher will measure how much the pupil has learned in a certain subject and will probably include in the assessment how the pupil compares with others in the same group. This type of assessment is rarely used in other services.

KEY TERM: Assessment

There are several ways of assessing and each has a different purpose. Formative assessment is aimed at deciding what to do next in the light of what you have found out about a child's present situation. It 'forms' your next action. Diagnostic assessment looks into a particular problem so as to target specific help. Doctors and speech therapists diagnose. Summative assessment is used at the end of a stage or period of study. Since all babies and young children develop at their own pace, it can be misleading to focus on how a child stands in relation to how most children of that age perform, as happens in the case of normative assessment.

The educator or doctor may collect a series of observations before coming to a decision, but the police and social services have much less leeway in deciding what action they can take. Their very strict procedures compared with those of other services may cause confusion in service users. Police and social workers are legally bound to take a particular action immediately in certain circumstances.

Two services working with the same family may have different values, procedures and approaches. This can create problems.

CASE STUDY:

DEBBIE

Debbie is a very young single mum with two small sons. She has been suffering from bouts of depression and mood swings and has had difficulty in coping with her younger son, an active 18-month-old called Tom. She went to her local SureStart staff to ask for help. She told them that Tom had not been sleeping and that he had been crying for two hours the previous evening. At the end of her tether, she had pushed him back into his cot and left him to cry. Next day she discovered that she had bruised Tom's arms when she had put him back into the cot.

Debbie was distraught about what she had done and wanted SureStart staff to help her to manage Tom's sleep problem.

The dilemma for the SureStart staff was how to help Debbie without losing her trust and also to follow the correct procedures to protect Tom. They explained that they had to inform the Child Protection team, but they reassured her that they would support her in every way they could. Debbie was adamant that she didn't want the social services involved and she became extremely distressed with the SureStart staff.

Tom was immediately taken into temporary care. Debbie went to see her GP and was prescribed anti-depressants and undertook a series of counselling sessions. Initially, Debbie felt very let down and traumatised. Tom and Debbie were reunited within a week. Tom has some respite sessions in a local nursery, but Debbie continues to need a lot of support and it will take her a long time to regain her confidence.

Debbie was surprised to find that in matters concerning child protection there are procedures that must be followed. In some sections of society there is a deep-rooted suspicion of authority figures. The childcare workers had seemed approachable, happy and welcoming, but in this case they were under a duty to alert the children's services. Sometimes childcare workers have to follow procedures which may not come easily to them.

FOCUS

How do you prepare for this? What support is available to you? If you are a manager, how do you find support for yourself?

Assertiveness

In this type of situation the childcare worker had to be assertive. Assertiveness is definitely *not* aggressiveness. It does not mean steamrollering over the other person. It means being neither condemnatory nor apologetic. It avoids expressions or indications of anger. It means giving direct, clear, concise and objective statements using sentences beginning with *I*.

Non-verbal aspects of the communication include being calm, keeping the voice level and avoiding excessive blinking, looking away or other signs of nervousness.

When you act assertively you recognise and respect the other person and you hope to be able to reach a satisfactory outcome for both of you.

Different approaches

Each service has its protocols about who can pass on what information, how, when and to whom. In some services the hierarchical structure is very strong; in others, more informality and a warmer relationship with service users is encouraged.

Each service has its own language; for example, education jargon includes *milestones, learning goals* and *SATs,* and the areas of the curriculum from three onwards are carefully demarcated. Services also differ in the amount of informality that is allowed. A police officer in uniform reading a book to a child is an unusual sight.

Each service has its own way of interpreting events. Watching a young child with clay, a person from one tradition may see the child exploring the feel and the malleability of the clay. Another may see the child working out some deep trauma or anxiety. A child using black for a painting may to one observer be enjoying the sharp contrast of black on white and the viscosity of the paint, and revelling in the sensory experience. To another, the child may be showing signs of being deeply depressed.

Other professionals such as police officers do work directly with young children

REFLECT ON YOUR PRACTICE

It is a skill to understand the viewpoint of the other services that have contact with the families and communities you work with.

What other services have contact with the families you work with? Are you able to direct parents to where they can get help or advice?

What can you learn about the procedures and structure of these services? How do they operate? What is their approach? What are their constraints?

Overcoming difficulties

The prosperity of a local area often depends on the availability of work. If work is not available (and there are areas where there are literally no jobs, and no public transport to travel to jobs elsewhere), people are more likely to become depressed and may then resort to drugs and alcohol to counter their feelings of alienation and depression. The work of the childcare team is more challenging in these circumstances.

The following case study offers a vivid first-hand description of how depression feels.

CASE STUDY: DEPRESSION

Depression is a niggling, annoying thing that's in people's heads waiting to destroy them and make sure that their everyday life becomes a struggle. It takes over your mind. You could say it's like aliens abducting your mind – the more you fight against it, the harder it tries to get you.

This is how my depression came about. I had depression when I was younger but I didn't realise it. I had my kids but couldn't cope, so they went to live with their grandmother. For a while I felt fine. I had my daughter living with me again and had another daughter on the way – everything was fine… The baby was born, but at 4 months she suddenly became very ill and was taken into hospital. There she had a second seizure.

Because her heart had stopped she ended up with severe brain damage and the doctor told me she'd never walk, talk or anything else. He said she'd be in a vegetable state for the rest of her life. While the doctors investigated the cause of what had happened to her, the social services placed my 2-year-old in the care of my Mum and my poor sick daughter in the care of a foster parent. The day the foster parent came to take my baby away I cried. After all that had happened to her, some stranger had my little girl, giving her hugs, kisses and putting her to bed.

➡

Eventually I got a job in a shop, which made me feel better. Then I became pregnant again.

Everything was fine until I left my job, and guess what? Social services told me I'd have to go through assessments in order for this baby to stay in my care. I got a midwife who didn't judge me, so that helped a bit. Near the end of my pregnancy I was told that the assessments couldn't start until my son was born. On 2 May my beautiful little boy was born. I spent a few days with him. Then I had to go to court, and got the worst news any woman could be told. My son was to go into the care of foster parents.

I went back to the hospital to get my belongings and to hold my son before the foster parents took him. I walked to my room expecting him to be in his cot, but he was gone and so were all his belongings. I broke down crying and screaming. Then I got my things and left the hospital.

I got up the next day and knew I had to do something positive if I wanted my son back. I co-operated with the social services and saw my son every day, and did all my assessments in order for my son to be returned to me. Finally, at 7 months, my little boy was returned under a supervision order to make sure everything was fine.

My depression had started to surface again so instead of going to the doctor's I joined the Community College drop-in study centre and my confidence improved. My depression hasn't come back since. I am a confident woman who can smile and talk to anyone. In my courses I have gone on to pass City & Guilds level 1 English, CLAIT, and am waiting for the results for my maths level 1 and English level 2. I start a pre-access course in September.

I won a hard fight. I see my children all the time. My little girl may have cerebral palsy but she's the light of my life and when I feel down I look at her photo and feel happy, as this little angel made me stop feeling sorry for myself and take a look at my life.

Sometimes the focus of support is in the setting; sometimes the nursery is only one of a team of services. In the case study above it was the contact with the childcare workers that helped the mother out of her depression by supporting her to build up her self-esteem. Childcare workers can and do make a difference to people's lives.

CASE STUDY:

EDWARD

We met Edward, aged one, in the nursery. He ate little, had no speech, was not interested in moving and was extremely passive. The mother was constantly at the health visitor's and the doctor's, saying the baby wasn't eating, was vomiting, had a high temperature, wasn't sleeping – anything and everything. Eventually she was struck off two doctors' lists.

We gave Edward a full-time place at the nursery and gradually realised that the mother's behaviour was the most likely cause of his developmental delay. We worked with the mother, building up her self-esteem while being fully aware of her tendency to try to get attention through the child's supposed illnesses.

An integrated approach such as Liverpool's Neighbourhood Early Years Service (NEYS) is valuable for children under five with special educational needs or disabilities. NEYS is a multi-disciplinary initiative resulting from partnership between Liverpool City Council, the primary care trusts and the Royal Liverpool Children's NHS Trust. They work in collaboration with other professionals from health, education and social services, and the NEYS team implements support agreements for children at home, in nursery or in reception class.

REFLECT ON YOUR PRACTICE

It is a skill to identify the sources of support in the local environment and to know when to refer a parent to another agency.

Are all members of staff aware of what is available? What are the procedures within the setting for raising an area of concern?

Sharing information

Research into how we can identify vulnerable children earlier has shown the urgent need for training in sharing information between services, voluntary organisations and charities working with families and children. Involving more people and services who work to support families would certainly identify children who are at risk earlier, but there are problems of training and issues around the development of trust between services. These problems focus on the issue of confidentiality.

CASE STUDY:

HEALTH VISITOR

A health visitor writes:

I am a qualified nurse and midwife, who chose to continue my training as a health visitor. I was attached to a doctor's surgery and used to carry out visits to families after 6 weeks when new babies had been visited by the midwife. From this to school age my job was to run clinics, encourage parents to take up immunisation, identify and work with post-natal depression and check the development of children at two.

I had a case load of children, some of whom had special needs, and I also responded to child protection issues. In my area there is a shortage of health visitors and therefore there is a lot of pressure. I also respond to requests from other professionals to visit the homes of children under four who are a cause for concern.

Now I am a member of a team of children's centre workers and I am also involved in running groups for parents and children such as Pamper Group, baby massage, dental services, school health fairs, weaning groups, speech and language groups such as Babbling Babies and Chatterbox, and the Five-a-Day Voucher scheme.

It is a different approach with new roles, and works now to child-centred approaches. For example, our oxygen-dependent baby has been supported in many other groups as well as the Baby Breathe Easy group, where the mother can get support from specialised services and other mothers.

We still have lots of challenges, such as information-sharing protocols, but we are working to towards having joint records.

The childcare worker is very close to each family attending the setting and has connections with all the other services involved with young children and their families. The childcare worker has information that the other services need. This information has to be readily available and it needs to be trustworthy.

Memories fade and mingle, but an important tool for the childcare worker is the written observations made of each child. These narrative observations must be made regularly and reflected upon regularly. They are primarily for the parent, but may be needed by other services. Kept in written form, they will be available to other services if required for evidence at a case conference. Each observation, however small, is a contribution to the work of the team within the setting and to the work of other services.

REFLECT ON YOUR PRACTICE

It is a skill to keep useful records of the development of each child in the setting.

Is each child observed regularly? How are your records made? Do they give a full picture of the child's interests and well-being at a particular time? Tick lists do not give sufficient detail.

How often are records made? Are the observations that have been made discussed with colleagues? Are they used in deciding on interactions with the child? What is the policy about sharing and keeping the records? How could you ensure that all staff are aware of relevant background information?

The role of the key worker is vital in any work with young children.

REFLECT ON YOUR PRACTICE

It is a skill to be able to take the lead in supporting children.

What is the role of the key worker in your setting? How many children does a key worker have responsibility for? What exactly is expected? How much contact does the key worker have with the children in his or her remit? Is the role mainly bureaucratic or do other colleagues talk with key workers about the children? Does the key worker have the opportunity to become a loving, familiar and supportive person in the child's life?

The theme of this chapter has been the importance of the role of the childcare service in supporting parents and sharing information. For a partnership, information must flow from home to nursery, and from nursery to home.

CASE STUDY:
USING TECHNOLOGY

One setting makes use of technology to do this. Using digital cameras, the staff take photographs of children throughout the day. They use sticky notes to capture what the children say. Each child has his or her own folder on the computer where work is stored. Two-and-half-year-olds can access their work at any time of the day, and they can bring up images of themselves if they wish. Younger children's work is documented in the same way but it is held in files until the children are able to manipulate the IT equipment in the same way. Parents can access their child's file at any time using a password. They can also contribute images and dialogues that the staff can use to stimulate conversation with the child.

This is a working model of how information can flow from nursery to home or home to nursery. A similar system to enable information to flow from service to service in the interests of the child and the community would be valuable. When this is achieved there will be a joined-up community that will nourish the people who live in it. The childcare worker will be at the heart of this network.

Conclusion

This chapter has discussed the contribution the childcare setting can make to the well-being of the families and community it works with.

The following skills have been highlighted:

◆ It is a skill to reassure parents about your role working alongside them in caring for their child.

◆ It is a skill to be aware of the range of feelings in the parents you work with.

◆ It is a skill to be able to read adults' non-verbal messages.

◆ It is a skill to recognise the signs of stress in yourself and to have strategies for dealing with it.

◆ It is a skill to know where to send parents for the help they need.

◆ It is a skill to arrange opportunities that will support parents' own development.

◆ It is a skill to empower parents to use their local environment for the benefit of their children.

◆ It is a skill to arrange opportunities to build a community feeling.

◆ It is a skill to ensure the childcare setting makes a contribution to the community in general.

◆ It is a skill to be aware of what childcare work now involves.

◆ It is a skill to understand the viewpoint of the other services that have contact with the families and communities you work with.

◆ It is a skill to identify the sources of support in the local environment and to know when to refer a parent to another agency.

◆ It is a skill to keep useful records of the development of each child in the setting.

◆ It is a skill to be able to take the lead in supporting children.

Chapter 6

Being a professional

In this chapter we draw together the implications of the material in the preceding five chapters. We will look at what it means to be a professional, the type of training that childcare workers require, and the first steps that can be taken by individuals on their own account.

This chapter is divided into the following sections:

- ◆ What is a professional?
- ◆ The childcare professional's service users
- ◆ The UN Convention on the Rights of the Child
- ◆ Indicators of quality provision
- ◆ Starting from where we are now
- ◆ Early years policy in the UK
- ◆ A profession for the future

What makes an early years worker a professional?

What is a professional?

The word *professional* has several shades of meaning. The first is that a professional is someone who knows his or her job. Professional musicians, tennis players and footballers claim the title. We expect good standards from them. They practise their skills and maintain them. They learn from watching others in the same profession. They keep in good condition to give of their best. Maintaining and enhancing their standards is their individual responsibility, and they retire when they find they can no longer reach them.

Doctors, lawyers, clergymen, chartered accountants, engineers and others claim the title of being professionals. They have undergone long and arduous courses of study. They provide specialist help when it is needed – often at times of crisis in their clients' lives. They can be relied upon to have the specialist knowledge needed to help their clients. As a group, they monitor each other to ensure that standards of knowledge and ethics are maintained. Incompetent doctors, lawyers or clergymen can be prevented from practising their profession because their professional bodies can expel members who do not meet the group's standards.

There are other professions, such as teaching and social work, which also serve society in a specialist way. High standards are expected of them too, but these are not self-regulating groups. They are less accountable to their colleagues than to the law. Court action is taken against them if they fail to meet the standards that are set for them.

All professionals are expected to have a body of specialist knowledge and to have high standards. They have to be aware of innovations in their field and changes in practice, through reading journals and keeping abreast of research. They exchange views with colleagues by attending conferences, courses, training sessions and seminars in order to enhance their understanding of advances in practice. They study the changing needs of their client group. They learn how to communicate better with them. They are all expected to do their best for their clients.

However, professional groups differ in the status they are given. Those we need less frequently tend to have a higher status than those who are more familiar to us. Status is often reflected in the money these professionals earn – compare a footballer and a teacher – and the clients they serve.

REFLECT ON YOUR PRACTICE

It is a skill to look beyond your workplace.

How do you keep in touch with research? Does your setting take *Nursery World* or a similar publication? Are there any books for the staff? Do you attend conferences? Are relevant official documents such as *The National Standards for Day Care* (2001) available for all staff?

FOCUS

How do you think a childcare worker rates in relation to the criteria mentioned above?
Have you:

◆ an important client group

◆ responsibility

◆ specialist knowledge

◆ special skills?

Do you update your knowledge regularly in the light of new information and attitudes?

Do you guarantee high standards of service?

Are you monitored by other colleagues in your profession?

Does your work bring you prestige?

Are your earnings high?

The childcare professional's service users

Professionals know and work for their clients. Previous chapters in this book have stressed the needs of your service users, children from birth to three and their parents. From birth onwards, babies need to feel they are welcomed into the world and that their needs are important to the adults around them. They need to sense that they can grow at their own pace and that they can express all their feelings. They need to be affirmed for being who they are.

In the second half of their first year, babies also need to feel that exploring is encouraged, that they can be interested in anything and that they can do things as many times as they need to. They need to be allowed to initiate activities, and they need to realise that they are loved as much when they are active as when they are quiet.

Later, from about 18 months on, children need to be appreciated for thinking for themselves, for testing limits. They need to be accepted for striving for independence, as well as for asking for help, and for their feelings as well as for what they are able to create.

How these needs are met varies from society to society. Children adapt to whatever they feel is expected of them. Some cultures focus on the need to be a social person. This is so in Japan, where the 'good' child is one who meets the expectation to be a compliant yet constructive member of society. In the US, the focus is on being independent and autonomous. Generally, however, these decisions are unconscious; we simply understand what everyone around us expects of children.

JACK

What are the expectations of this child?

Jack is four. He has been overprotected by his mother, who would like him to stay as a baby. He's been encouraged to use a bottle and a dummy all of the time. Jack has no front teeth and watches videos for long periods while sitting in his buggy. This has resulted in Jack having little or no language and very poor physical skills.

REFLECT ON YOUR PRACTICE

It is a skill to become aware of unspoken assumptions in the group we belong to.

What are the unspoken assumptions in the UK about children? How often are they excluded from public places, and catered for in poor premises, with unimaginative copies of Disney characters in the windows and on the walls, where the space inside is cluttered and the space outside minimal? Why are children so often seen strapped into undersized outward-facing buggies which do not allow for any communication with the adult, with dummies or bottles in their mouths, or clutching soft toys as a badge of their cuteness?

It is the task of this chapter to tease out what childcare work is about. Are childcare workers substitute mothers, caring for an unnatural number of children, in a worse plight than Mother Hubbard ever was? Are they instructors, transmitting specific skills to children, always with an eye on the following stage? Are they experts in their field? Are they a child-parking service? Are they a support for parents? Or are they something else? What would you say *your* purpose was?

There have been some attempts at government level to define how childcare workers should appropriately meet the needs of children in their care.

Children in Spain

Spain has been debating for several years how to meet the needs of young children under three, and now sees provision for these children as an integral part of the education system. Marta Mata y Garriga explains that in talking about education up to the age of six, 'we have a conception of the school that "educates" rather than instructs' (2000 page 75).

In Spain the focus is on the child's self-respect, identity, and personal independence. Social relationships and human activity are important, as is learning about the environment; developing communication and representation are vital. Fostering emergent literacy and numeracy, as well as art, music and dance, is fundamental. The role of the childcare worker (called a teacher in Spain) is to be a companion, minimising the use of authority and control over the children, to guide the children and to encourage their initiative, games, experiments, reasoning and social co-operation. Parents play an important role in the management of the nursery and are encouraged to take part in school activities. Children are also welcome and visible in the wider community, especially in restaurants.

REFLECT ON YOUR PRACTICE

It is a skill to recognise your setting's intentions.

Using the above description of the priorities in Spain as an example, analyse your setting's intentions and curriculum for under-threes. Compare your setting's intentions with Spain's. Are there any significant gaps in the provision on either side?

Children in New Zealand

In 1996, the government of New Zealand produced a document on a curriculum appropriate for under-threes. The document, called *Te Whariki* (a Maori word for a woven mat) is an indication of the New Zealand government's desire to take into account the community aspects of Maori culture.

Te Whariki says that for the first 18 months of life, in order to thrive and learn, an **infant** must establish an intimate, responsive and trusting relationship with at least one other person. Infants are able to develop close attachments with several people, but not with many people. To develop a sense of their own identity and the strong sense of self-worth necessary for them to become confident in relationships and as learners, infants must experience physical and emotional security with at least one other person in each setting.

The document describes children in their first 18 months as showing the following characteristics.

◆ Physical growth and developmental changes are more rapid during infancy than during any other period of life.

◆ Infants are very vulnerable. They are totally dependent on adults to meet their needs and are seldom able to cope with discomfort or stress.

◆ Infants have urgent needs that demand immediate attention.

◆ Infants need the security of knowing that their emotional and physical needs will be met in predictable ways.

◆ Infants are subject to rapid fluctuations in health and well-being.

In the light of this they require much more than a babysitting arrangement. They need:

◆ one-to-one responsive interactions (those in which the care-givers follow the infant's leads)

◆ an adult who is consistently responsible for, and available to, each infant

◆ higher staffing ratios than for older children

◆ sociable, loving and physically responsive adults who can tune into an infant's needs

◆ individualised programmes that can adjust to the infant's own rhythms

◆ a predictable and calm environment that builds trust and anticipation

◆ partnership between parents and the other adults involved in caring for the infant.

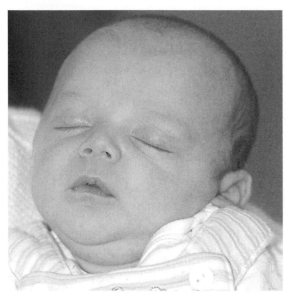

Infants are vulnerable, and totally dependent on adults

Turning to children from around the end of their first 18 months to the age of three, referred to in the document as **toddlers**, the document states that the behaviour and development of toddlers tend to vary, and swing back and forth much more often than is the case for any other age group.

These children, it is stated, are struggling to evolve a sense of self and to achieve independence from the adults to whom they are emotionally attached, while at the same time needing continuing emotional support. Their desire for independence, knowledge and increasing control over everyday life is often in conflict with their ongoing dependence on care-givers to make things happen.

Toddlers are rapidly acquiring physical, social, reasoning and language skills but these need a lot of practice. Toddlers tend both to resist and to find comfort in rituals and routines. Swings such as these can cause a wide variety of conflicting feelings, ideas and actions which challenge the resourcefulness and knowledge of parents and adults who work with toddlers.

Children from 18 months to 3 years are described by the New Zealand document as:

◆ energetic and always on the move

◆ gaining control of their world by checking out limits, causes and effects

◆ often ahead of their language and physical abilities to achieve what they want

- active and curious, determined to become competent and to make sense of happenings, objects and ideas.

It goes on to say that:

- their feelings are intense and unpredictable
- they thrive on opportunities and being encouraged into exploration and creativity
- they are impulsive and lack self-control
- they seek social interaction and learn by imitating others
- they learn with their whole body and learn by doing rather than being told.

Consequently they need a programme that is neither the specialised arrangements made for infants nor the independence and 'busyness' expected in programmes for those over three.

It is recommended that all children under three need:

- a secure environment and a programme that provides both challenges and predictable happenings
- opportunities for independent exploration and movement
- a flexible approach that can accommodate their spontaneity and whims at a pace which allows them to try to do things for themselves
- adults who encourage the toddlers' cognitive skills and language development
- responsive and predictable adults who both understand and accept the toddler's developmental swings.

The New Zealand curriculum is described in terms of being based on the principles of ensuring:

- empowerment
- the holistic development of the child
- respect for and involvement of the family plus the community
- constructive relationships.

There are also five interwoven strands. These are:

- **Well-being** – in terms of promoting health, emotional well-being and safety
- **Belonging** – there are links with the family and the wider world, children know they have a place in the community of the nursery, they feel comfortable with its routines and they know the bounds of acceptable behaviour
- **Contribution** – the children are affirmed as individuals and they are encouraged to learn with and alongside others
- **Communication** – children develop non-verbal and verbal skills, experience the stories and symbols of their own and other cultures, and are encouraged to be creative
- **Exploration** – play is valued, as are physical skills, thinking skills and observation skills.

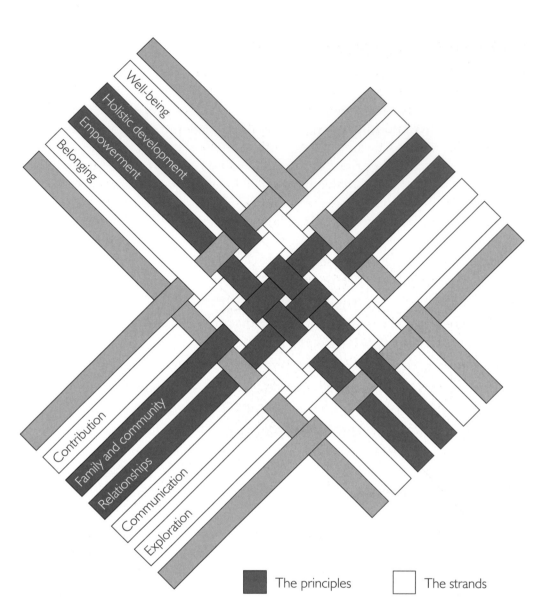

Well-being

Holistic development

Empowerment

Belonging

Contribution

Family and community

Relationships

Communication

Exploration

■ The principles   □ The strands

The Te Whariki *mat*

REFLECT ON YOUR PRACTICE

It is a skill to evaluate an expression of intention.

Is there any aspect of this curriculum that you would like to incorporate into your own setting? Are there any aspects that you already incorporate in your setting's practice? How do the strands relate to the *Birth to Three Matters* document?

What are the main differences between New Zealand's and Spain's stated intentions in their curricula?

Children in Italy: Reggio Emilia

Reggio Emilia is a prosperous town in the north of Italy, near Bologna. The development of provision in this local authority was inspired by the work of Loris Malaguzzi, who was a psychologist by training. Nurseries were set up after the Second World War, and from the beginning the parents were very much involved in their management. Children remain with the same staff members until they are three, then as a group they meet another staff team who stay with them until they go to primary school at six. Malaguzzi wrote: 'In our experience, for exchanges among children to become more co-operative, the ages and developmental levels of the children in the group should not be too different.'

Children benefit when their parents are closely involved in nursery management

About 40 per cent of children under three attend the *asilo nido* (which translates as 'the nest'), because the law recognises the right of any mother, working or not, to use state-supported day nurseries for children under 3 years of age.

The staff focus on the personal and social development of the child. There is a special room for resting away from the group and a child who is tired can go and lie down there. Often the beds in this room are at floor level, in the form of a very large basket with a low opening, rather like a dog basket. The children know their own bed and can access it.

The children are seen as a group who facilitate each other's learning. They act on each other and build knowledge together. The childcare worker leads the learning of a group of children by using individuals' ideas to frame group action. The ideas for the projects arise from the children (for example, one group of 3- to 6-year-olds had the idea of making a playground for the birds). The worker assists even the youngest children to listen to others' ideas, to take account of and respond to the things that are interesting them, for example, light and shadows, and to communicate successfully in all sorts of ways.

There are two childcare workers for each group. As in Spain, the role of the staff member in relation to the child is to be a companion and a facilitator. There is no hierarchy among the staff members; they work as a collective. The staff members are supported by a *pedagogista*, who looks after a group of nurseries. The *pedagogista*'s role is continuous in-service on-site training, based on the staff's close documentation of each child's development, with a visit to each nursery once each week.

The careful documentation of each child's work provides the children with a concrete and visible reminder of what they have achieved. It serves as a springboard for their next steps in learning. In Reggio, documentation is not about recording finished products. It is about tracking the development of ideas as they gradually emerge. It is constantly revisited and discussed and becomes the basis for continuing professional development for the staff. For the children it is a way of revisiting their experiences, stimulating conversation and building relationships.

The documentation also provides the public with detailed information about what is happening in their schools and it is a means of eliciting their reactions and support.

All the nurseries for children from three to six (and many of the first-stage ones too) have an artist (*atelerista*) working in them full-time. This person has the responsibility of working alongside the staff to develop the children's powers of communication through representing meaning in a wide range of media. Again, each child's development is carefully observed (rather than being directed), and the staff's co-operative maintenance and examination of the documentation (which includes noting children's comments while they are working) is regarded as crucial.

Parents play a large part in the running of each nursery and often come in and eat with the children at lunch time. They are asked to volunteer to contribute to the upkeep of the buildings and grounds, to repair and paint furniture and to make toys and equipment.

FOCUS

Make a list of the differences between the intentions of your setting and the intentions in Reggio Emilia.

REFLECT ON YOUR PRACTICE

It is a skill to be able to pinpoint the ideas behind one's practice.

Using the notes you have made as you read about the approaches in Spain, Italy and New Zealand, try to evaluate the approach you have in your setting. What is seen as the focus of *your* curriculum? What is seen to be the intention of the staff in your setting? Where do parents fit in, and what is the role of the community?

The UN Convention on the Rights of the Child

Professionals know and respect their service users' rights. They will act as advocates to ensure that rights are recognised. The rights of childcare workers' service users have been defined by the United Nations Convention on the Rights of the Child, 1989.

> **KEY TERM:** UN Convention on the Rights of the Child (1989)
>
> *Global standards for the recognition of children as citizens, expressed in 54 articles. Every country except the United States and Somalia has ratified the convention and has undertaken to change national law in accordance with it and to inform adults and children alike about the Convention. Governments have also agreed to report to the UN every 5 years about the progress they have made.*

The rights in the list vary – some are legal requirements, while others may only be goals to be aimed at, 'to the maximum extent of [each nation's] available resources'. Others may be conditional, affected by 'the evolving capacities of the child'. All rights claimed must balance with the rights of others.

The rights of one must balance with the rights of another

The UN Convention on the Rights of the Child considered three kind of rights: provision, protection and participation.

Provision

These rights include the right to:

♦ standards of care 'established by competent authorities particularly in areas of safety, health, and the number and suitability of their staff as well as competent supervision'

♦ a regular review of whether these standards are being met

♦ healthcare to 'the highest attainable standard'

♦ financial support and a good standard of living in regard to housing, nutrition and clothing.

The child has a right to education that is 'compulsory and free for all'. Education includes 'the preparation of the child for responsible life in a free society, in the spirit of understanding, peace, tolerance, equality of sexes, and friendship among all peoples'. The child has a right to rest and leisure, to engage in play, and 'to participate freely in cultural life and the arts'. Governments must undertake 'to make the principles of the Convention widely known, by appropriate and active means, to adults and children alike'.

REFLECT ON YOUR PRACTICE

It is a skill to use external criteria to assess your own experience.

Think of the locality you work in. Are these rights being met there? What are the standards of housing, nutrition and clothing? Do the parents in your area receive financial support to meet all their children's needs? What is the provision for play in your area?

Think of your workplace. Do the experiences you provide for the children meet all of the elements described for education? Is there too much emphasis on health and safety at the expense of the right to play? What access is there to cultural life and the arts? How can a children's centre contribute to this aim?

How can young children's responses to the provision that is made for them be measured? How much do adults and children know of these and the following groups of recommendations? How can your setting help?

Protection

A child has the right to protection against 'unlawful attacks on his or her honour and reputation', and against 'all forms of physical or mental violence, injury or abuse, neglect or negligent treatment, maltreatment or exploitation'. The UK's record on physical punishment was especially criticised by the UN Convention on the Rights of the Child.

Children's ethnic, religious, cultural and linguistic background shall be respected. This applies not only to children who are adopted or fostered but to children who are temporarily deprived of their family environment when they attend day care. Governments are required to 'encourage the mass media to disseminate information and material of social and cultural benefit to the child and in accordance with the spirit of the Convention'.

Participation

The child has a right to a name, nationality and identity. States should 'ensure recognition of the principles that both parents have common responsibilities for the upbringing and development of the child'.

Governments should ensure to the maximum extent possible the survival and development of the child. The child has a right to freedom of expression, 'including freedom to seek, receive and impart information of all kinds… through any medium of the child's choice'. The child should have freedom of information – to know what is happening, to be talked to, as well as freedom of thought, conscience, religion and association and peaceful assembly.

'A mentally or physically disabled child should enjoy a full and decent life in conditions that ensure dignity, promote self-reliance and facilitate the child's active participation in the community.'

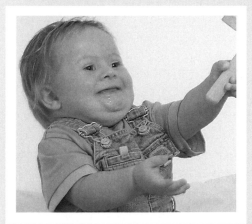

Indicators of quality provision

Professionals promise quality. Quality cannot ever be measured merely mechanically, but has to be assessed in different ways.

The first way relates to the use of the resources. It is easy to measure the space and list the resources within it. Making judgements on the quality of adult–child relationships and the amount of flexibility in the arrangements is harder.

Measuring cost-effectiveness is a double-edged sword: some results, for example community building and effecting social change or educational gains, may take years to become evident.

Judgements of quality can be made by a range of people who stand to gain from the provision. These include the following.

◆ The parents – does the programme fit their needs to work, to build a career, for respite?

◆ The siblings – do they get more quality time?

◆ The childcare worker – what are the working conditions like? Is there scope for career development?

◆ The producers of materials and the experts – do they find scope for their talents?

◆ The politicians – do they gain status or more votes for supporting the programme?

Views on quality will be held by all the people involved in the service. These include the following.

◆ The programme managers – what is their budget?

◆ The childcare workers – where do they get their perspectives on quality?

◆ The parents – what do they know and feel about the direction and intentions of the programme?

◆ The community leaders – are they committed and interested?

◆ The children – are they contented, stimulated or bored?

FOCUS

Try to answer the questions above in relation to your own setting.

Starting from where we are now

Professionals are aware of what is happening elsewhere. The Daycare Trust collated the following information in 2005 to compare the current provision in the UK with that in other places.

Denmark

◆ Public spending on early education and care is approximately 2 per cent of gross domestic product (GDP).

◆ Parents pay no more than 33 per cent of the cost of childcare, with reductions for more than one child and for children with special educational needs.

◆ Provision is available for all children over 8 months old.

◆ There are no waiting lists.

◆ There is no unmet demand.

◆ Staff are highly qualified and train to graduate level for 3½ years.

Sweden

◆ Public spending on early education and care is approximately 2 per cent of GDP.

◆ Parents pay on average 11 per cent of the cost of childcare.

◆ Fees are capped and parents spend a maximum of £93 per month for the first child, with decreased fees for subsequent children. There is no charge for childcare for the fourth child.

◆ There are highly qualified early years workers with strong teaching backgrounds.

◆ Access to childcare is considered to be a right.

Finland

◆ Public spending on early education and care is approximately 1.3 per cent of GDP.

◆ Parents pay approximately 15 per cent of childcare costs.

◆ Generous parental leave (about 11 months) and homecare allowance are given to parents until the youngest child is three.

◆ Childcare is considered a universal right, has qualified staff, and is based on partnership between local authorities, providers and parents.

Flanders in Belgium

◆ Public spending on early education and care is approximately 1 per cent of GDP.

◆ Early years workers are graduates and childcare workers undergo specialised training for 3 years post-16.

◆ Parents pay between £1 and £12 per day for childcare.

◆ There is a strong emphasis on diversity in the workforce, including more men.

New Zealand

◆ There is a 10-year vision and strategy for improving early education and childcare services, which has been in place since 2002.

◆ The vision is of a fully qualified workforce, affordable and universal access to early education and care, and the engagement of parents in services.

◆ There are financial incentives to providers to improve quality, for example by employing more highly qualified staff.

◆ The aim is for 100 per cent of early years workers to be graduates by 2012.

The UK

◆ Public spending on early education, childcare and parental leave is approximately 0.54 per cent of GDP.

◆ Parents pay 75 per cent of the costs of childcare. In 2005 the typical cost of a nursery place for a child under two was £141 per week – or £250 in London. Rates rise anually.

◆ There is one registered childcare place for every four children under 8 years old, and an acute shortage of places for children under two.

◆ The average gross pay of a childcare worker is £7,800 per year, compared to £22,662 for nursery and primary teachers. These figures reflect a range of qualifications and consequently status.

◆ The government's 10-year Strategy for Childcare, published December 2004, is aiming for childcare services that are the 'best in the world' within 10 years.

◆ The UK has anti-racism legislation.

REFLECT ON YOUR PRACTICE

It is a skill to examine alternatives and establish priorities.

If you could propose a policy for birth to threes for implementation in the UK, what would it be? Give two reasons for your choice.

Early years policy in the UK

Governments in the UK have tended to ignore children under school age. The Plowden Report (1967) recommended the establishment of educational priority areas and within them an expansion of nursery provision. A generation later, the Children Act (1989) provided guidelines for policy-makers, local authorities and practitioners to develop effective liaison, to ensure quality control, to recognise the importance of the curriculum experienced by the children and the training, status, conditions of service and recruitment of suitable staff.

A report prepared by a committee chaired by Lady Plowden for the government. The report recommended the setting up of educational priority areas and the expansion of nursery provision.

In 1990 the Rumbold Committee reported on the quality of the educational experience offered to 3- and 4-year olds. It introduced the notion of the curriculum being described in terms of six areas of experience and called for settings to have policies on equal opportunities, parental partnership, liaison with other institutions, quality control and staff development. It repeated the demand for the co-ordination of services made in the Children Act of the previous year.

In 1997 a Labour government came to power stating that one of its aims was the eradication of child poverty within 20 years. In 1998 it launched the National Childcare Strategy, providing free half-time nursery education for all 3- and 4-year-olds, creating 500 SureStart programmes aiming to reach one-third of the young children living in poverty, offering financial support for childcare costs and transferring childcare regulation and inspection to the Office for Standards in Education (OFSTED).

KEY TERM: OFSTED

The Office for Standards in Education, the schools inspectorate. Under the National Childcare Strategy it has also taken over responsibility for monitoring and inspecting children's services.

OFSTED produced the National Standards for Daycare in 2001, and they represent a baseline of quality below which no provider may fall.

There are 14 standards to achieve. Four of these focus on the child; the others concentrate on management requirements. The guideline was published in 2001 and it said that all supervisors must hold a level 3 or higher qualification and 50 per cent of staff must hold a level 2. However, the Children Act had stated that at least 50 per cent of staff should be qualified and most people at the time had assumed it meant that half of the staff should be qualified at level 3.

Birth to Three Matters

A new programme of children's centres was announced in 2002. That year also saw the publication of *Birth to Three Matters*, which broke new ground. For the first time ever, this document focused on the needs of birth to threes, a group that had previously not been included in guidance documents for education and care. Discussing learning, the document avoided prescribing a set curriculum or dissecting the child according to the conventional areas of physical, cognitive and emotional development. Instead, three clear principles were defined:

◆ learning is a shared process and children learn most effectively when, with the support of a knowledgeable and trusted adult, they are actively involved and interested

◆ children learn when they are given appropriate responsibility, allowed to make errors, decisions and choices, and respected as autonomous and competent learners

◆ children learn by doing rather than being told.

These principles have important implications for the adult's role. Adults need to respect the child's competence and remain flexible, responding to the child's rhythms and initiatives. The document stressed that relationships with other people are of crucial importance and that relationships with a key person at home and in the setting are essential for young children's well-being. Further information on the *Birth to Three Matters* framework can be found on the SureStart website at www.surestart.gov.uk.

Every Child Matters

In the following year, *Every Child Matters* was published in response to the death of the abused child Victoria Climbie in 2002. Her plight had been ignored by 12 different professionals. This document has particular relevance to children from birth to three, with its emphasis on better prevention, earlier intervention and stronger support for parenting and families.

It starts by naming five desired outcomes for young people:

◆ being healthy

◆ staying safe – being protected from harm and neglect

◆ enjoying life and achieving skills for adulthood

◆ making a positive contribution to the community and society

◆ not being prevented by economic disadvantage from achieving their full potential.

It proposes action in four main areas:

◆ supporting parents and carers

◆ early intervention and effective protection

◆ accountability and integration – locally, regionally and nationally

◆ workforce reform through a common core of training for all who work with children and families, and common occupational standards and pay.

Training

Apart from the money spent on childcare services, there appear to be two linked issues for the government in the UK. One of the issues that must be addressed is training. In Denmark, staff are skilled professionals in early education and care who are concerned with helping the child to live a good life as part of the community. Their training involves studying the characteristics and needs of young children and preparing for work in the community. It includes aspects of social work and theoretical and practical preparation for working with other adults. Besides being trained to work with and support the child's parents, they are prepared for liaising with other professionals, for example with medical staff and educational psychologists who are involved with children with disabilities, and for work in case conferences and meetings concerned with child protection.

In contrast, initial training for work with young children in the UK is in a state of transition. There are few graduates entering the profession. Few trained teachers are trained specifically for early years work, and there are fewer still whose training includes work with the under-threes. There is a post-graduate Certificate in Montessori Education, and there are foundation degrees, including one from the Steiner Waldorf Foundation. University courses in childhood studies, while giving a perspective on childhood, include very little, if any, practical work.

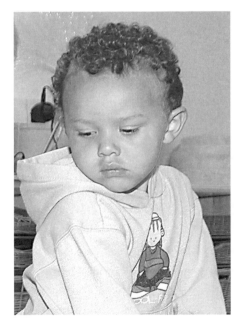

Training for work with young children is mostly assessed in the workplace

Most training is through National Vocational Qualifications (NVQs), which were introduced in 1986. They are work-related, competence-based qualifications. They reflect the skills needed to do a job effectively, and assessment takes place in the workplace. There is very little time for the underpinning knowledge base against which practice can be interpreted.

NVQs are offered at five levels. Competence in routine and predictable work activities is expected at level 1. Level 6 expects the ability to work in a wide and often unpredictable variety of contexts with substantial personal autonomy, with responsibility for the allocation of resources and for the work of others. The SureStart Childcare Approval Scheme document shows seven courses at level 4 that are relevant to under-threes. They come under the banners of CACHE, the Montessori College and BTEC. There are 35 level 3 courses, with titles as diverse as degree, diploma and certificate, offered by nine bodies. NVQ level 3 is required for a post as nursery supervisor, pre-school leader, crèche leader, playgroup leader, toy library leader, nursery nurse, nanny or childminder. Level 3 focuses on planning for children's development. In the National Qualifications Framework, the expectation is of a wide and varied range of work activities, considerable responsibility and often the ability to offer guidance to colleagues.

At NVQ level 2 there are 41 courses offered by providers. NVQ level 2 is accepted for a post as nursery assistant, pre-school assistant, crèche assistant, parent/toddler group assistant, toy library worker, Homestart worker, mother's help, or babysitter/au pair. Level 2 is intended to support children's development. In the new framework, the preparation will be for a significant range of activities and some individual responsibility. Collaboration with others is expected.

NVQ courses are linked to workplace experience, which is an attractive idea, but in practice a person's training may be patchy, depending on the needs and priorities of the particular workplace and the possible difficulty of getting staff cover. NVQs are accessible because they are offered in many places, but problems have been found in relation to standardisation. In 2004 the Joint Awarding Body, the QCA, reported:

> The project has found that typically internal verifiers focus on the first strand [sampling assessments] and little time is given to the other two [monitoring assessment practice and standardising assessment judgements]. In some instances the full scope of the internal verifier's role is poorly understood and centres have failed to allow sufficient time and resources to facilitate anything other than portfolio sampling.

Most childcare workers have a level 2 or level 3 qualification. One problem is that the sharp demarcation between the levels may produce a hierarchy, which could act as a barrier to personal development and growth. The differentiation between the levels seems to parallel the classroom situation of the teacher and the nursery nurse, where often very competent nursery nurses' skills are under-used.

Peter Moss (2000) refers to the work of Carr and May (1993), who question the very idea of concentrating on competencies. They criticise the separation between units and levels, and see development not as merely adding extra pieces of information in measured steps. They pinpoint the difference between merely transmitting knowledge and constructing knowledge in a collaborative way. They see development coming through people challenging their previous assumptions, and considering new ideas and skills. It is harder to measure these subtle, ongoing changes that arise from recognising and considering problems and dilemmas.

The proposed level 3 in Children's Care, Learning and Development is a nine-unit qualification comprising five core units and four option units. One of the mandatory units, 'Reflect on and develop practice', would seem to be a step in the direction of encouraging workers to become **reflective practitioners**, as Carr and May were advocating.

KEY TERM: Reflective practitioner

A person who keeps reappraising his or her practice and keeps on trying to find ways to improve it.

A further issue is that for some time there will be few people with the full range of experience (for example, in collaborating with other professionals or working closely with the community) who can provide the type of training that, as we saw in Chapter 5, is now needed. That is why it is important for colleagues to share their professional experience with others in their workplace or nearby.

Other in-service training is patchy. A recent survey of the courses on offer in one area showed that of 240 courses on offer, only 43 had links with extending knowledge of working with young children. Most of the courses were for one day only. A high proportion were on topics such as food hygiene, first aid, safeguarding the disabled, moving and handling babies and children aged five and under, behaviour management, play work, and school-related topics. As Cathy Nutbrown commented, 'It is not enough to simply change the label and call all training "professional development". The content must be examined and a clear decision made about what is offered to early years educators' (1998 page 34).

Manning-Morton and Thorpe looked at what is required for being a key worker, and found it was not an easy role to fill appropriately, because of time constraints and the tendency to provide 'factory line' care. They found children were often treated as a group rather than as individuals, and that the fostering of attachment with a particular staff member was not regarded as important. Staff were often regarded merely as cogs in wheels and consequently morale could be low. So they set up an accredited course of training to help practitioners to address the emotional issues of working with very young children and collaborating with their parents.

FIND OUT MORE

Manning-Morton, J and Thorpe, M (2003) *Key Times for Play: The First Three Years*, Open University Press

Elfer, P, Goldschmeid, E and Selleck, D (2002) *Key Persons in Nurseries; Building Relationships for Quality Provision*, NEYN

Status

A second problem is the perceived status of the work, even sometimes among childcare workers themselves. Helen Penn interviewed the childcare students in training in two inner London colleges of further education in 1996–97. She found that the students she spoke to had limited horizons. They had chosen the work because they felt that they brought intrinsic talents (patience, kindness, understanding, consistency, reliability) to the job of childcare, and that this talent was at least as important as, if not more important than, any knowledge they acquired in the course of training.

Responding to the government's Children's Workforce Strategy, the Pre-school Learning Alliance said that the government must address pay and conditions in the early years sector as a matter of urgency. Low pay equates with low status. Until there is a more coherent pay structure linked to qualifications, experience and responsibility, the work will be unattractive.

Penn concluded at the end of her report:

> Without further interventions in social policy, conceptions of work in this sector will remain narrow and gendered, women carers' pay and conditions of work and career mobility will continue to be limited, and their lack of voice will be conspicuous… If professionalism is a goal for those working with young children… common sense would suggest that the more lively and enquiring the workforce, the better the support they receive, and the more training they have, the better will be the outcomes for the children for whom they care (2000 page 129).

FIND OUT MORE

Penn, H 'Is working with children a good job?' in Penn, H (ed) (2000) *Early Childhood Services*, Open University Press

A *profession for the future*

Crèche workers don't just 'look after' children

Professionals extend their expertise in response to new initiatives. Changes in several jobs are happening because of the shift in perspectives brought about by the SureStart initiatives. Overleaf are descriptions of some of the jobs that childcare workers involved in a SureStart area and a children's centre now do.

CASE STUDY:
CRÈCHE WORKER

The crèche worker in one area's SureStart team writes:

When I left school I did an NVQ level 3 in Childcare. I have worked in a lot of private day nurseries. At my last nursery I was in charge of the toddler room – this was the age group I liked the best. I was beginning to get bored with my job and some of my friends had got jobs with the local SureStart programmes. Their jobs sounded more interesting than working in a nursery every day. The last time SureStart advertised I was lucky enough to get a job and I am now working as a crèche worker for the local programme.

I find the work very different from the private day nursery. We just looked after the children and we didn't have to think about the families at all. In SureStart we are dealing with the whole family and trying to give them all opportunities. In the crèche we look after children while their parents are on training courses. Lots of parents left school without any qualifications. Some of them are doing starter courses and some are working towards maths, English and IT qualifications. In the short time that I have been working for SureStart I can see that some of the parents are really enjoying their courses and they are hoping that they will eventually get jobs.

The SureStart team also organises a lot of groups where the parents and children can do things together. We have 'Stay and Play' groups and lots of language development groups. I work with some of the groups and I have found I can use my training and knowledge in different ways from working in a day nursery.

My relationship with parents has changed and I feel I am much more involved with the whole family, and I also understand their problems more than I used to. Sometimes when I worked in the day nursery I got very cross if the parents turned up late or didn't reply to one of our letters. I now think I have a better understanding of the pressures that our families face.

I really enjoy my job. I think it has broadened my horizons. I think that all childcare workers should have the opportunity to work in different ways and to see different settings such as SureStart. I hope when we change to a children's centre I will be able to have the same challenges in my job.

CASE STUDY:
CHILDCARE DEVELOPMENT WORKER

A childcare development worker writes:

I began nursing in 1984 after gaining my NNEB. I chose to apply for jobs within the education sector as I felt that was where my skills would be most useful, and I enjoyed working with this range of children.

I left nursery nursing in 1998 as I felt it was time to move on. I retrained as a childcare tutor but found this was not the direction I wanted to take. I then applied for a post with SureStart and have never looked back. I am a childcare development worker and thoroughly enjoy working with the families in the SureStart area, setting up various activities such as Rhyme Time, Babbling Babies and Chatterbox. It is such a pleasure to see the children progressing from baby to toddler and then 'big boy or girl'. This work is extremely rewarding and I have enjoyed working in the SureStart setting.

CASE STUDY:

OUTREACH WORKER

The outreach workers attached to SureStart programmes have a varied role. Home visiting is a key role for this team, and every family with a child reaching the age of 5–7 months is visited by an outreach worker. The family can then be given the latest information on the groups, training and activities run by the SureStart programme or the children's centre in the area, and they are given the opportunity to discuss their views and to comment on the services they receive.

Each outreach worker has a designated locality and school. They do a lot of networking with the professionals connected to that area. These include health visitors, social workers and learning mentors. They also work closely with organisations and charities in the community, and liaise with housing associations.

Their job description is:

- to ensure that all parents in the area know what is happening in the children's centre, to network with parents and other agencies to ensure that parents, carers, grandparents and children are able to access all the services that are on offer easily

- to set up a parents' forum in the children's centre area

- to build relationships with parents to ensure that all parents are aware of the full range of services and how to access them

- to direct families to appropriate services, such as health, education or training

- to ensure all parents receive home support if necessary

- to support the delivery of core services

- to listen to parents' and children's views and concerns and to ensure that the team are aware of the issues involved, if and when appropriate

- to monitor the effectiveness of the service by listening carefully to how parents experience the delivery of the services on offer

- to be an advocate for parents and children in the local area.

REFLECT ON YOUR PRACTICE

It is a skill to assess professionalism.

Look back to the beginning of this chapter and list activities that have been described in this section which can be rated as involving a professional stance.

Do any of the jobs that have been described remind you of the approaches in other countries that you have read about in this chapter? Do any of the roles described here differ from those in other countries? Can you think of an explanation for this?

Professional qualities

The notable features that emerge from these accounts are as follows:

- the personal qualities, enthusiasm, commitment and flexibility of the people who have told us about their jobs
- the concern for the child in the family
- the concern for empowerment of the parents
- the concern for the child and family in the community
- the frequent references to teamworking
- the lack of references to rigid structures
- the sense of personal responsibility.

A new initiative such as SureStart initially attracts people with vision. Maintaining the momentum begun by these innovators is obviously going to put heavy demands on both trainers and the supervisors of services. Normally trainers are those who have personal experience of the area they teach. What will the trainers teach? The fact that there is as yet no accepted training or agreed standard of achievement for this profession works against the professional ideal of continuous updating and peer review. How do practitioners become aware of their personal strengths and weaknesses and their contribution (or the reverse) to the profession? Where is the forum for exchanging views with colleagues? In a new area of working such as this, who provides quality assurance for the training? Who monitors or evaluates the outcomes of the provision? By which standards, and at which stages will this be done? Which are the areas on which research will be focused?

Before a group of people can make a joint claim to be professionals, there needs to be an agreed body of knowledge, which does not remain fixed and unchanging but which reflects the shared experience they have jointly considered as equals. Large-scale research projects cost money, but every member of the profession can contribute to the profession by being a **reflective practitioner**. That means being a person who takes time to reflect on aspects of what they do. Many of the tasks in this book, especially those that begin with the words **It is a skill to...**, are designed to encourage you in this professional practice.

Another strategy is to undertake a small piece of **action research**. Action research means focusing on one small area of your normal activity. You may decide to make one small change that you think might be helpful. You decide how you'll do this task differently. You say for how long – a week, a month, a term – and then at the end of the specified time, you check to see whether you still think it's a good idea. Has anything improved?

As a member of a profession you should share your findings with your colleagues. This approach is not dramatic, but it keeps you thinking and developing, which is another characteristic of being a professional. You should aim to do one piece of action research as you do your normal job each year. It is important that you share your findings with your colleagues, and listen to their experience too. In every other professional area, all lasting changes are built on the accumulated experience of workers in the field.

As a profession we need to investigate the boundaries of how and where we work.

◆ Is it possible to keep our vision both global *and* relevant to our particular context? This requires all the members of the childcare profession to be aware of the international perspective of the UN document and of practice abroad. It is impossible to transplant foreign structures unchanged into the UK. But aspects of best practice can be adopted, for example from Reggio Emilia the use of careful documentation, including snatches of conversation, photographs and examples of work. The idea of staff working as a collective is also an appealing one.

◆ How can we keep in mind both the past *and* the future? The innovators of the past have insights that are still valuable (for example, Margaret McMillan's view of the importance of improved health arising from children being able to be active outside, and her work with parents), but the future holds new challenges about building communities and sharing cultures.

◆ Can we work both for children *and* the community? Both children and the community require our help, and ultimately, as Bronfenbrenner pointed out, children can only be helped by improving the communities in which they live. This requires us to act as citizens. But it also provides us with the challenge not to neglect the children's interests while we work in the community.

◆ Can we combine the idea of the child being a participant in society *and* a person needing nurture? Our current thinking is more about protecting children from danger than about children being helped to take some responsibility for themselves and being responsible citizens. More research would seem to be needed into how to help the child to become socialised. To change adult perceptions – from seeing children as helpless to seeing them as resourceful beings worthy of respect and able to take on appropriate responsibilities – is an enormous challenge involving influencing the media.

◆ How can we help the child to be both socialised *and* an individual? This is related to our definitions of being socialised and of self-actualisation. In fact, self-actualisation only comes about through being open to others. The Reggio Emilia approach has a lot to offer us, but it demands a radical rethink of our practice.

◆ How can we be both proactive *and* reactive? Many of the challenges we face require urgent action (as in some of the case studies you have read), but it is easy to lose sight of the bigger picture if we only react to immediate circumstances and lose the long-term view.

We have to be members of a team to manage to do anything. It requires great skill to hold one's own in a team and ensure self-actualisation for everyone. Only if we take care of each other as professionals and share our skills and understandings will we be able to be effective as a group. The case for appropriate continuing professional development, as compared to the half-day 'trainings' now in vogue, is overwhelming. Again it is up to you, the professional, to articulate your needs and to take steps to have them met.

Seeking for quality is a personal and professional life-long quest. It will emerge as the result of personal reflection and collaborative learning.

Children are individuals and *social beings*

Conclusion

In this chapter we have considered various approaches to the task we share with educators the world over. Although the cultures we work in may differ, the young human beings we work with have much in common with each other. There is much to be learned from examining other points of view and other practices.

The following skills have been highlighted:

◆ It is a skill to look beyond your workplace.

◆ It is a skill to become aware of unspoken assumptions in the group we belong to.

◆ It is a skill to recognise your setting's intentions.

◆ It is a skill to evaluate an expression of intention.

◆ It is a skill to be able to pinpoint the ideas behind one's practice.

◆ It is a skill to use external criteria to assess your own experience.

◆ It is a skill to examine alternatives and establish priorities.

◆ It is a skill to assess professionalism.

Running record

Name	Sam	Date of birth	10.06.02
SCHEMA		On top of	
Date	Event and context		Signed
28 April 04	In the nursery today I saw Sam really concentrating on putting the lids on boxes. Does he do anything like this at home?		Katy
1 May 04	*He seems fascinated with lids. 'Lid-on' has been one of his favourite words for a while now.*		*Sally*
17 May 04	*At his Grandmother's birthday today he carefully replaced the wire cages from the top of champagne bottles back on the empty bottles.*		*Sally*
9 Sept 04	Today I saw Sam with a hat on. He then put a row of toys along the top of the window sill, and looked delighted with what he'd done.		Katy
4 Nov 04	*He's still into hats, putting them on all his toys. He puts mugs onto coasters.*		*Sally*
17 Jan 05	Sam climbed to the top of the climbing frame, balanced there and said 'I'm on top.' He did this several times.		Katy
20 Jan 05	*At home he makes a pile of cushions and does the same thing. At the weekend we visited what they call The Pudding Basin and Sam climbed to the top of it.*		*Sally*
22 June 05	Today Sam made a model. He put an upturned yoghurt pot onto some cardboard, then put a cylinder on top of it and told me it was a cake, with a candle on top.		Katy
19 July 05	I've sent home the painting Sam did today – a face. He said 'And that's the hair on top.'		Katy

Schema	Available in room	Books and rhymes	To obtain	Local visits
Rotation				
Enveloping				
Horizontal trajectory				
Vertical trajectory				
Transporting				
Connecting				
Going through a boundary				
Enclosures				
Transforming				
Grids				

Transcribed and analysed dialogue

The two boys are getting ready for bed. Sam is just four, Robbie is two and a half.

Speaker	Utterance	Description
Sam	Watch Robbie jump. Robbie jump for Mammy	Directing
Robbie (jumping)	Ooh, hit my head	Reporting
Sam	He's doing this (jumping)	Reporting
	Like a monkey Robbs	Comparing – logical reasoning
Robbie	Ooo Ooo Ooo Me bunkey	Reporting and imagining – immature grammar (use of *me* instead of *I* and no auxiliary verb) and articulation
Mother	No, no, not on the bed	
Sam	Why?	Asking for a reason – logical reasoning
Mother	Well why?	
Sam	I don't know	Self-maintaining
Mother	Because you might fall on the floor, and then what might happen?	
Robbie	On floor	Predicting; two-word utterance – location
Sam	I never fall on the floor, do I Robbs?	Self-maintaining; tag question
Robbie	Fall on floor Sam, Sam cry mammy, Sam cry, Sam you cry, Sam floor Mammy, Sam floor	Reporting – immature grammar, but uses *you*
Sam	Can I brush my hair?	Self-maintaining
	Can I borrow one of your brushes?	Directing

(Sam rushes out of the room to get the brush)

Robbie	Me brush, me brush Mammy	Self-maintaining; two-word utterance
Sam	I'm going to watch Scooby Doo now	Predicting
	Come on Robbie	Directing

(Sam runs downstairs)

| Robbie | Me DooDoo well Mammy, Me DooDoo well | Self-maintaining; immature grammar; shortened forms; reduplication; articulation |

Continuing Professional Development

A summary of the *It is a skill to…* sections mentioned in the text. The skills have been arranged under the headings of **Attitude-related, Self-knowledge**, **Professional Competences** and **Specific knowledge and skills**. These groupings are to help you to decide where you want to begin your individual journey in continuing professional development.

Attitude-related skills include:

◆ respecting children by planning opportunities for them to take appropriate responsibility for themselves

◆ respecting parents as the child's first educators

◆ recognising people's strengths

◆ being aware of the prevalence of gender stereotyping

◆ being aware of the unspoken presumptions of the group you belong to.

Self-knowledge skills include:

◆ one's own expectations of and responses to children

◆ one's own habitual ways of responding

◆ managing one's own emotions

◆ developing one's vocabulary and communication skills.

Professional Competences include the ability to:

◆ help children to control their responses and to talk about their emotions

◆ help children to develop trust in the carers at the center

◆ provide sensory experiences for babies

◆ provide treasure baskets and heuristic play

◆ support toddlers' sense of mastery

◆ support schemas

◆ share knowledge of schemas with parents

◆ use the environment indoors and out and help children to develop their understanding of the world in which they live

◆ nurture a child's drive to learn

- meet individual learning needs
- provide materials to support learning
- tell stories and read stories
- share your knowledge of language development with parents
- make children aware of the use of symbols in our culture
- help children to learn to pretend
- provide appropriate props for pretending
- choose children's books
- help children learn about literacy in an informal ad hoc way
- demonstrate literacy and numeracy in use and encourage mark making
- provide an environment in which emergent literacy and numeracy can grow
- read adults' non-verbal messages
- help community building
- ensure the childcare setting makes a contribution to the local community
- keep useful records of a child's development
- evaluate an expression of intention underlying a curriculum
- pinpoint ideas underlying your own practice
- evaluate your own practice
- examine alternatives and establish priorities.

Specific knowledge and skills needed include:

- an understanding of schemas
- the ability to analyse stages in a child's development of language
- the ability to describe a particular child's use of language
- a knowledge of nursery rhymes, lullabies, counting rhymes and traditional stories
- the ability to recognise themes of play in stories
- the ability to explain what literacy is and how it develops
- the ability to explain what numeracy involves and how it develops
- the ability to describe spatial relationships
- the knowledge of sources of help for parents
- the ability to empower parents to use their local environment for the benefit of their children
- a knowledge of the changes in childcare
- a knowledge of the viewpoints of the professions you collaborate with
- a knowledge of what quality relies on
- a knowledge of what being a professional involves
- the ability to take the lead in supporting children.

References and further reading

Abbott, L and Langston, A (eds) (2005) *Birth to Three Matters*, Open University Press

Ainsworth, MDS, Blehar MC, Waters, E and Wall, S (1978) *Patterns of Attachment: A Psychological Study of the Strange Situation*, Erlbaum

Arnold, C (1999) *Child Development and Learning 2–5 Years: Georgia's Story*, Paul Chapman Publishing

Athey, C (1990) *Extending Thought in Young Children*, Paul Chapman Publishing

Bartholomew, L and Bruce, T (1993) *Getting to Know You*, Hodder and Stoughton

Bettelheim, B (1976) *The Uses of Enchantment*, Thames and Hudson

Bowlby, J (1953) *Childcare and the Growth of Love*, Penguin

Bronfenbrenner, U (1979) *The Ecology of Human Development*, Harvard University Press

Bruce, T (2004) *Developing Learning in Early Childhood*, PCP

Bruce, T (2001) *Learning Through Play: Babies, Toddlers and the Foundation Stage*, Hodder and Stoughton

Bruner, J (1974) *Beyond the Information Given*, Allen and Unwin

Buss, A H and Plomin, R (1986) 'The EAS approach to temperament' in Plomin, R and Dunn, J (eds) (1986)

Campbell, D (2002) *The Mozart Effect*, Hodder and Stoughton

Campbell, R (1998) 'A three-year-old learning literacy at home' in *Early Years* Volume 19 Number 1, Autumn 1998, 7–89

Carr, M (1999) 'Being a Learner: Five Learning Dispositions for Early Childhood', *Early Childhood Practice: The Journal for Multi Professional Partnerships* 1 (1), 81–100

Carr, M and May, H (1993) 'Choosing a Model: Reflecting on the Development Process of Te Whariki, National Early Childhood Curriculum Guidelines in New Zealand', *International Journal of Early Years Education* 1 (3), 7–22

Caspi, A (2000) 'The child is father of the man: Personality continuities from childhood to adulthood', *Journal of Personality and Social Psychology* 78, 158–72

Chisholm, K (1996) 'A three-year follow-up of attachment and indiscriminate friendliness in children adopted from Romanian orphanages', *Child Development* 69, 1092–1106

David, T (ed) (1993) *Educational Provision for Our Youngest Children: European Perspectives*, Paul Chapman Publishing

DES (1967) *Children and their Primary Schools: The Plowden Report London*, HMSO

DES (1990) *Starting with Quality: Report of the Committee of Inquiry into the Educational Experiences Offered to Three- and Four-Year-Olds: The Rumbold Report*, HMSO

DfES (2001) *National Standards for Under Eights Day Care and Childminding*, DfES Publications

DfES (2002) *Birth to Three Matters*, DfES Publications

Doherty-Sneddon, G (2003) *Children's Unspoken Language*, Jessica Kingsley Press

Dunn, J and Wooding, C (1981) 'Play in the home and its implications for learning' in Roberts, M and Tamburrini, J (1981) *Child Development 0–5*, Holmes McDougal

Edwards, C, Ghandini, L and Forman, G (eds) (1994) *The Hundred Languages of Children – the Reggio Emilia Approach to Early Childhood Education*, Ablex

Elfer, P (2005) 'Observation Matters' in Abbott, L and Langston, A (eds) (2005)

Elfer, P, Goldschmeid, E and Selleck, D (2002) *Key Persons in Nurseries: Building Relationships for Quality Provision*, NEYN

Erikson, E (1964) *Childhood and Society*, Penguin

Fantz, R (1961) 'The origin of form perception', *Scientific American* 204, 66–72

Gardner, H (1982) *Developmental Psychology*, Little, Brown

Gelman, R and Gallistel, C (1978) *The Child's Understanding of Number*, Harvard University Press

Gerhardt, S (2004) *Why Love Matters*, Brunner-Routledge

Goldschmeid, E and Jackson, S (1994) *People Under Three: Young Children in Day Care*, Routledge

Goleman, D (1996) *Emotional Intelligence*, Bloomsbury

Goleman, D (1999) *Emotional Literacy*, Bloomsbury

Greenberger, D and Padesky, CA (1995) *Mind Over Mood*, The Guilford Press

Halliday, MAK (1975) *Learning How to Mean: Explorations in the Development of Language*, Arnold

HMSO (1989) *Children Act*, The Stationery Office

HM Treasury (2003) *Every Child Matters*, The Stationery Office

Hodges, J and Tizard, B (1989) 'Social and family relationships of ex-institutional adolescents' *Journal of Child Psychology and Psychiatry* 30, 77–98

Howes, C et al (1992) *The Collaborative Construction of Pretend*, SUNY Press

Hutt, SJ, Tyler, S, Hutt, C, Cristopherson, H (1987) *Play, Exploration and Learning: A Natural History of the PreSchool*, Routledge

Johnson, MH and Morton, J (1991) *Biology and Cognitive Development: The Case of Face Recognition*, Blackwell

Kagan, J (1997) 'Temperament and the reactions to unfamiliarity' *Child Development* 68, 139–143

Kochanska, G, Coy, KC and Murray, KT (2001) 'The development of self-regulation in the first four years of life' *Child Development* 72, 1091–1111

Kochanska, G (2002) 'Committed compliance, moral self and internalisation. A mediational model' *Developmental Psychology* 38, 339–351

Laevers, F (ed) (1994) *The Innovative Project 'Experiential Education' and the Definition of Quality in Education*, Katholieke Universteit

LaGasse, LL, Gruber, CP and Lipsitt LP (1989) 'The infantile expression of avidity in relation to later assessments of inhibition and attachment' in Reznik, JS (ed) *Perspectives on Behavioural Inhibition*, University of Chicago Press

Lewis M, Alessandri, SM and Sullivan, MW (1992) 'Differences in shame and pride as a function of children's gender and task difficulty', *Child Development* 63, 630–38

Livingstone, T (2005) *Child of our Time*, Bantam Press

Manning-Morton, J and Thorpe, M (2003) *Key Times for Play: The First Three Years*, Open University Press

Marta y Garriga, M (2000) 'The future of infant education' in Penn, H (ed) (2000)

Maslow, AH (1970) *Motivation and Personality*, Harper and Row

McGuinness, H (2003) *Baby Massage*, Hodder and Stoughton

Maclellan, E (1997) 'The importance of counting' in Thompson, I (1997) *Teaching and Learning Early Number*, Open University Press

Meggitt, C and Sunderland, G (2000) *Child Development: An Illustrated Guide*, Heinemann

Miller, L et al (eds) (1989) *Closely Observed Infants*, Duckworth

Miller, L (2002) *Observation Observed: An Outline of the Nature and Practice of Infant Observation* (videos and booklet), The Tavistock Clinic Foundation

Ministry of Education (1996) *Te Whariki* Wellington, New Zealand

Morris, D (1991) *Babywatching*, Jonathan Cape

Moss, P (2000) 'The Parameters of Training' in Penn, H (2000) op cit

Murray, L and Edwards, L (2000) *The Social Baby*, CP Publishing

Nutbrown, C (1998) *The Lore and Language of Early Education*, The University of Sheffield

Nutbrown, C (1999) *Threads of Thinking*, Paul Chapman Publishing

Opie, P and Opie, M (1963) *The Puffin Book of Nursery Rhymes*, Puffin Books

Opie, P and Opie, M (1951) *The Oxford Dictionary of Nursery Rhymes*, Oxford University Press

Ouvry, M (2000) *Exercising Muscles and Minds*, Early Years Network

Paley, VG (1986) *Mollie is Three*, University of Chicago Press

Paley, VG (1988) *Bad Guys Don't Have Birthdays*, University of Chicago Press

Penn, H (1997) *Comparing Nurseries: Staff and Children in Spain, Italy and the UK*, Paul Chapman Publishing

Penn, H (ed) (2000) *Early Childhood Services*, Open University Press

Piaget, J (1953) *The Origins of Intelligence in the Child*, Routledge and Kegan Paul

Plomin, R and Dunn, J (eds) (1986) *The Study of Temperament*, Erlbaum

Plomin, R and Walker, S (2003) 'Genetics and educational psychology', *British Journal of Educational Psychology* 73, 3–12

Robinson, M (1989) 'Bookspeak' in Hall N (ed) *Writing with Reason*, Hodder and Stoughton

Rothbart, MK, Ahadi, SA and Hershey, KL (1994) 'Temperament and social behaviour in childhood', *Merrill-Palmer Quarterly* 40, 21–39

Rovee-Collier, CK (1999) 'The development of infant memory' in *Current Directions in Psychological Science* 8, 80–85

Rymer, R (1994) *Genie: A scientific tragedy*, Harper Collins

Schore, A (1994) *Affect Regulation and the Origin of the Self*, Lawrence Erlbaum Associates Inc

Sheridan, M (1978) *Children's Developmental Progress from Birth to Five*, NFER

Thompson, R (2000) 'Seeing Double', *Nursery World* 27.01.2000

Tizard, B (1977) *Adoption: A Second Chance*, Open Books

Tough, J (1977) *Listening to Children Talking*, Ward Lock

Trehub, SE and Henderson, J (1994, July) 'Caregivers' songs and their effect on infant listeners', *Proceedings of the Meeting of the International Conference for Music Perception and Cognition*, Liege, Belgium

Vasta, R, Miller, SA, Ellis, S (2004) *Child Psychology*, John Wiley & Sons

Vygotsky, L (1978) *Mind in Society: The Development of Higher Psychological Processes*, Harvard University Press

Wade, B and Moore, M (2002) 'A Sure Start with Books' in *Early Years* Volume 20 Number 2, Spring 2000, pp 39–46

Wells, G (1985) *Language Development in the Preschool Years*, Cambridge University Press

Whalley, M (1998) *Learning to be Strong*, Hodder and Stoughton

Whalley, M and the Pen Green Team (2001) *Involving Parents in their Children's Learning*, PCP

Whitehead, M (2002) 'Dylan's routes to literacy: The first three years with picture books', *Journal of Early Childhood Literacy*, Volume 2, Number 3, 269–289

Whitehead, MR (1997) *Language and Literacy in the Early Years*, PCP

Winnicott, DW (1974) *Playing and Reality*, Penguin

Wood, D (1988) *How Children Think and Learn*, Blackwell

Wood, D, McMahon, L and Cranstoun, Y (1980) *Working with Under Fives*, Grant McIntyre

Websites

Day Care Trust www.daycaretrust.org.uk

Literacy Trust www.literacytrust.org.uk

QCA www.qca.org.uk

The Centre for Children's Books www.sevenstories.org.uk (tel: 0191 276 4289)

Glossary

Accommodation The word given by Jean Piaget to the process of having to take account of an example not exactly similar to those you already have. This leads you to adjust your mental categories.

Adjective A word identifying an attribute of a noun, e.g. the *big, red* truck; the *slow-to-warm-up* baby. You can usually add *-er* or *-est* to an adjective to indicate the degree of the attribute, e.g. *redder, bigger* when comparing two items, or *reddest, biggest* when comparing three or more. Some comparatives are irregular, e.g. *good, better, best*.

Adverb A word that describes the kind of action expressed by a verb, e.g. the child played *happily*.

Amniotic fluid The fluid that surrounds the foetus in the womb.

Articulation Production of the sounds of speech by movement of the jaw, lips, tongue, and vocal cords.

Assessment There are several ways of assessing and each has a different purpose. *Formative* assessment is aimed at deciding what to do next in the light of what you have found out about a child's present situation. It 'forms' your next action. *Diagnostic* assessment looks into a particular problem so as to target specific help. Doctors and speech therapists diagnose. *Summative* assessment is used at the end of a stage or period of study. Since all babies and young children develop at their own pace, it can be misleading to focus on how a child stands in relation to how most children of that age perform, as happens in the case of *normative* assessment.

Assimilation Named by Jean Piaget, the process of recognising a similarity and allocating a new object easily into an already existing category.

Attachment A long-enduring, emotional tie to a specific individual. The baby's urge to form an attachment has a biological function – the need to survive. The urge also has a psychological function – the need for security.

Axon A strand in the brain extending from the neuron, which carries information out from the nerve cell.

Baby massage Used with babies under 18 months to soothe them with gentle touches. Some believe it aids their digestion.

Baseline assessments A set of measures taken of the child's knowledge, especially in the areas of literacy and numeracy, on entry to formal education.

Body language Facial expressions, eye contact, body posture, the distance people maintain between each other and gestures used by people for telling or responding in a face-to-face situation.

Cardinality principle The understanding that the last number used for the last item of the group that has been counted indicates the number of items that there are in the group.

Compliance A child's willingness to go along with a care-giver's expectations, which Mary Rothbart saw as an important element in a child's temperament.

Control group Experiments investigating people are generally measured by having two matched groups. One group receives the special treatment, whether it's a medication or an opportunity to use extra resources. The other, the control group, is similar in all respects to the experimental group but does not receive the treatment. The two groups are measured at the beginning of the experiment and at the end to see whether the treatment has had the effect of making a difference between the experimental group and the control group.

Conversation The exchange of ideas, feelings or information in speech between two or more people. Conversations require that participants are aware of each other, listen to each other and respond to what they have heard. They require turn-taking. Babies begin to learn about how conversations work from a very early age, long before they can speak.

Cortisol A substance produced by the body from the adrenal glands in response to stress.

Creativity The ability to use objects or ideas in an individual way. To do this requires the ability to make connections and the confidence to consider things in new relationships with each other.

Curriculum 0–3 The only appropriate curriculum for children up to three is one that is based on a close and affectionate relationship with a familiar carer, who is skilled at observing both spontaneous and repeated interests and who can provide appropriate support and experiences to enhance those interests.

Curriculum areas In the UK, the early years curriculum has been described in the document *Desirable Outcomes* as centring on six areas of experience and learning: language and literacy, numeracy, knowledge and understanding of the world, music, physical skills, personal and social development.

Dendrite In the brain, branching strands extending from one side of a neuron which receive information for that neuron across a synapse from the axons of a neuron nearby.

Dyad A close pair, e.g. mother and child.

EAS model Robert Plomin proposed that temperament could be described in relation to the factors of *emotionality*, that is the amount of negative emotion displayed in response to a stimulus, *activity*, the amount of energy a child displays, and *sociability*, the amount of pleasure the child derives from being with people.

Emotional intelligence, emotional literacy Terms describing the ability to recognise and deal with one's own and other people's emotional states.

Exploratory play The type of play in which the child's chief purpose is to discover the characteristics and potential of something, such as water, sand, clay, paint, sound, a new toy, etc.

Extended family The wider family including grandparents, aunts, uncles and cousins, etc.

Frontal lobes The parts of the brain concerned with planning and attention.

Gender identity Recognising oneself as male or female.

Gender role knowledge Knowing what is expected of a boy or girl, man or woman.

Gender stereotyping Having fixed expectations of how boys and girls are likely to behave and encouraging them to behave in these ways. Gender stereotyping may inhibit a child's potential by closing off areas of activity.

Grammar The study of words in sentences.

Heuristic play Sessions recommended by Elinor Goldschmeid to enable toddlers to examine the properties of a range of materials.

Inhibition A general wariness in all challenging situations (Jerome Kagan), being ill at ease in society (Avshalom Caspi).

International Phonetic Alphabet A system first devised in 1888, which has a symbol to identify and describe every sound of every language, e.g. for the nasal sound *-ing*.

Intonation A distinct pattern of pitch in a sentence, which is used grammatically to indicate meaning or context.

Irregular verb A verb that does not behave as the vast majority of verbs do, for example by adding *-ed* to indicate the past tense. Instead, in some verbs the vowel changes in the past tense, e.g. *ring* becomes *rang*. Other verbs change their shape entirely to indicate different persons or tenses, e.g. I *am*, she *is*.

Key Stages The National Curriculum for England and Wales is divided into stages and the children are assessed at the end of each stage in the core subjects of English, maths and science. Key Stage 1 is ages 5–7, Key Stage 2 is 7–11, Key Stage 3 is 11–14, and Key Stage 4 is 14–16.

Key worker A member of staff whose responsibility it is to know specific children (their temperaments, learning styles and stages of development) and to be available to respond to their needs in a sensitive way. The key worker is also responsible for maintaining good contact with the parents of the children in their charge. The key worker role is particularly crucial for children under three who all need the security of a strong relationship with an interested loving carer who knows them, affirms them and can respond appropriately to support them in their learning.

Literacy The ability to cope with written language by reading and writing it.

Ludic play The type of play in which children are exploiting what they have learned through exploratory play and feel confident enough to be able to make fanciful adjustments to what they know is reality.

Motherese The name given to the way people talk to very young children. Outside the UK it is sometimes known as *caretaker speech* or *baby talk*. Many adults use it instinctively and even children as young as four use it to younger children.

MRI scan A medical scan making use of the properties of magnetism to look at areas of activity within the body's tissues.

Myelin A white substance coating the axon which speeds the flow of information from one neuron to another in the brain.

Negative Ways of expressing 'No'. For example, the positive statement *I like it* is changed in the negative to *I do not like it*. Young children often take time to learn to use the negative form correctly.

Neurons Nerve cells that pass information from nerves, glands and muscles to the brain. The most important are those in the brain and in the spinal cord.

Neurotransmitter A chemical substance released to aid the transmission of messages across synapses from nerves, glands and muscles to the brain. It usually works in the presence of substances released either by hormones or the endocrine glands.

Non-verbal communication Communication that does not rely on words. It includes facial expressions, gestures and body language.

Noun A word used as the name of a person (*Mary*), place (*kitchen*) or thing (*stove*). Some nouns are about things you can see or touch (*car*), while others name abstract ideas (*beauty*). Most apply to individual items, but some name collections (*herd, army*). Nouns function as the subjects or objects of sentences.

Nuclear family The smallest family unit – parents and children.

Number sentence The list of the names we give to numbers, e.g. *one, two, three, four...*

Numeracy The ability to cope with numbers, to count, to use numbers in measurements, and to do calculations.

Nursery rhymes Traditional rhymes passed on from carers to children. Many go back hundreds of years; the first collection was printed in England in 1744.

Object permanence The fact that objects continue to exist even when they are out of sight. Adults take this idea for granted. Jean Piaget traced the way the idea gradually dawns on the child, usually between 6 and 18 months of age.

Occipital lobe The part of the brain concerned with the understanding of visual images and the interpretation of written words.

OFSTED The Office for Standards in Education, the schools inspectorate. Under the National Childcare Strategy it has also taken over responsibility for monitoring and inspecting children's services.

One-to-one principle Matching one number name to one object when counting. This understanding is built on the experience of putting one car in each garage, one doll in each bed or one button in each division of an egg tray, etc.

Open group That part of the young child's vocabulary that is continually expanding when the child is at the stage of two-word utterances.

Order irrelevance principle In counting, the principle that the objects to be counted may be counted in any order.

Palate The arched bony structure in the roof of the mouth, divided into the hard palate and the soft palate. The soft palate is nearer to the back of the mouth.

Parasympathetic nervous system The system producing bodily sensations when a person is thinking of transgressing a code he or she has accepted.

Parietal lobe The part of the brain concerned with touch, body-part awareness and visual–spatial thinking.

Phonology The study of the sound system of a language: the sounds the language uses, and the way syllables are stressed.

Pivot group The closed group of useful words that can combine with any word in the child's open group at the stage of two-word utterances, e.g. *no, more, allgone, that*.

Play A child's self-chosen activity, whether it is exploratory, or involves pretending. Children may be seen playing by themselves, playing alongside others but without interacting with them (*parallel play*) or jointly pretending with all involved in taking a specific role (*sociodramatic play*).

Plowden Report (1967) A report prepared by a committee chaired by Lady Plowden for the government. The report recommended the setting up of educational priority areas and the expansion of nursery provision.

Polyad A small, closely connected group.

Possessives Words that indicate ownership, e.g. *mine, hers, his*. Possessives are also formed by adding an apostrophe and *s*, e.g. *Tom's house*.

Pragmatics The study of the range of language uses available for various types of interaction, e.g. in social interactions remembering to say *please* and *thank you*.

Prepositions Words that indicate position (e.g. It's *in* the box *under* the bed *behind* the door) or give more information about the details of an action, e.g. Give it *to* me and go *with* John.

Pronouns Words that replace the name of a person or thing (a noun), e.g. *I, me, he, him, it, them, those*.

Proto-literacy The stage before the complete understanding of reading and writing, when children have realised that print carries meaning and that there are literary conventions, e.g. that stories often have a formal beginning and ending.

Reflective practitioner A person who keeps reappraising his or her practice and keeps on trying to find ways to improve it.

Role play The type of play where a child plays out a role, e.g. a mother, a builder. The purpose is to have an opportunity to think about what it must feel like to be this person. In that sense role play is a version of exploratory play.

SATs Standard Assessment Tests in English, maths and science, taken by all children at the end of the Key Stages of the UK National Curriculum. They are used to evaluate the system as a whole and to assess the effectiveness of individual schools.

Schema Jean Piaget noticed that children have schemas or patterns of action, e.g. sucking or grasping, which they adapt in various ways as appropriate. Chris Athey followed up this idea and watched how young children focus for a while on a particular phenomenon, which can be seen repeated in many guises in the world around them, e.g. circles or enclosures.

Self-actualisation The stage when an individual has an efficient and accurate perception of who they are, their strengths and weaknesses. It is marked by the courage to think independently, to resist pressure and to accept responsibility.

Self-regulation The ability to control one's actions and emotional responses.

Sensorimotor stage Jean Piaget's name for the way the child operates in the first two years of life. It is the time when the baby or toddler gathers information through the senses of taste, smell, touch, sight and hearing, and through his or her actions.

Single-word utterances The first stage of using words to communicate, most noticeable between 12 and 18 months. One word, or a phrase used as one word e.g. *all-fall-down*, carries meaning. Most words used at this stage are the names of people, food, clothing or household items.

Social referencing The action of a baby who is crawling about and exploring but looks back at an adult for approval or permission to continue. Doing this shows that the child is aware that there are boundaries to be observed.

Sociodramatic play Play in which children assume roles and agree on a storyline to develop with other children. This type of play usually begins when a child is over three. It requires language skills and the ability to negotiate.

Speech therapist A person trained to diagnose, assess and treat speech disorders.

Stable order principle The principle of always using the same number sentence for counting, even though at an early stage it might not be the conventional one.

Strange situation procedure A procedure devised by Mary Ainsworth to test the response of a child aged 12–18 months to being left alone with a stranger. The child's response when the mother returned gave an indication of the child's relationship with the mother.

Subitising Correctly recognising the number of units in a group without having to count them one by one.

Subordinate clause A clause that contains a verb, but cannot stand alone; it needs to be associated with a main verb in a sentence to make complete sense, e.g. The baby, *who had just woken up*, began to cry.

SureStart A government programme to deliver the best start in the UK for every child. It brings together early education, childcare, health and family support.

Syllable One of the units that combine to make up a word, acting as a unit of rhythm. It contains a vowel, either alone, as in the first syllable of *a/bout*, or within consonants, as in *seg/ment*. In a word of several syllables some are given greater stress than others.

Synapses In the brain, junctions or fluid-filled gaps between dendrites of one neuron and the axon of another. Information is passed from cell to cell by chemical activity in this fluid. Those synapses that are frequently used grow in size.

Temperament A characteristic approach to life.

Temporal lobe The part of the brain concerned with the understanding of sounds, spoken words and meanings.

Treasure basket A low, handle-less basket filled with a variety of natural and everyday objects for a sitting or supported baby to explore.

Two-word utterances A way of speaking that begins to be used about the age of 18 months. The child has two classes of word, *pivot* or *closed* class and *open* class. Pivot words are only used with open words. Two open-class words can be used together.

UN Convention on the Rights of the Child (1989) Global standards for the recognition of children as citizens, expressed in 54 articles. Every country except the United States and Somalia has ratified the convention and has undertaken to change national law in accordance with it and to inform adults and children alike about the Convention. Governments have also agreed to report to the UN every 5 years about the progress they have made.

VAK Short for the visual, auditory and kinaesthetic modes of experiencing, remembering and representing experience.

Verb A word referring to an action (*to walk*), an event (*to wake up*) or a state (*to know*). It changes to show differences in time (tense), person and number.

Vocabulary A collection of words.

Vocal cords Two muscular folds in the larynx which vibrate as a source of sound.

Voicing The change in the quality of a sound as a result of the vibration of the vocal cords, e.g. the difference in sound between *f* and *v*.

Index